Dave Masiak, once the "strongest man at Baker," is now pitably broken by diabetes, hypertension, and arthritis. The health problems which dominate his life have been attributed chiefly to his inability to cope with the plant closing.

And there's Baker's last production manager, Lloyd Shearer, who today denies the sequence of the closing and hasn't had a visitor in his house since the closing.

During the two-year closing, fully half the men studied were beset by problems such as ulcers, arthritis, hypertension requiring hospitalization, alcoholism, depression requiring medical help, even hair loss--all precipitated by the plant closing. Of Baker's seven salesmen, three died during closing.

The report isn't one-sided, however. Slote also interviews management, both at Baker and the parent plant, to give a fair, balanced view.

TERMINATION is an indictment of society's indifference to the influence of social and economic anxieties on the mental and physical health of its members. Inspired and guided by research conducted by the Institute for Social Research, this cogent sociological study is also a skillfully written narrative more readable than many novels.

ALFRED SLOTE is a novelist and children's author and is executive producer at The University of Michigan Television Center.

TERMINATION

The Closing at Baker Plant

TERMINATION

The Closing at Baker Plant

ALFRED SLOTE

WITH A FOREWORD BY SIDNEY COBB, M.D.

The Bobbs-Merrill Company

INDIANAPOLIS/NEW YORK

The Bobbs-Merrill Company, Inc.
A Subsidiary of Howard W. Sams & Co., Inc.
Publishers / Indianapolis — Kansas City — New York

50984

AUTHOR'S ACKNOWLEDGMENTS

This book could not have been written without the cooperation of the following groups of people:

the men of the "Baker" plant, hourly and salaried, who let me into their homes and talked openly and frankly about the closing of a plant they loved;

the officers of the West Side Local and the International Union who gave me access to records and told me the story of the closing as they saw it;

the executives of the "Pennsylvania Corporation" who welcomed me and talked frankly about their reasons for how and why they closed the plant;

the staff of the Institute for Social Research, nurses and interviewers, who were generous beyond the call even of compassion in making themselves available for consultation and questioning.

This book was inspired by the research being done by Dr. Sidney Cobb's group at the Institute for Social Research of the University of Michigan. The research study, begun in 1964, was supported by the United States Public Health Service, grant # 5-R01-CD00102.

Although in most cases the names of people, companies, and places have been changed, and some incidents, conversations, and meetings changed in order not to embarrass the relevant parties, the story of the death of this factory (which I have called the Baker plant) and of the people I have talked to and described herein, is true.

I went down, down, down to the factory
Early on a Monday morn.
When I got down to the factory
It was lonely, it was forlorn.
I couldn't find Joe, Jack, John or Jim;
Nobody could I see:
Nothing but buttons and bells and lights
All over the factory.

I walked all around, all around, up and down
And across that factory.
I watched all the buttons and the bells and the lights—
It was a mystery to me.
I hollered "Frank, Hank, Ike, Mike, Roy, Ray, Don, Dan
Bill, Phil, Ed, Fred, Pete!"
And a great big mechanical voice boomed out:
"All your buddies are obsolete."

from "Automation,"
words and music by Joe Glazer
Copyright: Joe Glazer

All man has to do is stay smarter than a machine.

NAM pamphlet, October, 1957

   I am a son of God, a husband and father, a man, and a pipefitter. It's because I'm a pipefitter that I'm not worried about
this plant closing.

Walter Jahnke,
hourly employee of the Baker Company,
in the summer of 1965

MAJOR PERSONAGES
IN THIS STORY,
IN ALPHABETICAL ORDER

Wysse Allen—former vice-president, Coatings and Resins Division, the Pennsylvania Corporation, and the man who made the decision to close down Baker.

Louis Arnot—chief salesman for original finish at Baker, who dreaded driving back and forth to Cleveland.

Jefferson Barret—former supervisor at the warehouse and the only Negro in a supervisory position at Baker. A man liked and admired by everyone.

Henry Burns—former hourly worker (jitney driver) at Baker, nervous and worried and bitter, who lived across the street from a beautiful stand of oak trees—at one time.

Will Calloway—a popular salesman for refinish at Baker—the only man who actually died on the job.

Perry DeMoss—the union rep from West Side Local, tough, intelligent, honest, a former long time employee of Baker himself, which perhaps didn't help him during the closing negotiations.

Neil Esslinger—former hourly worker (warehouse checker) at Baker. An honest, slightly self-righteous type who has his doubts about the origin of the great explosion.

Tom Frohman—vice-president, Manufacturing and Equipment, the Pennsylvania Corporation.

Matt Gargan—supervisor, shipping and receiving at Baker who went from hourly to salary, an old-timer admired but also distrusted.

Howard Green—divisional director, industrial relations, Coatings and Resins Division of the Pennsylvania Corporation, and a former plant manager of Baker. The only man in the General Office who felt personally involved in the Baker closing.

Mike Harrah—assistant general counsel, the Pennsylvania Corporation. A sharp, tough, and shrewd Irishman who looked more like a union lawyer than a corporation counsel.

Willis Ingram—former hourly worker (canning machine operator) at Baker. An ex-tuberculosis patient who fooled some people by coping successfully with his job loss.

Lee Jones—manager, industrial relations at Baker before the closing. Fired by Frank Robertson, who felt he could not close the plant decently with this man there.

Cal Koonz—regional director, UAW. A man with an impressive office and an inadequate file.

Ike Kraeger—general manager, production, the Pennsylvania Corporation.

Dave Masiak—former hourly worker (janitorial duties) at Baker. Fat, toothless, perhaps the saddest case, though once he carved lovely totem poles.

Jerry McNerney—former hourly worker (kettle operator) at Baker, who opted for security and became imprisoned as a prison guard.

Harley Merritt—plant manager at Baker before Frank Robertson. In the view of General Office, not the kind of executive to close a plant.

Tom Morgan—Baker's last industrial relations manager. Easygoing, an ex-athlete, an old-timer, popular, though held in friendly contempt by the union committee.

Otto Mueller—last superintendent of the resin plant at Baker, who drives a school bus now and wonders why Frank Robertson wonders what has happened to him.

Ralph Muzetti—vice-president in charge of industrial relations, the Pennsylvania Corporation, a man prone to lecturing on the 'big picture.'

Duane Paddleford—former hourly worker (lab assistant) at Baker. Nobody should have to lose his hair twice, but Paddleford did.

unemployment is more complex and stems from several lines of research and theoretical development in social psychology. First, though it has long been recognized that man has more complicated ways of adapting to his environment than other animals have, it is only recently that there has begun to be some agreement on terminology. For example, when faced with more work than he can finish in a day, a man could react by attempting to change his environment, e.g., asking the boss to reduce the load or give him an assistant. This is called "coping," whether successful or not. Or the man might try to change himself, e.g., take some sort of training to improve his skills so that he could keep up with the demands of the job. This is called "self-development." Or, thirdly, the man might deny that he is unable to keep up, and thus protect himself from the drop in self-esteem that would be caused by his admission that the job is too tough for him. This is called "psychological defense" and may involve distortion of the perception of self, or of the perception of the environment, or both.

Willis Ingram in this book had what was probably the toughest situation of anyone in the Baker plant for he lost both his job and his house within two weeks, yet he coped extraordinarily well. A good example of self-development is Glen Littler whose story is told briefly in the chapter titled *Winners and Losers*. Littler used his three weeks of vacation time during the closing to get training in the driving of semi-trailers. And finally, Lloyd Shearer, who kept the rain-soaked author fascinated for thirty minutes while he denied the reality of the closing through a crack in the front door, is an outstanding example of the use of psychological defense. So the various patterns are not only there, they are all represented in this book.

Second, we must attend to developments in role theory and self-identity theory. In this area the most relevant statement is almost an aphorism; it simply states that a man becomes what he does. Actually it is not quite as simple as that, for the theory is only fully true for flexible individuals. The rigid have difficulty changing what they do because they have difficulty making the necessary changes in self-identity that are related to a change in role.

When you combine these two concepts with the obvious fact that the unemployed role is one that is looked on with disfavor in our society, it is not surprising that some people prefer to move into the sick role and accept the identity "sick" in preference to the identity "unemployed." These persons must be among the more flexible and presumably will have had recent experience with the sick role. This is in fact what we find and Big Dave Masiak is a good illustration of what can happen.

All this is one way of accounting for the increase in sick benefit payments after the closing of the Studebaker plant in 1963. Now, what about an increase in actual sickness? This takes us into the area of psychosomatic disease or stress-related disease, where knowledge, though limited, is beginning to grow. First, there are few, if any, diseases for which the cause is entirely psychosocial, but there are many for which we have evidence that certain environmental stresses when brought to bear on susceptible people will substantially increase the likelihood of illness. For example, from the work of Dr. Hinkle of Cornell we now know that when people become depressed their nasal mucous membranes become pale and somewhat swollen. These pale and swollen membranes are more susceptible to the invasion of respiratory viruses, so when a virus and depression hit together the likelihood of a cold is materially increased. Of course it goes without saying that plenty of people get colds without being depressed. In other words you don't have to be depressed to get a cold, but it helps.

In rheumatoid arthritis, my own work would suggest that conflict over the expression of aggressive feelings, plus tissue damage from infection or trauma, provides the climate most likely to set off an attack of rheumatoid disease in a susceptible person. Duodenal ulcer, by contrast, seems to appear in susceptible individuals with greater frequency when their psychological need to be nurtured or even mothered is unmet. With regard to high blood pressure the situation is less clear but it seems likely that frustration, resentment, unexpressed anger and dissatisfaction have something to do with it. Finally, *alopecia areata*, or the falling out of hair, is a rare disease associated with acute anxiety. The fact that not all who suffer with acute anxiety lose their hair strongly suggests that there are some major components in an individual's constitution which act as contributory factors in this disease.

All of these diseases seem to be associated with the loss of a job and might be looked on as prices paid in the course of adaptation to change, and all of them appear in one or another person in this

TERMINATION

The Closing at Baker Plant

Baker, 1968

Wyoming Boulevard in Detroit: factories, truck depots, pizza places, a motel on the corner of Michigan and Wyoming, gas stations, seat cover shops, a funeral home looking neat and incongruous.

Suddenly, without warning, Wyoming becomes residential: neat little two bedroom houses, pedestrians, small stores on the corners. The avenue goes on this way for a few blocks and then the residential area culminates in McKenzie High School, a large red brick building with an athletic field alongside. A right turn onto West Morton and there are factories once again, bars and grills, gas stations, and in the middle of the next block—the Baker paint plant.

Across the street and slightly to the west of the Baker plant is the Compton Industrial Clinic, a low orange-colored brick building Next door to the clinic and directly across the street from the plant is the Skyway Cocktail Lounge, to which the hourly rated employees retired on the last day when Ned Rockwell personally bought Frank Robertson a drink. "Going out," as Ned said, echoing Robertson's words, "with our heads up."

Abandoned factories should look like abandoned factories—desolate, haunted, with broken or boarded up windows and crude schoolboy sayings painted on the walls. The Baker paint plant, abandoned now for three years, looks neat and tended. Jack Whitsell, who is in charge of the grounds, has kept his promise to Frank Robertson, the last plant manager, to "keep her face clean." The grass alongside Building 2 is mowed, the little hedge border is neatly clipped. There are no broken or boarded up windows. Whitsell is surprised that anyone is surprised at how neat the deserted plant looks.

"We're trying to sell it for one thing," he says. "We damn well better keep her face clean."

Right now the company is using the empty buildings as a tax write-off, but soon the price is expected to go down and they will be able to sell the old plant. Also, as Whitsell points out, Building 1, the main office building, is still used by the sales staff. "So we keep it neat for our morale as well," he says.

From the outside, the only real sign that this plant is abandoned is the large empty parking lot with its small white signs scattered about: 8 A.M. Shift Park Here Only. 2nd Shift Parking Only. There are a dozen or so cars in a lot that can handle up to five hundred. A wire fence separates the parking lot from the large concrete yard and the plant buildings. The yard, with its smokeless stack and absence of people, has a flat two-dimensional appearance.

Whitsell admits us, or rather tells the guard to admit us. My guide is Tom Morgan, the last industrial relations manager for Baker. Morgan took early retirement and says he is pleased with it. A lanky former athlete who took a factory job back in the depression, Morgan is pleased now to go fishing with his son up north in the summer, and travel to Florida in the winter. I have managed to catch him between trips.

"I don't miss Baker one bit," he says. "I'm probably different from the other people you've been talking to. I'll go along with them that it was a good place to work. Maybe too good a place, but all in all I'd rather go fishing."

Morgan is a little annoyed that the guard at the main gate insists on telephoning to Jack Whitsell to let him in. "I worked here 35 years," he says, "and this is the first time I couldn't walk right in. How long have you been here?" he asks the guard.

"Six months," says the guard, waiting on the phone.

Morgan turns to me. "The last few months of the closing we had our most experienced guards on. The stuff they tried to take out under their shirts you just wouldn't believe."

"OK, Mr. Whitsell," the guard says, and turns to us. "He says it's OK, but he wants to come down to say hello to you. I'll call the ADT right now."

"That's the alarm system downtown," Morgan explains. "He's got to let the protection people know that the photo-electric beams are going to be tripped."

It is a windy afternoon in January, strangely warm and uncomfortable. As we walk across the plant yard, the wind blows dust and dirt over our shoes. The rails of a railroad spur are covered with dust and silt. They emerge gleaming for a few feet and then dive down beneath the dirt. A dead pigeon lies rotting on the ground.

"It sure looks like hell, doesn't it?" Morgan says, and shakes his head. "You're not getting the right picture. You should have come here when this yard was filled with trucks going back and forth, guys with dollies. We always had a lot of fork trucks moving around. It was one of the signs the place was obsolete too," he adds, grinning. "We had to carry things from building to building. But it sure made it a jumping place. Noisy too. This is Building 2. A very important building. Our main production building and we've got our testing labs in here too. Ugh..."

Condensation from the ceiling has created pools of water on the floors. The ovens in the testing lab are rusted. Morgan stares at it all for a moment. Then he tugs at an oven door. Nothing happens. He pulls with two hands and slowly, noisily, the door squeaks open. "Jesus," he says, "and we used to be so damn proud of this room."

There are several small ball mills in the room, used for testing colors. Now they are covered with a fine brown rust. According to Morgan at one time each ball mill was filled with a ton of tiny steel balls that ground the pigment powders with resins and solvents.

"The floor used to be covered with these steel balls. Maybe I can find you one."

He looks around, and locates a small steel ball, brown, a half-inch in diameter, covered with a soft coating of sludge. Beneath the soft sludgy surface you can feel the steel.

"Keep it as a souvenir."

I put it in my pocket and follow him around a pool of dark water that has white flecks of paint from the ceiling floating in it.

In all, there are seventeen buildings in the Baker plant—eighteen, before the great explosion in August of 1964. Building 2, the main production building, was the sole building forty-two years ago when the company began to concentrate solely on automotive finishes and refinishes. The Baker Color Company had begun as a family business in 1901 at another location, turning out japan colors for horse carriages. It was natural for the company to start making paints for automobiles. In 1924, the Baker brothers sold the business to two partners and in 1925 the partners sold it to the Pennsylvania Corporation, which has owned and operated it ever since. In December of 1965 the corporation closed the Baker plant down (with the exception of the the office building, still occupied by the industrial and distributor sales force) and moved the production facilities to a new and automated plant in southern Ohio.

The new plant is a single building with raw materials coming in at one end and cans of paint going out at the other. It is just the opposite of the Baker plant with its seventeen separate structures —each one ultimately a nail in its coffin. Baker was a plant that grew as the automobile industry grew, that added buildings much as rooms were added to nineteenth century American homes as the families inside them grew larger.

"We could never stop production long enough to modernize," Morgan explains. "There were always crises, emergencies, production schedules to fill. And then one day it all caught up with us and they decided it was cheaper to start new somewhere else, with new people, than to rebuild the old. And that's where the hard part started. We wanted to keep making paint, closing down one plant and opening another a long distance away at the same time. We did it too, and there aren't many plants that could have got away with it."

"What do you think made you succeed?"

"Frank Robertson—and a certain amount of loyalty from the men. Maybe loyalty's not the right word. Maybe it's just that all of them knew there wasn't ever going to be another place as good as Baker to work and they didn't want to leave it till the very end. Most of them stuck it out right to the end. They wouldn't take other jobs. This was their place, their home. . . ."

We walk from building to building—seventeen obsolete buildings, and now in each one the cold damp smell of rust. The big machines are still there: ball mills, mixing tanks, filling lines, a small assembly line that didn't go anywhere—"an experiment in modernization that failed," Morgan says, with a half-grin—electric kettles, storage tanks. And there are numerous small items: buckets, scales, a few paper cartons that got left behind, safety posters, and, posted near the door on every floor of every building, evacuation route maps.

"We were the most safety-conscious paint plant around," Morgan says with a rueful shake of the head, "and yet we had the biggest explosion of any of them. But we came back from that too. You heard the word 'sabotage' but there wasn't any sabotage. There wasn't a man who worked here who would have wanted to hurt this place. Their fathers worked here, their cousins, brothers, uncles, aunts. And when it was closing they just couldn't believe it. They wouldn't believe it. Hell, I should have known, and part of me

Harold Peterson—Baker's sales manager in charge of refinish sales. A hard-driving man whose death haunts Frank Robertson.

Arthur Phelan—assistant general counsel, UAW. A tweedy, pipe smoking, articulate lawyer who looked more like a corporation counsel than a union lawyer; he knew it was a desperate and delicately balanced line he was treading—threatening legal action angrily with one hand and extending the olive branch of collective bargaining with the other.

Jack Ramsay—former hourly worker (truck driver) at Baker. Crazy about his dog Tina; together they visit their doctors regularly.

Doris Robertson—the wife of Frank Robertson. Childless, she collects miniatures.

Frank Robertson—Baker's last plant manager. The man who buried his beloved factory and is haunted to this day by it, who has gone down to Arkansas to hide. A proud, complex little man.

Ned Rockwell—the last chairman of the union plant committee, an hourly worker (tank house attendant) at Baker. Rockwell, another proud man, helped Robertson bury the plant with love and now looks back in bitterness.

Lloyd Shearer—Baker's last production manager. A southerner liked by black and white hourly workers, who today denies the sequence of the closing and hasn't had a visitor in his house in two years.

Peter Thompson—president, West Side Local, a man with stories to tell about other closings.

Stepan Toucek—former hourly worker (truck driver) at Baker. A bantam hard-nosed type who prides himself on his hard-headedness: he told them where to stick their severance pay.

* * *

Dr. Sidney Cobb—of the Institute for Social Research at the University of Michigan. His study of the "Baker" plant provided much of the material for this book; indeed, it was his idea to write this book.

Health programs for industrial workers have obvious humanitarian objectives but on the whole their initial acceptance was occasioned by management's hope that they would reduce the amount of sick absence and required disability compensation. One seldom, if ever, sees evidence that the first objective, reduced sick absence, has been accomplished. On the other hand, if one thinks in terms of disability due to toxic substances generated in the environment one cannot help but be impressed with the improvement.

Lung disease from dust, especially silica dust, remains a problem in our mines and factories, but things are certainly better now than in the flint mines of northern Italy in the 16th century when, we are told by Agricola, it was not uncommon for a woman to lose seven successive husbands to the breathlessness engendered by continuous exposure to the silica-containing flint dust. By the same token, much progress has been made in the prevention of lead poisoning since 1786 when Benjamin Franklin, writing to his friend Benjamin Vaughn, recounted "the mischief . . . occasioned by . . . that use of lead" in distilleries, printing houses, among plumbers, glaziers, painters, and even soldiers and stonecutters, and concluded "that the opinion of this mischievous effect from lead is at least above sixty years old; and you will observe with concern how long a useful truth may be known and exist, before it is generally receiv'd and practis'd on . . ." Despite Franklin's pessimism, since his time progress has been made in the control of a whole host of industry-created toxic substances.

It is only recently, however, that the more subtle issues of the influence of the social environment on the health of employees have come under scrutiny and so far very little has been done with the information that is available. This is the major focus of the current research conducted by my immediate colleagues and myself at the Institute for Social Research of the University of Michigan. Though we started some years ago looking at problems of shift work, of work overload, and of status in the organization as these factors relate to mental and physical health, we soon came to realize that we didn't know enough about what it meant to have or not to have a job. So we turned to an examination of health problems at the work-no-work boundary. This involves one study that looks at the transition from school to work, another that concerns the effect of job loss in middle life, and perhaps a third on retirement. TERMINATION is concerned with one of the plant closings that was investigated in the course of the second of these studies.

In order to understand this study's significance, it is important to look at the scientific setting in which it appears. That is, we must trace some developments in a variety of fields which have made this complex, yet integrated, study possible. For generations there has been an impression that the unemployed and impoverished have more illness than the well-to-do. At first it was assumed, probably quite correctly, that money was the issue. It did not seem unreasonable to suppose that those who were, in New Deal language, "ill housed, ill clothed, and ill fed" should presumably, as a consequence be more frequently ill. It is only since we have had adequate welfare programs, and hence little starvation among the unemployed, that we have begun to realize that there may be some fundamental issues other than the simple problems of hunger, cold, and unsanitary conditions.

I recognized this first in connection with the 1963 closing of the Studebaker plant in South Bend, Indiana. When this plant closed, the union negotiated a continuing health insurance coverage for the men who remained unemployed. This was to be paid for by the company and the fee to the insurance carrier was to be renegotiated monthly based on the number covered and the illness experience. The fee rose so rapidly to what were described as astronomical levels that the company balked at payment, although of course when the appropriate legal pressures were applied the company faced up to its responsibility. In checking around to see if this was an isolated instance, I found that it was an accepted fact at the Detroit Metropolitan Hospital that admission rates go up during layoffs and model change-over times. The theory at this hospital was that this was a matter of convenience for the men. Specifically they came at those times for elective surgery because it would save them being off work during busy times. Surely there was some of this motivation but my theory was and is quite different.

My theory about the rise in sick role behavior during times of didn't believe it either. Lloyd Shearer, who was the production manager at the end, didn't believe it either. It was just one of those things you didn't want to accept, I guess. Hell," he kicks at some papers and debris that blows into our path, "it was like your family closing up on you. Your father throwing you out of the house. That's what this place was for forty years—one big family. We carried everyone. Goldbrickers, goof-offs, crooks. We had picnics, bowling leagues, softball teams, chess teams, hardball teams, tennis tournaments, bridge tournaments. We were hiring Negroes before it was fashionable.

"Maybe it wasn't all with the best motives in the world—we couldn't afford slowdowns, strikes, walkouts. We couldn't afford trouble. We were always counterpunching to the big Chrysler and Ford plants, but especially Chrysler. At the end it was a real juggling act that Frank Robertson put on. He did what no other man could have done, closing this plant and keeping it going too. And now he's paying for it. He's sick. He's down in Arkansas, sick as a dog, I understand, but he brought off a miracle. To close a plant, get people jobs, keep the place going, make paint, make money, ship out machinery, not a single work order missed, and on top of that—half the plant blows up on him a year before it closes. If all that isn't a miracle, then I ask you, what is?"

Darkness has fallen as we walk back across the yard. The lights of the office building where the sales staff still works are on. We walk toward them. Behind and around us the factory buildings melt into the night. To our right there is the snap of loose papers hitting against the wire railroad fence. Tom Morgan turns up his collar.

"If you want to know what it was all about, go down to Arkansas and see Frank Robertson. He was the key to it all. I'm sure he'll talk to you. This plant was his family. He never had any kids of his own. And I'm sorry for him right now. Watch it!"

We stop. An empty carton skids by us. Tom Morgan shakes his head. "They'll have to do a lot more cleaning up before anyone would buy this place now."

The Plant Manager

Name: Frank R. Robertson
Age: 63
Married: Doris Howell 9/11/26
Children: None
Religion: Protestant
Employment: 1922–23, school teacher, lower grades—Iowa
　　　　　　　 1923–24, cowboy, farmer, truck driver—Wyoming
　　　　　　　 1924–25, school teacher, lower grades—Iowa
　　　　　　　 1926–65, Baker Color Company, Detroit
　　　　　　　　　　　 laborer, technician, foreman, supervisor, in-
　　　　　　　　　　　 dustrial relations manager, production man-
　　　　　　　　　　　 ager, plant manager
　　　　　　　 1966, retired
Residence: Rt. 1, Booneville, Arkansas
Health: suffered extreme weight loss during plant closing, from 164
　　　 pounds to 116 pounds. Pain and fever attacks during final
　　　 week of closing, diagnosed as mucous colitis, presently on medi-
　　　 cation for this.

To get to Booneville, Arkansas, by plane you take a Central Airlines
DC3 from Saint Louis and two hours later get off at a hilltop airfield
at Harrison, Arkansas.

You rent a car from "Smitty's Car-Boat-Plane Rental Service"
and, on a cool spring day, you drive some 50 miles through winding
hill country with stands of scrubby pines and signs pointing toward
lakes, hunting lodges, boat rentals, through towns like Yellville
("Home of the National Wild Turkey Calling Contest"), through
Cotter, past billboards proclaiming Bull Shoals Cavern ("The Cadil-
lac of the Caves," "Visit Caves in Sunday Clothes"), past Pyatt,
Ark., pop. 144, with a second sign pointing toward the "Business
District," past a plain straightforward sign that says "Arkansas—
Where the People are Friendly" and finally through Booneville

which consists of a post office, a general store and gas station, and a half dozen houses. The Robertsons live two miles outside of Booneville on a narrow but paved road that ultimately leads north into the Ozarks and Missouri.

The house, a rented one, is a low yellow wood and gray brick modern ranch set back about one hundred feet off the road and sits on an acre of land. It looks west over fields with the rolling Ozark hills to the north. The nearest neighbor is a gas station about a quarter of a mile down the road. It is a far cry from the Detroit neighborhood the Robertsons lived in for forty years.

Neither Frank Robertson nor his wife Doris is well. Mrs. Robertson has had an ulcer for over five years now which, according to Robertson, acts up every fall. This past fall she was in the hospital for six weeks. Complicating this is a hypoglycemic condition, in which a malfunctioning pancreas produces too much insulin, drastically lowering the sugar content of the patient's blood stream. It is a kind of reverse diabetes and can have serious consequences.

An accompaniment to, and perhaps partly a cause of, her ulcer and hypoglycemia is an emotional problem she has had for a number of years. She had been getting psychiatric help in Detroit, but here in Boone County there are no psychiatrists. According to Robertson, she gets help from a local general practitioner. Robertson is protective about his wife and her illnesses and he partly blames himself for them. "We never had children. My own life was wrapped up in the plant. Baker was my family. Doris had nothing."

Although he himself hadn't been sick one day in Detroit from the time he first arrived in 1925 to the final week of the plant closing in December of 1965, during that last week Robertson had attacks of pain and fever. His doctor examined him and, finding nothing, concluded it might be a virus and gave him some antibiotic. The fever did not clear up. Massive doses of antibiotic were administered. After a few days the fever went down but the stomach pain and bowel disorders lingered. Robertson went into the hospital for some tests the day after he retired in February 1966, and his illness was then diagnosed as mucous colitis—a persistently irritable colon which, according to medical literature, is mainly caused by tension associated with feelings of guilt. Robertson was told that his mucous colitis was caused by a reaction to the antibiotic. He was also told to expect to take medication for it for the rest of his life.

Whether his illness is a reaction to drugs or to tension and guilt symptoms, Robertson concedes that today he feels guilty about his role in the closing of Baker. "I had a dream," he says. "I wanted to see that place grow. More than I ever wanted anything else. There were good people in that plant. People who were proud of what they were doing. No man, no company, ever had the right to expect the loyalty and sincerity that those men gave me. Right up to the last day. I hope to God they're all right now."

But he's not so sure, and medical studies on physical changes in the hourly rated employees during and after the closing done by Dr. Sidney Cobb's research teams from the University of Michigan's Institute for Social Research would reinforce Robertson's sense of guilt.

As a salaried person, Robertson was not part of Dr. Cobb's study —a fact Cobb regrets, for there is mounting evidence that middle and top management people are often hit harder by a plant closing than are hourly workers. Certainly Frank Robertson was a man who was hit hard, though it might be more accurate to state that Robertson hit himself hard.

Robertson's phenomenal feat of keeping a plant going for two years after its closing was announced was due mainly to the fact that he cared about his people and was able to communicate his caring. It was also this caring which later produced, in Dr. Cobb's words, "uncontrollable feelings of guilt, which, in turn, contribute to Robertson's colitis."

Two years after the plant's gates have finally shut, Robertson senses the box his caring built for him and for some of the Baker men. And yet what choice did he have?

"I guess I made it too good a place for them," he says. "But a plant is made up of people, and people come first, don't they?"

He pauses, waiting for reassurance and quickly gets it. For we both know, on that coolish spring day in Arkansas, that what he says is true. He did make it a good place to work. He carried the lame, the inefficient, the goldbrickers and the sick, and carried them because they were "his" people. But we both know there is also the possibility that he may have carried them because it was good business to do so. The automotive paint business is a pressure business, re-the table and Tom said, "You won't need that, Frank. Not yet anyway. A decision was made less than 24 hours ago about the Baker plant."

My heart skipped a beat. I knew what was coming.

"You all know about the 1958 product alignment study and we all know how obsolete the plant was 20 years ago. Well, a decision's finally been made to close the Detroit plant. We're going to build a new, completely automated plant. We don't know the location yet. It'll handle the automotive refinish that you were doing in Detroit, but it'll also take on Newark's appliance finishes and Atlanta's can coatings. Cleveland is going to be enlarged, remodeled and new equipment put in, and they'll take care of Detroit's original finishes."

No one said anything. I was shocked. Stunned. I knew it was coming, but I was stunned anyway. Even the way he never said Baker but always said Detroit, just making it a little item going to be taken off a peg. One of many items; one of many pegs. I looked around the table. Merritt was frozen-faced. But it didn't mean a damn thing to him. He wasn't a Baker man. He'd been with one of our competitors when Ike had hired him. I looked at Ike Kraeger. He was fiddling with a pencil on a piece of paper. I found out later he'd heard about it an hour before.

What was there to say? To think? We'd always been living on borrowed time. That product alignment study of 1958—I could have written its conclusions ten years before that. The company has 14 plants producing paints and each one was producing a like product in industrial coatings and finishes. Each plant was duplicating the others in sales, research and development, service, production. Duplicating expensive equipment, personnel. The study had pointed out that one new modern automated plan could take over certain operations from all the plants. So one plant was being closed. And it was Detroit because Detroit was old, 18 buildings, high cost, and because, under Merritt, General Office had been allowed to bleed it. But Detroit wasn't Detroit—it was Baker, and two or three generations of men and women had worked there. Seventy-five percent of the people at the plant had been there for 15 years or more. I felt sick.

For some reason Tom kept looking at me. His voice was soft. "Our timetable is tentative at the moment, but the task force to engineer the new plant and the improvements in Cleveland is being set up. It's too early to set target dates right now. Frank, are you with me?"

"Yes," I said.

"I've got something I know you'll be interested in. We want you to take over the Detroit plant as of Monday, April first."

I stared at him. After 37 years at Baker, I was finally being offered the top job.

I don't know how long the silence lasted. Frohman was waiting for me to say something and my first instinct was to say, *No, I don't want it; you want to bury it. I won't do your dirty job for you. Merritt was good enough to bleed it. Get someone else to bury it.*

But I didn't say anything. I just sat there. And Tom went right on. Harley was being transferred back to General Office as a process engineer. Everyone agreed that I was the only man who could do it. He realized he was putting me on quite a spot. No one knew exactly how long it would take to finish the new plant. It would have to be no later than December 31st, 1965, when the union contract at Detroit ran out. That was about two and one-half years from now. In these two and one-half years I had to keep Baker going, lay off people, terminate and bury and show a profit too. I knew the Baker people, he was saying. There were men there I'd started work with 37 years ago. They trusted me.

"I know I'm putting you on quite a spot, Frank," Tom repeated.

I nodded. "It's a spot," I said.

"Do you want to think about it? Take a moment and think about it?"

Take a moment? I didn't even think I needed that. I believed in growth, the future. I was no undertaker. That plant was everything to me. The men in it were everything to me. I'd seen plants close before, even within our own company. I'd seen things fall apart, seen the chaos. As I thought about that —I knew suddenly I'd accept the job. Someone was going to have to do it; and it ought to be someone who loved the plant and the men. You don't want to be buried by people who don't know you. In the single moment that I rejected the assignment, I accepted it.

I heard myself saying: "It's a poor thing, Tom, but if you feel I can do it, I'll consider it. But I'd like to ask a few questions."

Tom said: "I'd be surprised if you didn't have any questions."

"This first question might surprise you even more. Do you want, does the company want to keep the original finish business? It's just that simple."

Tom said: "Oh, my God, yes. Everybody down here wants that original finish business."

And I said: "Well, would you want to fight for it? Work for it? We're on our way out right now as a major supplier. We've gone way down from No. 1 in Chrysler ratings and way down in Ford ratings till we're almost out of sight. Will you help me get those ratings up?"

"Yes," Tom said, "I'll help you get the ratings up." Then I knew I'd get the $140,000 for the ball mills and the grinding equipment.

But what madness. To accept a job to terminate a plant, and then fight to get more money to make the plant productive again before it dies.

"OK, item No. 2," I said. "What about my future, Tom? I want to know what's in it for me."

He knew I'd put in for early retirement, retirement at 60. That was next year. Tom hemmed and hawed and looked at Harley and Ike and said we'd talk about it and annuities and pension and looked at his watch, jumped up and said it was time for lunch.

So we all got up and rode the elevator down and walked through the tunnel to the Hilton and went into the dining room there. Tom tried to make a big thing of it. A drink to the new plant manager. I lifted my old-fashioned and drank but there wasn't any lift, any elation. I was scared deep down. And it was unreal. A couple of minutes ago my life had changed and I wasn't sure to what.

After lunch we went back to Kraeger's office and then Merritt got a call to go down to process engineering and Kraeger and I went back into Tom Frohman's office and we went over my financial arrangements in detail. I wanted it clear that my annuities and pension would begin when Baker closed. I said, "I'm going out with Baker."

We argued that back and forth and finally he agreed. Then we talked over my role in the planning of the new plant. He wanted a smooth transfer of operations. I said I couldn't guarantee anything. It would depend on the men, the speed with which the new plant was built.

He told me they had options on land in three different places for the new plant. At York, Ohio; Smithtown, Indiana; Newtonville, Ohio. I told him I'd help in planning the new plant, but I wasn't going to guarantee anything about keeping Baker going. The whole thing could fall apart in my lap.

The next move now was to get out a press release of my appointment for plant consumption. Ike would write it. I was to go back to Detroit and take over. How long should Harley stay? I made my first decision as plant manager: Merritt goes in one week.

Then I got my briefcase out and we went over plant improvements. Tom agreed to them all. Also a new salary program, freedom to move certain people. It was good to get lost in details. I almost forgot that I was hired to terminate the plant. About 3 P.M. the phone rang. It was Wysse Allen, Tom's boss, the vice-president in charge of all operations of the coatings and resin division. He wanted to see me.

I could tell that Tom and Kraeger were surprised. They hadn't known this was coming, but I also knew that if anyone made the decision it would have to be Allen.

Wysse Allen's office was down the hall. Not as posh as Tom's,
more homey, like a den in your house. But there was nothing
homey about Wysse Allen. A year younger than I, he's not
a big man but wiry, thin gray hair and pale cold eyes. He was
trained in business administration at some small Indiana
college, had started out with the corporation as a salesman and
had worked his way to almost the top. Like Tom he'd married
into the ———— family. He was a hard, cold man, but honest.
You never had the slightest doubt where you stood with him.
He cut through words, got to the essence of things; he wasn't
afraid to make a decision and he wasn't afraid to lay his own
job on the line. I was a little afraid of him, and I respected
him a lot. He always looked right at you when he talked to
you.

When I got into his office he motioned me to a chair without
saying anything and just looked at me for a few minutes. Then
said: "Robbie, you don't know how happy I am you've taken
it on. This is the dirtiest, toughest job I ever handed a man.
I know you're the only man who can do it. And I can understand your emotions. All I can say is thanks. And tell you that
any facility, anything you need out of General Office is yours."

I didn't say anything.

"Robbie," he said, "you're going to walk alone."

He swiveled around and looked out the window. "This is one
of the biggest moves we've ever made. There are dangers in
it. It could be a fiasco, and we could pay for it with our stockholders. But Baker is and always has been a high cost plant.
If we're going to survive in the automotive paint business
we've got to start somewhere."

He looked at me.

I didn't say anything. I was thinking, *You bastard, you could
have started ten years ago by putting some money in as well
as taking it out. You let it get cancer and now you're curing
it by killing it.*

"How do you feel, Robbie?" he asked.

I shrugged. "Scared as hell," I said, though at that moment there was a kind of peace inside me. He was a big man, Allen, and I was doing something for him and the company that no one else could do. I was a little proud even, God help me.

"Lots of things are going to happen, Robbie. Lots of things we haven't thought of. We don't know what we're getting into. A lot of it will have to be played by ear. But I'm here to help you. Whatever you need, just pick up the phone or come down to see me."

He stood up and we shook hands and I left, thinking he respected me and all I'd really said was that I was scared as hell.

I went back to Kraeger's office and he and I discussed some of the mechanics of the appropriation for the ball mills. We got Harley on the phone and he and I met in the lobby and took a bus out to the airport. Harley turned to me during the bus ride and said: "Well, how do you feel about being plant manager at last?"

I didn't answer him. He wouldn't have understood. He never was a Baker man. I changed the subject and all the way back and in the plane, too, we talked about other things. And all the way back I was thinking why did I reject it and then an instant later accept it? And, what was I getting into?

Harley and I walked to our cars; I remember they were parked near each other. We stopped by my car and Harley turned to me and said: "You coming in tomorrow?"

"No."

"I am. I want to turn over to you all my cost accounting figures."

Harley had always done his own cost accounting. He didn't have to, but he'd always done it.

"Forget about that," I said. "I trust Don Cates and our whole accounting department. Their figures have always looked right to me. I don't want to see your figures.'

"I worked a long time on these figures, Frank."

"You did it for yourself then, Harley. Not for the company or for me. Listen, I don't know if Tom or Ike told you but you've got one week here."

He didn't say anything. And I never found out if he was hearing it for the first time. I didn't much care either. I got in my car and drove home. Doris was watching television. She kissed me and searched my face. You get to sense things after 37 years, but she didn't understand what she read there. I told her the plant was going to close and she looked shocked. I told her that starting Monday I was the new plant manager and she was pleased. "I'm so proud of you, Frank," she said.

"No," I said sharply, "it's not good news, and there's no time for pride or celebrating. No time for that at all."

Sunday. Went to church, something I haven't done in a long time. Went to church and prayed for help. I don't want to see anyone hurt in this thing. God, *help me put this plant to bed, gently and painlessly, for all of us,* I prayed.

"You Can't Carry A Loser in Business."

Name: Arthur Wysse Allen
Age: 62
Married: Patricia Wyatt, June, 1928
Children: Ellen, 28—Mrs. Robert Simes; Ted, 25; three grandchildren
Religion: Protestant
Born: Fort Wayne, Indiana
Education: Hillsdale College, Hillsdale, Michigan, A.B.
Occupations: 1936–37, Pennsylvania Corporation
                salesman; sales manager; general manager, sales;
                divisional manager; vice-president, paint and brush
                division
                1967, retired
Residence: spring and fall: Pittsburgh; winter: Winter Park, Florida;
        summer: Bridgeman, Michigan
Health: good

The road to Bridgeman, Michigan, is a four-lane freeway—Michigan's answer to the Ohio and Indiana tollroads. Bridgeman itself is a small summer community on the shore of Lake Michigan, about ten miles south of Benton Harbor. A left turn at Bridgeman's only stop light takes you onto a macadam road and a second right off the macadam road takes you onto a dirt road. There are two signs at the entrance to the dirt road. One says: "Woodlea Shores." The second sign, set back slightly, says: "Private Property, Restricted, Members and Guests Only, Police Patrolled."

The dirt road loops downward with unostentatious but expensive cottages nestling a few yards back in the pines. Allen's cottage, set below the road, fronts on the immense blue of Lake Michigan. On the other side of the cottage is tall grass, sloping down to a sandy beach and the lake.

The cottage is large and summery: wicker chairs, lived-in family furniture, calendar art on the walls, a few books and paperbacks in an unpainted bookcase, summer things collected over a number of years which have finally come to rest in a handsome retirement cottage. An Irish setter walks across the bare maple floor wagging its tail. Allen orders it from the room and the dog turns and walks off with an easy red grace.

Allen, incredibly, is dressed all in black and white. Black golf shirt, black shorts, black socks, white tennis sneakers. He smokes a cigarette in a long black holder. His eyes are a frosty blue, colder than the blue of the lake, and his hair is silver. Hollywood would cast him as a West Point general. He is trim, erect, a 60-year-old man in good condition. Frank Robertson called him the hardest looking man he'd ever seen; Allen looks as though he has worked hard on that image.

"I retired June 25th," he says tersely. His voice has a rasp—too many cigarettes, too many conferences; he has had to take command so often. "I told them I was going to take early retirement. They didn't believe me. When I did it, they acted as though I'd raped a six-year-old girl." He smiles. "For the first time in thirty years I don't have to take sleeping pills or drink—what's that stuff? —alka seltzer. For thirty years I left my house at six-thirty to be at the office at seven. I made fourteen trips to Europe last year. I was gone twenty-five weekends out of the year. Now . . . I sleep as late as I want, I play golf every afternoon, and I've that to look at the rest of the time."

He nods toward the porch and the immense blue lake that rises half-way on the windows. There is a cloudless blue sky and is nothing as far as the eye can see but lake and no land, no sail, no ship— only a beautiful blue expanse.

"What's on your mind?" he asks.

"Exactly when did the company decide to close down the Baker plant?"

"The company didn't decide. *I* decided." He pauses, blows out smoke. "I was put in charge of the paint and brush division in 1959. It didn't take long reviewing studies and figures of operations to see that we had a real loser in the Baker factory. And this in spite of the fact that the automotive finish operation was a money-maker for other companies."

"Weren't you making money?"

"We weren't making enough money."

"Does a company ever make *enough* money?"

"Of course it does," he snaps. "Given the nature of its operation, capacity, investment. Baker wasn't doing what it should have been doing. It was a loser. And in business you don't carry losers."

The dog walks back into the room, looks at Allen who shakes his head. The dog turns and goes away again.

"I had 17 factory operations under me in the United States and four overseas and Baker was the weak sister of the bunch. It had to go. It wasn't a snap decision. I had a pretty good idea what was involved in closing up a plant. I'd closed two other smaller plants which weren't making profit. I had the big report of 1958 which showed the way to a corporate reorganization. I came into my job in 1959, a new vice-president, a new broom; I had an idea what was expected of me, but I didn't make a snap decision; we worked on it carefully."

Allen recalls the time in 1960 when he was invited to address the Baker management group in Detroit. It consisted of every level of salaried employee from foreman on up to plant manager. They had a big dinner at a motel and after the twenty- and thirty-year wrist watches were presented he talked about the state of the paint industry in general.

There was no discussion of Baker in particular, Allen recalls. But the moment he was finished a supervisor got up and asked if there were any plans for closing the Baker plant. This was 1960, three years before the decision was finally made. They knew too. Everyone knew. It was obvious.

"I told that man and the others that at that moment there were no plans. But, I said, I'll be frank with you people now and say right out that the Baker operation is not a satisfactory one, and unless something different happens, we at General Office will have to consider alternatives.

"Someone else stood up and said—he didn't ask, he said—the real problem was the low markup on automotive finish. They were not making anything profitable at the plant. If we in General Office put a profitable product in, the company would then see a satisfactory sales operation.

"That kind of thinking always goes on in a losing operation. The

fact of the matter was that for nine months, against my better judge-
ment, I put a trade sales product into the plant. A resin. It didn't
help. In fact, it lost us money because it could have been produced
more profitably elsewhere. You can't save a plant with a product.
You can't expect one product to bail out other products. Every
line has got to pay. Otherwise you erode the profit of other plants.

"Baker had to close. I was divisional vice-president; it was my
responsibility, my obligation to the stockholders to see that there
was an adequate return on investment. That's what business is all
about. If there isn't an adequate return on investment there's no
business. So I made the decision to close. But the decision to close
that one plant also meant the decision to open another one. Whenever I hear people talking about automation causing job loss, I say
bull. Automation is opening up all kinds of new jobs. It's true a lot
of older workers aren't going to be able to make the switch. And
that happened at Baker. Besides the layout of the place, which
was impossible, there were the people—sloppy, inefficient, not giving a damn about quality or production. It was the fault of management partly and partly just long-ingrained, sloppy work habits.
Baker had a tradition of goldbricking that went back forty years.
That was one of the reasons we didn't build a new plant in Detroit.
We wanted to get away from the past. We wanted to start new.
You can't ask people who've goldbricked for twenty or thirty years
suddenly to go to work with new methods, new techniques, new
machines.

"Sure, there's hardship on some of them. I know that. We all
knew that. The government has a role to play here. Unemployment
compensation, job retraining programs. That's not the private corporation's responsibility. You can't expect a company to subsidize life
tenure for an employee. Any employee has got to realize that if he
doesn't produce effectively he can lose his job, and if the job
changes, he can lose his job.

"We've got to have that freedom, that option if we want our
economy to move ahead—if we want to keep our nation strong. If
we didn't have that freedom, we'd be like England or any of your
socialist countries where private enterprise is hamstrung by government regulations. That's one of the reasons England's in trouble
right now. Too much government interference; a company there is
not free to change and grow.

"Let's get the record clear: closing Baker was a gamble. It meant putting ten to twelve million bucks into a new facility. But now— two years later—it's paying off. We won the gamble.

"It wasn't without worry. I had plenty of sleepless nights, believe me. I wasn't afraid of a strike, because a strike would have been illegal. We could have collected damages. We were more afraid of production loss during the changeover. Afraid people would leave on us. That's where the severance pay came in; it was designed to keep people at their jobs till we no longer needed them.

"We didn't have to pay severance pay; we suggested it before the union did. We had a good relationship with the union. We went to great pains to point out to them that the closing of Baker was not a union problem. We've never had any trouble with the UAW. Other unions, other factories—yes. But not the UAW.

"This isn't to say we always saw eye to eye with them, because we didn't. But we worked together to close this plant and their cooperation was invaluable. Let me tell you something about unions: They make problems, but they have their values. As companies get bigger and bigger, management tends to lose touch with its lower echelon workers. That's where the union can be helpful. It helps give you effective control of the men. Naturally the UAW fought to prevent the closing, but when they saw there wasn't anything they could do, they worked with us to make the closing as effective as possible. I understand some of the hourly workers think the union could have prevented the closing in the first place. This just isn't so. But I can tell you why they think that."

He pops another cigarette into the holder, a silver lighter flashes in the sunlight. His voice is harsh. The smoke drifts in the sunlit air in front of him.

"They've been sold a bill of goods that the union is their Big Daddy. Once, a long time ago, I was a union man myself. I got thrown out because I didn't conform. Union members today knuckle under to union leadership in a way they never knuckled under to management leadership. They think it's immoral to knuckle under to the work boss and moral to knuckle under to the union boss. Well, now they're paying for it. They've relinquished their personal initiative; they're just like sheep led to slaughter by the judas sheep. The union is supposed to be able to take care of them in all situations. Union power? It's there all right. I've seen it and I won't deny it, but it's not there in every situation. It wasn't there to prevent the closing. The men don't realize this. They think the union can do anything it wants. Well, no one on God's earth can do whatever he wants."

Allen sits back. In another room, someone—perhaps his wife—is moving about. But he or she does not enter. Allen is silent a moment, listening too. Then he says softly:

"I'm a grandfather. I've got three grandchildren. I worry about this world as much as anyone. Those riots in Detroit. That kind of thing spells the end of our nation. That's anarchy and it's been coming for a long time. I'm a Presbyterian. My minister, he's a young fellow. We don't see eye to eye on many things. A year or so ago he went down to the Selma march to break some so-called unjust law down there. I tried to make him understand that when you break a little law in one place you can break a lot of law in other places. Those Detroit riots started in Selma. They started in every place people broke the law no matter what the reason. Once you turn something on, you better damn well be sure you know how to turn it off. No one's sure anymore. The country is drifting into anarchy.

"I believe in law and order. As a businessman I've got rights, but I've also got obligations. I was responsible to my boss, to the stockholders of the company. And I had obligations to the people who worked at Baker. I tried to do everything right. I complied with every provision of the law as I was familiar with it. During the long and difficult time of the closing I never saw any word of criticism in the public press. Our customers never complained. During the throes of moving people and equipment there was no sabotage, no resentment on the part of people. If there'd been a great uproar, the public would have got into the act. We'd have had trouble.

"Part of it was luck. Times were good and the plant was located in a big city. If we'd been a large plant in a small town, there'd have been an uproar about the loss of taxes and so on. We were in a big city and the economy was going great in Detroit. The auto industry turned out nine million cars that year, I believe. It was the ideal time to close a plant. At the same time, though, we ensured our luck. We worked to make this change as humane as possible. We gave the men ample warning. Wouldn't you say that two years was a lot of warning? We gave severance pay—we didn't have to do that. Sure there was a large amount of self-protection in the severance pay, but it was still a decent thing to do.

"I also pride myself on picking the right man to close the plant— Frank Robertson. I picked him because he was an old-timer. He had compassion for the men. And he was a good businessman. A damn good businessman. Do you realize for over a year that old obsolete Baker plant was closing and producing at the same time.? We made more money than we lost. And when we sell the old plant we'll make still more."

Smoke wreathes Allen's face, sunlight gleams on the black cigarette holder. He looks reflectively toward the lake. A gull has swooped into the picture window, skims the water and flies off. On the distant horizon a Great Lakes freighter has appeared and is slowly working its way across another window.

"You know," Allen says quietly, as if the idea were occuring to him for the first time, "someone could buy the old Baker plant now and have a fine little paint factory. You couldn't duplicate those facilities for five million dollars."

The Irish setter comes back into the room, and this time Allen nods. The dog stays. The interview is over.

The New Plant Manager

4/1/63

For Frank Robertson, Allen's new plant manager, the seven months between April, when he assumed his new duties, and November of 1963, when the men were notified of the plant closing, were to be the worst months of his life. He had no hint of that, however, when he arrived at work Monday morning, April 1, at 7:30 A.M. He began his day as he usually did as production manager—before going to his office he looked in on a part of the plant where there had been some trouble earlier. On this Monday Robertson went to the grinding department where an altercation between two employees had delayed production on Thursday. Everything was running smoothly now, but from the curious looks he received from the men he knew there had been intense speculation about the reason for his and Merritt's trip to Pittsburgh.

He couldn't help smiling. There was always speculation when the two top men went down to General Office. Indeed, rumor and Baker had gone together for years. For almost as long as he could remember, men had talked about this crazy quilt of a plant being obsolete, and every trip of his or Merritt's to General Office always kicked off another intense round of rumors.

Robertson greeted a few men in the grinding department and then walked over to maintenance—his favorite department—and looked in on the men there. These were the elite of the hourly workers, men who could be counted on in any pinch, men who would stay till the very last day and who would be easily placed in other factories. Robertson stayed in maintenance for about ten minutes listening to stories of April fool jokes they had played or had had played on them, and then went along to his own office. No sooner had he sat down at his desk than his phone rang and it was Harley Merritt wanting to go over the announcement of his appointment.

It would be the last time that Merritt would ever summon him. Robertson walked down the hall to the plant manager's office with the eight-foot-long desk and its eighteen coats of hand-polished lacquer. That desk, which the Baker company had bought from

28

Detroit Edison in 1931, had served four plant managers, and now in one week's time he would be sitting behind it.

Merritt handed him the copy of the announcement that he and Kraeger had worked out in Pittsburgh. Robertson studied it carefully. He nodded. "It seems OK."

"Then I'll call in Mrs. Parkinson and have her type it up."

The plant manager's secretary came in and Merritt gave her the announcement. Mrs. Parkinson was an older woman. Like the desk, she had served four plant managers. As she read the paper, her eyes widened.

"Have it mimeographed," Harley said curtly, "and give copies to Lee Jones or Charley Burns for all the bulletin boards."

"Yes, Mr. Merritt." She turned to Robertson and smiled. "Congratulations, Mr. Robertson."

Robertson remembers the smile, and her saying that—the first set of congratulations he received and it felt like getting hit in the stomach. It should have been a warning to him.

Before the day was out, his hand would be pumped a hundred times as hourly rated workers and salary people alike, congratulated him and swore loyalty to him and told him they'd work for him as they'd never worked for anyone before. After all, as one of the foremen said, he was one of them, he'd started from the bottom himself thirty-seven years ago, and he knew the plant as no one knew it. Robertson had to look them in the eye and accept their congratulations and promises of help and devotion and thank them and know he could not tell them the truth—that he had been chosen to bury the plant.

"No man should be made to deceive people like that," Frank Robertson says today. "With that morning began the most degrading and unhappy time of my life. I had never lived a lie. Always I had deep resentment for people who did. But to have that announcement go out, and the reaction that took place was so tremendous and the congratulations, and, on the surface, the happiness and pleasure at my taking over was so overwhelming, and to accept their congratulations and promises of help and devotion—I think that was one thing, in the next few days, that almost got the best of me. It's difficult to look into someone's eyes and listen to them and know that in due time you'll have to tell them the truth."

It would be seven months and ten days before Frank Robertson and General Office would tell them the truth. That day, to each person he merely said what he said to Mrs. Parkinson, his new secretary, when she congratulated him: "Thank you. I know I can count on you to do your best."

Production records testify that in the months that followed, everyone did do their best for the new plant manager. Eighty-five percent of the cost of a gallon of paint is in the materials, 15 percent in the labor. It was in the labor margin that the Baker company showed an immediate improvement after Robertson took over. Costs went down as efficiency went up. Bickering stopped and ideas, good ideas, started pouring in. It became a happy factory. People were kidding and working as they did in the old days, a situation bound to give satisfaction to any plant manager. But it gave no satisfaction to Frank Robertson.

"It made me feel guiltier than hell," he says, looking out his window at the brown Arkansas hills, "and that guilt is with me today. I recognize what I'm doing: I'm hanging onto the guilt. Sometimes I feel guilty by just going out and riding on a beautiful lake and doing nothing. But I can't kid myself. I know what I'm going to remember. People worked for me while I lived a lie for them. That's inside me as big as life."

While Frank Robertson lived the lie, he also threw himself heart and soul into the job of running the plant while he could. He had waited a long time to become plant manager and he knew immediately what was needed. In the week that followed his appointment, with concrete promises of new equipment from general office in hand, Robertson paid three visits to the top management of Chrysler and Ford plants.

He spoke to the managers of the change in Baker and said he wanted to serve them. They sent him to the engineers, men he'd known for years. They had already heard of the change. The chief engineer at one of the Chrysler plants said: "This gives me great pleasure, Robbie. You know Baker's ratings have gone way down. You're on the bottom of the totem pole. But if you tell me you'll take care of us, Robbie, we'll give it a real whirl."

Within ninety days, Baker had more business than it could handle.

Robertson made few internal changes. The day he returned from visiting the Chrysler plants and the Ford plant he held a meeting of top technical people, quality control people, production and sales personnel. He told them what he wanted to do, what the automobile people had said, and what was needed. The past was dead, he said, they all had only one object: to build business, to make Baker number one again. "We can do it," he said, "if we all row together. If you don't fit, you'll get moved."

That day Robertson "moved" two people—a salesman and a quality control engineer. He also appointed Lloyd Shearer to his old position of production manager. Shearer was an old-timer, a fair man, liked and respected by the hourly and salary people alike. He was a Tennessee man originally, but the Negroes, to a man, trusted him. Installation of new equipment began in ten days time, and the plant was off running.

All this time, with Merritt now gone to Pittsburgh, out of the more than 550 people in the plant only Robertson knew that Baker was to be closed. In all of Detroit only two people knew: Robertson and his wife. And for once Baker brought them together.

The Robertsons lived in the northwest section of Detroit in a comfortable red brick and frame house on a small lot among elms and basswood trees. Inside, their house was almost antiseptically neat. Wax fruit on a glass table, a plastic cover over the portable television set. Mrs. Robertson subscribed to six magazines and their latest issues were carefully laid out on the coffee table. On the walls hung landscapes painted in muted colors. There were interesting looking dolls and miniature tea sets set on the built-in book shelves.

Childless, Mrs. Robertson had one passion: collecting miniatures. Her collection was well known in southeastern Michigan. Robertson encouraged his wife in this hobby and sometimes went out weekends with her hunting miniatures in antique shops in Wayne and Oakland counties. Long ago he had promised her that after his early retirement, he would build her a gift shop wherever she wanted it, and from which she could sell miniatures. One of the first things they did when they moved to Arkansas was build a miniature gift shop out of sugar cubes that would be the exact model of the gift shop he would build for her in the tourist region of Arkansas where they now lived.

During the years at Baker when Robertson was industrial relations manager and later production manager, they never talked about the plant. They always talked about miniatures or gardening. Mrs. Robertson hated Baker. It was her husband's passion, the other woman in his life. His true family, she felt, were the men and women who worked there.

However, the day he came home from Pittsburgh and told her he had been appointed plant manager and the plant was to be terminated, things changed. From this point on, Frank Robertson found his wife keenly interested in Baker. She took to asking him all sorts of questions about the plant—the mechanics of closing, how he could keep things going and shut it down gradually, when and how people were to be notified, who was to be transferred to Cleveland, who was to go to the new plant, what would happen to the others. Baker was dying, and Mrs. Robertson couldn't hear enough about its death throes. Saddened, Robertson could also understand his wife's reaction and was, in a sense, grateful for it. For he needed to talk to someone about the closing. It was increasingly difficult to keep his feelings bottled up.

As production increased, business was booming, more orders were coming in and Baker's ratings were going up, Frank Robertson found himself becoming increasingly bitter toward the corporation. Here he was, proving this plant could compete. It was in the black now, contributing to the company pot. Production had come from an average of 22,000 gallons a day in 1962 to more than 35,000 gallons a day during 1963 and early 1964. Indeed, from June, 1963, to August, 1964, production figures would show that Baker contributed more to the corporate profit picture than it ever had before.

In short, the plant did not have to die. It would always have been a high-cost plant because of its age, but it could have competed if the company had kept it up-to-date. Robertson was demonstrating this in the first months of his tenure as plant manager. If, in the long-range view, a new plant had to be built, it should be built in the same area, Robertson felt, near the source of demand. It was true land costs were higher in Michigan than Ohio, where the new plant was eventually built; the tax structure of Michigan was not as favorable as Ohio's, and there was a union problem. (Even though the company was to state repeatedly that union and labor costs in general were not a factor in its decision to relocate, the union, Robertson insists, is always a factor. Witness the fact that the new plant in Ohio is not unionized.) Despite all this, Robertson acting on a day-to-day basis to automobile factory demands. Baker could not afford a strike, and grievances had to be settled before they got out of hand. Baker had to be a good place to work if it was to survive at all. Baker never had a strike; grievances were always settled. Working at the Baker plant was a lot like working in a family. When the pressure was applied from the auto companies, men worked harder than their union rules called for. And Robertson today may be plagued by the suspicion that what he explains to himself as caring, was taking advantage of "his" men.

"I guess some of them are not doing so well," he says softly, "but I'm not doing so well either. I was sick emotionally and physically when I came down here. I'd done just what I'd advised people for years not to do when they retired. I burned my bridges." He pauses again, to gauge the impact of these next words. "But there are just some bridges that won't burn, aren't there?"

He stands up, walks over to the window overlooking the fields and the Arkansas hills, the sun making a pretty sunset behind them.

"This acre of ground outside. It was a patch of weeds and a god-send. I worked on it from dawn to dusk when I first got down here. I worked on it trying to shut the long and sordid story of the closing out of my mind. But at night it would catch up with me. I'd lie there in bed and go over it again and again, what had happened, why I'd done what I'd done, would I do it again? Could I have done it differently?

"Some nights would be worse than others. The nights were always worse than the days."

He turns and faces me, his face a study of resentment and relief.

"And now you've come down here, and you want me to go through it all again. I don't know if I can. I don't think you know what you're asking me to do. You say I can help other people. Yes . . . maybe I can. This thing is going to be a problem all over America. Plants closing, automation, progress, human beings. Maybe I can help." He pauses, and adds softly: "Maybe I can help myself too. Maybe the only way I'll get rid of this thing is to go through it again. All right, where do you want to begin? In Iowa where I was born? Or in Detroit where I went to work as a man? Or do you want to start when it really started, on Thursday, March 28, 1963, at 9 A.M. when I got a call from Harley Merritt, who was plant manager then. . . ."

From the Recollections of Frank R. Robertson

3/28/63

Thursday. The big item today was a call from Merritt. Called me into his office to say he just got a call from home office and we're both to go down to Pittsburgh tomorrow. A 10 A.M. meeting, which means we can go down in the morning rather than tonight. Good old Northwest Flight 314, how many times have I taken it? And since it's a Friday meeting, it also means a one-day meeting. I asked Merritt what it was about, but Harley got that non-committal look in his eye which usually means he doesn't know. My hope is that it's about the long-delayed appropriation for the new ball mills and grinding equipment for Building 5. There's been no new equipment in the plant since 1960, the year Harley took over. They are quite openly and cynically bleeding us to death. At any rate, hoping against hope, I've put all the cost statements into my briefcase. It comes to a piddly $140,000 which would let us stay competitive for the moment.

Friday. Doris was still sleeping when I left. She had a restless night again. I kissed her on the forehead and left about 6 A.M. to have an easy drive to Metro and get some breakfast there. I met Harley at the airport a little after seven. He looked remote and uneasy and something told me it was going to be a serious meeting. Was he worried about being canned? He had every right to worry. He was no businessman. Why in hell Kraeger ever put him in charge I'll never know. They were both ex-Air Force colonels, maybe that was it. Both big leader-looking type men. Anyway, he just greeted me at the gate and hardly talked all the way down in the plane. He just read a magazine. Didn't even glance over when I took out the cost statements and went over them. At that, I didn't have to do it. I'd gone over them so many times, it was just gilding the lily now. It was a beautiful, crisp, clear sunny day.

Plane got in about nine, on time, and we took a taxi to 1 City Center. Harley didn't say a word and I wondered if he *knew* he was going to be canned or was just guessing. I couldn't help hoping it was the former.

Rode up to the 16th floor and went in to see Kraeger. On the way to the elevator Harley gulped one of his blue pills. I turned away. Harley once actually swore that there wasn't an executive of worth in America who didn't take tranquilizers before meetings.

Kraeger's secretary sent us right in and there was Ike looking, as usual, slightly larger than life with those damned awkward feet of his. His shoe budget, he once told me, was over $500 a year. Ike and Harley shook hands, two St. Bernards, the same age, the same backgrounds, mechanical engineering and the Air Force. I watched them.

We were all the same age: 59. Ike looked a little tense, I thought. He didn't ask us to sit down, and that made Harley even more nervous. "We're going to meet in Tom's office," Ike said. I asked him what it was about, more hopeful now about the appropriations showdown since Tom Frohman was vice-president in charge of manufacturing and equipment and no new equipment could go into any plant without his OK. Frohman had his soft spots, but you could do business with him; he was a wheel in the company. He'd been under Kraeger just a couple of years ago and now was way over him. Marrying into the ——— family hadn't hurt.

I was always impressed with Frohman's office. It was big and it had windows on two sides. One side you could see the river, the downtown buildings, and the highway coming down out of the hills with cars moving in a steady stream. The other side you could see the canal and barges and more downtown. Paintings on the wall, lots of books, a nice thick carpet. I couldn't help comparing it with my office or Merritt's in Detroit. We faced out onto the factory that made all these paintings and books possible.

Tom is tall, lanky, a Texan originally. He's got a lazy way of talking but he always gets right to the point. He's fifty and looks forty. Ike hates him, I know, but Tom is moving up fast in the company so Ike just suffers.

"Sit down, Harley, Ike, Frank," Tom said, and we all sat down around the round table by the bookcase. I put my briefcase on study seriously was a delusion. It was too late for studies now; someone in Pittsburgh just ordered it to cover his tracks when Detroit's increased production and efficiency started raising eyebrows down there. Nevertheless it was something positive Robertson could do—there was always a chance. And so with his two young engineers and Steve Heiser, he began a marathon, working 15 hours a day, 7 days a week, sketching out rough flow patterns, major innovations, new equipment, which buildings would have to come down, which had to be revamped. He costed it out. For a little over two million dollars, he figured, they could make Baker efficient and competitive for the next 12-15 years.

On a Saturday afternoon less than two weeks after the request from Pittsburgh he took the plans home with him. They were in longhand, with corrections and duplications still in them, but there was no time to lose. He called up an engineer friend who did not work at Baker and they got together the next day—Sunday —and went over the plans in detail. The friend made two good changes but as a whole he liked the plans as they were. Monday morning Robertson called Pittsburgh.

That same afternoon the corporation's chief engineer flew down. Robertson and his two young engineers and the maintenance supervisor, met with the chief engineer in the back of a public restaurant on Grand River Avenue, a few blocks from the plant and they went over the plans. The chief engineer was enthusiastic. He liked the plans; he wanted to rebuild it. The hopes of the young engineers bloomed. And Robertson knew that they too had suspected the plant was scheduled to be closed down. With the flush of excitement caused by the work itself now over, Robertson found himself, he says, still skeptical.

The chief engineer took the plans back to Pittsburgh and when he called two mornings later he greeted Robertson with: "Well, Gloomy Gus, my whole engineering staff thinks you've done a great job."

But, of course, the final decision lay with the people upstairs. It hung fire for more than eight weeks. During that time business continued to improve, morale was good, and Robertson felt less tormented about the deception he was living, and about having to notify his people. Perhaps, just perhaps, Pittsburgh would see the good sense of keeping the plant near the source of demand.

Pittsburgh had never understood the automotive paint industry, its problems, the way it had to react day to day to demands of an automobile factory ten blocks away. The Pennsylvania Corporation lived in a skyscraper 400 miles away and overlooked more than 45 paint and glass plants throughout the world. They never understood how finely attuned Baker was to the specialized, pressurized demands of the automobile industry. Still, the study—the first complete study that had even been made of Baker—plus the fine production records they were making in the past few months, could wake them up. They could change their mind. They had a responsibility toward their stockholders; a new automated plant in another state was a big investment, a gamble, while Baker, if properly managed and cared for, was a sure thing. There was a good chance. No—a better than good chance.

Then on August 31, one week before Labor Day, the bubble burst.

Robertson's phone from Pittsburgh rang, a direct line that did not go through the Baker switchboard.

On the other end of the phone was Tom Frohman. "Frank," he said, "that was a damn fine study, but we're going ahead with our original plans."

That was all he said.

Frank Robertson said: "Very good, Tom," and that was all he said, and after exchanging a few words about the weather in Detroit, they hung up.

That was it, and the net effect of the emergency engineering study had been to delay even longer telling his people the truth. Angry, bitter, Robertson was now determined to get that process started, and to hell with what Pittsburgh thought about it.

From the Recollections of Frank R. Robertson

August, 1963

Wednesday. Thirty-seven years with the company and this is the first time I'm doing things against their express wishes. But I'm the man on the spot. And I know what's best for

Baker and for the men, and for me too, for that matter. And so today, drove over to the old deserted Whearley Machine Shop on 7 Mile and took George Whearley, now retired, into my confidence about Baker. It took him by surprise. Heard we were doing well, but could understand that unless the company took the bull by the horns and built a new plant in Detroit, the old crazy patchwork of ours had to go sooner or later. Because of his experience with closing and relocating his own 350 employee plant, George was pessimistic about my chances of a smooth transfer. "People'll get mad at you, Robbie, and the first thing you'll find is an assembly line breaking down. It'll be a bent part or something. Then just as you're about to make a delivery to Chrysler, a truck'll have a flat tire. Grievances you should be able to contain will get out of hand, and you'll be spending three days out of six in arbitration." George's advice: don't tell them till three weeks before. It sounds hard, George said, but if he'd given three weeks' notice instead of 90 days, he would have saved a lot of money. He lost over $100,000 in the transfer of operations. Play it close to the vest was his advice. When I told him I was talking about two years' notice, he thought I was out of my mind. Maybe I am.

Friday. Bought Oscar Potts lunch at the Dearborn Inn today to find out how his closing had gone last year. Oscar was industrial relations manager of Ace-Marvin, auto parts company. They had about 400 employees. He was surprised too about Baker. Made him sad. Felt Baker was as much a part of Detroit as Briggs, Vernors, Burroughs, the auto factories. He just sat there and shook his head. I asked him how his closing had gone and he said: "Poorly, Robbie, but that's because we didn't prepare the men. There weren't any strikes or sabotage, but a lot of people took off right away to hunt for new jobs. Times were good, the way they are now. That works against you." It turns out Oscar gave his people two months' notice which he thought was just about right. He lost money on the transfer of operations but wouldn't say how much. He thought that you could close a plant and open a new one and make it a smooth transfer and not lose money, but the odds were against you. When he helped close Ace-Marvin he read some literature on the subject and saw somewhere a statistic that said two out of three plants went to pieces in a closing that lasted longer than two weeks. Just the same Oscar didn't think there was any God-given economic rule that said a plant had to go to pieces while it was closing, though as an old personnel man and contract negotiator he didn't see how you could do the decent thing by the men and work for the corporation at the same time. When I told him we were thinking about final closing in December, 1965, more than two years from now, he agreed with Whearley. "It's too long, Robbie. They'll blow up the place before that." I was to think about those words of his the following August when part of the plant did blow up. I wondered if old Oscar Potts was remembering his prediction then.

Monday. I went to the public library and asked for any materials they had on plant closings. The material, about woolen mills closing in Massachusetts, made depressing reading. Notice was given to the men and the plants closed up months before their target dates. Everything seemed to bear out Ike Kraeger's warnings. I returned to the plant more undecided than before.

Tuesday. Bill Marciniak, maintenance supervisor on the 2nd shift, came in to see me. "Frank," he says, "there's rumors flying about that they're going to close down Baker."

"Hell, Bill, those rumors have been flying about for years."

"Yeah, I know, Frank, but my wife wants a bigger house. We've spotted one out in Livonia. It's going to take all our dough and I want to know how sure my future is here. Do I go ahead and buy that house?"

Well, here it was. Right on the spot. And not a damn general reassurance did I have the right to give Bill. He'd worked at Baker for more than 15 years. One of the most devoted people we had. What was I supposed to tell him? I said: "Bill, I've heard the rumors too. Why don't you sit tight for a while till I try to get at the bottom of them?" He looked at me, and he knew what I knew he knew. We were both not fooling anyone. He shook his head glumly. "Thanks, Frank, I guess I put you on the spot." He went out, a very sober man. Pretty soon another rumor would be on its way. Old Robertson told

Marciniak not to buy a house: Baker's going to fold soon. And, by God, that wasn't far from the truth.

Other people have been coming to me. People wanting to buy homes or to remodel them or to invest money in this or that. Are they serious or are they testing out the Marciniak rumor? The plant is filled with rumors. What do I tell them to do? I can't go on much longer like this.

Friday. I dialed Howard Green's number in Pittsburgh. Howard is industrial relations manager for all of the corporation's plants in the coatings and resin division. He'd been plant manager here from 1945-50. He knew the men here as well as I did. He knew the plant. He'd handled all the contract negotiations. If I couldn't get Howard to see the inhumanity of this, then no one would.

"What's up, Frank?" he said.

"Howard, the men are working like hell here for the company."

"I know that, Frank," Howard chuckled. "You're making some people here look pretty foolish."

"Howard," I said bluntly, "we owe them the truth about the plant. I think the men ought to be notified soon. Rumors are flying all around. People are coming to me wanting to know whether they should buy new houses, remodel old ones. They want to know about their future. They've got a moral right to be told, Howard."

"Frank," Howard said guardedly, "I guess you know that Ike, Frohman, and I have talked about this."

"I know you have, Howard. I spoke to Ike last week, but I'll tell *you*, and then I'll tell the rest of them right up to Wysse Allen: I'm not going to be responsible for this place or the company's image if we don't let them know soon. I don't like living a lie, not in front of men I've worked with all my life. Howard, you know these people as well as I do. Damn it, Howard, these are decent, loyal, human beings."

"Frank," Howard said, "let me call you back. I'm going to set up a meeting with Allen and Frohman. The decision will have to come from them.

"Will you back me up, Howard?"

He hesitated a second and then he said: "I'll back you all the way, Frank."

I hung up feeling better for the first time in weeks. There are good and bad things about Howard Green, but he's first and foremost a Baker man. Anyone who ever worked here: hourly or salary, is a Baker man for the rest of his life.

Tuesday. Howard called back this afternoon. A meeting to consider the timing on notifying the men has been set up for a week from tomorrow. I'm to come down and plead my case.

Thursday. We're number one in Chrysler ratings again. I got word from Chrysler management this morning. Also word from cost accounting that we've gone from nine gallons per man-hour to twelve gallons. Which fits in with our overall production figures and will make good ammunition in Pittsburgh next week.

Friday. Problem at 11 A.M. Lee Jones and Harry Teed came to me very upset. It seems that Farkas, our Hungarian DP filter press operator has quietly gone and bid on a job as kettle operator helper in the resin department, which would pay him five cents more, but it is a job he has neither seniority nor qualifications for. Unfortunately, no one else has bid on it and he has somehow slipped in. It would be all right except that the men in the resin department hate his guts. He's lazy and arrogant and turns his English on and off. He thinks the world owes him a living because he was a freedom fighter in Budapest. Lee Jones has been trying to fire him for over a year now. Harry says none of the men in the resin department will work if he starts operating a kettle. In fact, they're sitting on their hands right now. Jones says we could drum up an excuse and fire him. He can get a guard to swear he saw him taking out tools last week. Typical Lee Jones thinking. That's something else I have to ponder. How to close up this plant with a human being like Jones in charge of personnel? Anxious to fire everyone in sight. Another military godsend from Ike Kraeger. Another ex-colonel. God protect us from these ex-colonels. But this is a genuine problem. And I tell Harry to tell his boys in the resin department that Farkas won't be working there yet, and I tell Jones to ask Perry DeMoss to come over Monday afternoon so we can talk this thing out. Perry, the union rep, has been pretty reasonable on most things.

Monday. In the afternoon Perry DeMoss came over and we talked about the Farkas case. Perry's back was up. Ned Rockwell sat with him. On our side of the table: Lee Jones, Charley Burns, and me. Jones, for once, shut up. Rockwell glowered at him. Charley presented our side of the case. The men in the resin department won't work with Farkas. I spoke about Farkas's peculiar personality. Maybe it was that way with all Hungarian freedom fighters. Perry didn't say anything. Sat there silent and grim. Then all of a sudden he exploded.

"He bid on the job the way he was supposed to and he got it," Perry said. "I don't see the problem. A bunch of guys in the resin department don't like the way he looks. I'll take care of them. What's the problem?"

No one said anything. I said softly: "No problem, Perry, if you'll see that the work goes on in the resin department. We don't want a grievance as you know. The plant's going full blast and I don't want to see any of the men lose work."

"They'll work," Perry said grimly, and he and Rockwell got up to leave, but not before Ned got in a parting shot at Lee Jones and me. "You bastards always think the union can be had, don't you?"

And out they went. Jones was furious but Charley and I laughed. Ned had a foul tongue and as chairman of the union committee within the plant he used it every chance he got. Charley was dubious about DeMoss' chances of calming the men down, but I thought he would. He's got to. He's put himself on the line. As I think back on that little incident, our mistake with Perry, *my* mistake, was in bringing up the fact that Farkas was a Hungarian and no one liked him. A little like saying someone was a Negro and no one liked him. But Perry should have known better. Baker had never been that kind of plant and he, a Negro, and a Baker man for more than 20 years, knew it better than anyone. Still, Perry has always had a chip on his shoulder and beware the man with a chip on his shoulder who gets power. He becomes a real dictator. Perry DeMoss has it in him to become a real dictator if he ever rises in the union. For his sake and for the sake of the people he represents, I hope he doesn't.

Tuesday. I was going over some production figures from accounting to take down to Pittsburgh tomorrow when Harold Peterson came in my door looking distraught. Harold was sales manager in charge of refinish. His hair was all over his face and I thought: *Oh God, not now.* Harold had had problems in the past and I went through a lot of them with him then, but I didn't have time for it now.

"Frank," he said, "you're going down to Pittsburgh tomorrow, aren't you?"

"Yes," I said, wondering how he knew, and then thought that probably everyone in the sales division—both original finish and refinish—must know more than they gave out. They were constantly in touch with Pittsburgh and they must have been getting now the kind of tip-off questions that accounting got three months ago.

"Frank," Harold said, and his hands were moving all over the place—and I was thinking, *Not now, Harold, not now*—"let's have lunch together."

"Sure, Harold," I said, thinking that I could spare time very poorly indeed. But I couldn't have Harold cracking up at this time.

We ate at the Terrace Lounge on Greenfield, and I bought him a drink. He calmed down a little, but he'd heard from Maxwell in Pittsburgh that Baker was on the skids. And what was going to happen to him? He was fifty-four years old, making good money here, had lived all his life in Detroit, his boy in Milwaukee depended upon him, and on and on Harold went and talked about his wife's extravagances, their summer home up in Tawas and his boy in Milwaukee again—I thought we'd straightened out the boy in Milwaukee over a year ago. The "boy" was thirty years old and was a Baker salesman under Harold. Harold had carried him on credit and the "boy" ran up a bunch of bills and Harold had to take an enforced vacation from work because of worry and tension. I put the "boy" on a cash basis, and advised Harold to get himself another salesman in Milwaukee, which he hadn't done yet. I was willing to go a long way with Harold because he was a great sales manager, and he knew the paint business and the people a sales manager should know in the auto plants. But it struck me as he poured out his woes that Harold was going to be a problem during this closing, when he didn't necessarily have to be one. There were no plans to move refinish sales out of Detroit. Original finish would stay here too and report to Cleveland. Lou Arnot was in charge of that. Lou could take this in stride. Harold would report to the new plant in Ohio. All that meant was lifting up a phone.

I thought of all this as I listened to him and understood from his nervous conversation that he thought I was going down to Pittsburgh tomorrow to get the final decision on whether or not Baker was to close. I decided to play along on his misinformation.

"Harold," I said, "you and I know something like this has been in the cards a long time, and there's nothing anyone can do about it. The corporation has an obligation to its stockholders and that's all there is to it. But I'm pretty certain that any relocation won't affect you. What the hell, we're still in the automotive paint business and the automobile factories are still largely right here in Michigan and we're selling to them in Michigan. You're not going to be moved anywhere."

He heard me and nodded, and kept stirring the ice in his glass with a spoon. But after a while he calmed down enough to talk about a problem he was having with his northern California salesman and did I think it might be a good idea to bring him back for a brush-up course? As he got lost in the specifics of this tiny problem, his nervousness left and he was

himself again. But it was a close thing. Harold has been in and
out of institutions at various times in his life. The next two
years was one time we could not afford a prolonged rest for
him.

Home late, and Doris and I went out to dinner. She wanted
to know about the plant, about Harold Peterson, about Lee
Jones, the Farkas problem. She can't get enough of it. It sad-
dens me.

Wednesday. The same early morning flight to Pittsburgh, and
a cab to 1 City Center.

This time to Howard Green's office. Howard and his assistant,
Ralph Muzetti, were waiting for me. They both looked grave
though Muzetti, a lawyer and a rising star in the corporation,
didn't look as concerned as Howard. Which was natural.
Howard was a Baker man. He looked as though he hadn't
slept for a few nights running and his eyes were a little blood-
shot. Howard had had a drinking problem in Detroit that we
both worked on, and it was supposed to be solved by now. He
was a tall man, and had put on weight lately; he didn't look
good at all. I felt sorry for him. I never thought he belonged in
the corporate world, but a man doesn't turn down a promo-
tion. We made small talk about Detroit for a few seconds and
then went right up to Wysse Allen's office. No dilly-dallying
around this time. Allen's office was filled with people and
you could feel the tension. It scared me a little at first. I'd
brought this meeting on and I think at this moment I first
began to realize the power I wielded over the corporation. I
could damn near put them out of the automotive paint business forever if I messed up their closing. Once they lost Chrysler and Ford orders in this year of plenty and pressure, they'd
never get them back. Especially not from Ohio. The Baker
plant was supposed to fold, but the Baker label was to go on
and on. Detroit had to keep going till Ohio was ready to take
over. And to make this work, they had to have a plant manager who was with them heart and soul, which at this moment
I was not.

Wysse Allen in bow-tie, hair neatly combed, chain-smoked
and looked cold-eyed at everyone. Tom Frohman slumped in
a chair, relaxed but solemn. Ike Kraeger stared mournfully at

his feet. Besides Howard Green, Muzetti, and myself, there were three new people. Not new to me, because they'd been in on our contract negotiations last year, but new to the closing. Dave Lloyd, corporation counsel, Mike Harrah, a bright young lawyer, a protege of Dave's and rising fast in the company's legal department, and a man named Porter, an actuary.

Allen began by stating that I wanted to notify the Baker people about the plant's closing and what were the reactions of the other people to this?

One after another they spoke against it. The same litany. Records show that two out of three plants go to pieces if men are notified too early. They couldn't afford to take the chance. Sabotage, slow-downs, union problems. Then Howard Green up and spoke his piece. He said that Robbie thought it was the right and moral thing to do and he agreed with me, but that he also agreed with everyone else here that it was a gamble. And that's how Howard Green backed me up. I couldn't help smiling. Finally Wysse Allen turned those eyes on me. "Robbie?" he asked.

I was calm. All my nervousness had fled. I was on the firing line and they were not. They needed me; I didn't need them. I was talking from a position of strength, and if the others didn't know it, I knew that Wysse Allen did. I said softly: "I think our people should be notified because it's the right and decent thing to do. They have been loyal to us over the years and we owe them that. Right now they know something is fishy, and it's a good question how long you can expect anyone to run a business when a wide-open farce is being played out. If the plant falls apart through misunderstanding and mistrust, I will not be responsible. The company has an image in Detroit, and I presume it will have one in Ohio. It's not going to have much of an image anywhere if this goes on much longer. You're still something to respect and admire, but if we play this game out much longer you'll be nothing. It's a gamble, I know. I'm gambling on the men being loyal, and you're gambling on me. I think we can all make it work if we're honest. If we're not honest we're dead."

That's what I said. Maybe not in those words, but it was like that, and when I finished no one said anything. Allen just

smoked and looked out the window. Ike sighed and Tom
Frohman had his eyes closed. Howard Green was studying
his papers. I noticed Harrah, though, was looking at me curiously. He was a tough young man and was to play a big part
in the closing.

Finally Allen said: "I think we all respect your feeling for
Baker, Robbie. At the moment I'm inclined to believe we
should notify the men." He glanced at his watch. "A final
decision will be made on this before Friday. Thanks for coming down."

And that was that. A flight down for a one minute speech.
Well, I spent the rest of the morning talking with Frohman
about equipment problems, and talked with Howard Green
about possible personnel problems that could come up. As I
was leaving I passed Harrah in the hall. He's short and stocky
and wears red suspenders, and he has a derisive cocky air
about him. He looks oddly like a union lawyer. He clapped
me on the back and said: "See you soon, Mr. Robertson."

And that was that.

Two days later Howard Green called me and said Allen had
decided to go along with me and notify the people. "Frank,"
said Howard, "they're taking a big trust in you."

"Not in me," I said, "in my people. And we'll repay that trust,
Howard. Don't you worry."

"I know that," Howard said.

Brave words. Braver than I felt, but I felt better as I saw that
my days of deceiving were coming to an end.

Before the Letter

Although he didn't know it at the time, Frank Robertson still had to go through two months of deceiving people when he returned from Pittsburgh. It was to take about seven weeks to compose the first letter notifying the men of the possibility of the plant closing. On September 15, Robertson received from Howard Green a first draft of the notification. Robertson felt it was a complicated legal letter, and worse, cold. It had been drafted by six people: Green, Harrah, Lloyd, Porter, Frohman, Kraeger, and Muzetti—and looked it. It was supposed to be signed by one man—Frank Robertson.

Robertson sent it back to Green with a note saying "If this is the final draft, it better go out under a signature other than mine."

So Pittsburgh went to work again and three weeks later Green called again and read Robertson another draft, slightly longer than the first but more personal. Robertson immediately objected to one part, a sentence that said the company was considering terminating its Detroit operations because the plant was "obsolete and worn out."

"Howard," Robertson said over the phone, "we're making more money than we ever did before. We're number one in Chrysler ratings and still moving up in Ford's. That line will make us the laughing stock of the paint industry in Detroit."

In fact, at the meetings of the Paint Club in Detroit, an informal social group of paint executives who met once a week to drink and play cards and billiards and discuss mutual problems, Robertson was being toasted as the miracle maker. The man who brought Lazarus back from the dead. Robertson accepted their joshing in good spirits, but winced at what their reaction would be to a letter saying that Baker was worn out.

Howard Green agreed to have another go at it.

About a week later Mike Harrah, the young lawyer, called Robertson and told him he was coming down from Pittsburgh with what he thought might be the final letter.

They met at a Holiday Inn motel and Robertson read the letter that would go out under his name. He made a few minor changes

47

to phrase it more as he himself would write it, but he said it was all right. He and Harrah had a drink together. Harrah said he thought it was still too early to notify the men but Robertson insisted it be done now.

Before "now" could occur, Harrah had to go back with Robertson's minor changes and show them to the committee for approval.

Pittsburgh, of course, took their time approving of the minor changes and ten days later Green called to say he and Harrah would be bringing the letter down on Monday, November 10, for Robertson to sign, and would he line up a mimeographing service downtown to run it off and supply them with name and address plates? Green expected that he, Harrah, Robertson, and Lee Jones would stuff and mail the envelopes themselves.

Early on the morning of the 10th, Robertson called Lee Jones, his industrial relations manager into his office and told him what was happening. Thus Jones, a man Robertson personally detested, became the first Baker employee to be officially notified of the closing. Jones pretended that he knew all along and Robertson thought that just might be so since Jones was in direct contact with Howard Green on industrial relations matters.

Harrah and Green arrived about 11 A.M. with the final letter which was dated Wednesday, November 13. Robertson read it through and signed it. Then the four men took it downtown to the Echelon Printing Service on Fort Street and had 600 copies mimeographed. They had taken a Pitney-Bowes stamp machine with them from Baker and Robertson knew at that moment that rumors would be spreading behind them like wildfire.

While the letter was being mimeographed, the four men had lunch at the Shelby and discussed procedure from now on. Harrah said that after the letter went out they would have to wait for the union's reaction, taking it one step at a time. Robertson's first move should be to get word to Perry DeMoss, the union rep, through the shop committee to meet on the morning of the 13th. While the meeting was going on, or soon after, the letter should be posted on all bulletin boards, along with a notice that copies of this letter were being mailed that morning to all Baker personnel.

Harrah was going back to Pittsburgh, but suggested that Green stay on to be in on the meetings with the supervisory personnel. However, he felt neither he nor Green should be at the first meeting with DeMoss, the union rep.

Frank Robertson remembers asking at this time if the company had gone into their strategy for collective bargaining on the closing. Were they going to give severance pay, for example? If so, how much? What about the pension plans? The insurance plans? Sickness and accident plans? What about the early retirement people?

He was particularly worried about people like Otto Mueller, supervisor of the resin department, who would miss early retirement by one year; with no union to represent him, he would lose out on his pension and he'd be too old to start anywhere else.

Harrah replied that he was certain that all these matters were being discussed at high levels and that a severance pay agreement was definitely under consideration even though there was nothing in the union contract that called on them to pay it, but for God's sake, Robertson was not to mention severance pay in the first meeting. Robertson was to do no more than read the letter. Management was putting them on notice, taking this one step at a time.

"What about the meeting with the supervisory personnel?" Robertson asked.

"Howard will be there with you," Harrah said. "My advice, for their sake as well as yours, is to play it the same way. Just read the letter."

After lunch the four men returned to the printing company and stuffed envelopes. It took them most of the afternoon. Then he and Green drove Harrah out to the airport. Lee Jones was to set up the meeting with DeMoss on Wednesday the 13th at 10 A.M.

All day Tuesday, the 12th, Howard Green hung around the plant, visiting various departments, chinning with some of the old-timers. He and Tom Morgan, now supervisor of the second shift, and Robertson had dinner together that night. Green drank too much and Robertson was certain then that the closing of Baker was having an effect on him too.

During the dinner Robertson broke the news to Tom Morgan about the closing, the letters that were being mailed the next day, and the meetings with all the supervisory personnel, sales and office staff he had set up for early morning.

Tom took it well. A 1965 closing would give him the early retirement he always wanted. Though Morgan along with Matt Gargan, Lloyd Shearer, and Robertson himself had been responsible for the relaxed atmosphere of Baker, the plant had never been

more than a second best bed for him. Morgan had a college degree; he had a teacher's certificate he never used, for he graduated
in the depression when no jobs were available. He would have
made a splendid high school coach, and one of the best-run industrial recreation programs in Detroit was the one Morgan ran
at Baker when he had been industrial relations manager there.
But Tom's weakness as a negotiator had prompted Howard Green
to bump him from the industrial relations job to superintendant
of the second shift. Tom Morgan disliked Green intensely and
vice versa.

But Robertson knew that easygoing Tom Morgan was the kind
of industrial relations manager he'd ultimately need to close the
plant successfully, and that was why he asked him to dinner with
Green that night.

Wednesday morning Robertson remembers as a rainy morning.
His wife got up with him but before she could say anything, Robertson said: "Now don't worry about me. We've prepared well for
this day."

He didn't want a repetition of what happened the first day he
went in as plant manager last April. Sometimes during the morning
then a huge vase of flowers had been delivered to his office. He had
looked at it, astounded. The note with it said "Congratulations,
Robbie," and was signed by his wife. After all he'd told her—
that it was no time for celebrating—she had sent him flowers! She
had understood absolutely nothing of what he was going through.
Much later, when Robertson was feeling truly sorry for himself,
he would compare the arrival of those flowers to the arrival of
flowers in a funeral parlor and then it would not seem so unfitting.

Now, although of course she wouldn't send flowers, God knows
he didn't want her calling him to "see how the men were taking it."
He told her brusquely that he'd fill her in on all the details that
night.

He picked up Howard Green at the Holiday Inn at 7:30 A.M.
Howard had the box of envelopes with him. They drove to the
branch substation on Woodward and dropped all the letters in
an outside box. Then they drove to the plant. It had been agreed
when Harrah was present that Green was to break the news to the
supervisory force, and Robertson to the office and union committee,
but now Green said he thought Robertson ought to do it all.

When Robertson protested, Green replied: "All you've got to

do is read them the letter. You started this whole thing, damn it."

Robertson was silent. He could see how badly Green felt and it was true that he had brought it on.

When they got to the plant, Green went to Robertson's office to wait while Robertson made his customary early morning visit to one of the departments. This morning he went to shipping and receiving where they were loading a truck of original finish for Chrysler. He stayed a few minutes and then walked back to his office, arriving at 8:30 A.M. Then he and Green walked to the big color conference room which ordinarily was used for sales conferences. There were twenty people in there waiting that morning. Men Robertson had known all his adult life. Men he'd started work with. Lean, humorous Will Calloway, who had started at Baker just fourteen months after Robertson and who had risen from clerk to salesman and stayed there; there was Matt Gargan of S and R, another old-timer, and Lloyd Shearer, his new production manager and one of his oldest friends. There was Steve Heiser, supervisor of maintenance. All the supervisors were there—from Grinding, Mixing and Blending; the stock control manager; both sales managers, Harold Peterson of Refinish, Lou Arnot of Original Finish; the office manager, Jack Whitsell; the process engineers; Lee Jones and Lee's assistant Charley Burns; Tom Morgan, superintendent on the second shift; the technical director of research and development—every department head in the plant was there, sitting around the long oval table, surrounded by glossy color charts, shiny plastic models of all 1963 Ford and Chrysler cars, and a map of Baker's sales regions.

Robertson remembers: "I stood there a minute and all I could see were wide open questioning eyes staring back at me. I sat down and said I regretted having to call this meeting, but it was on a subject that affected us all. As they knew, in 1958 the company had undertaken a big product alignment study which pointed out certain facts that had long been obvious to most of us old-timers: the plant was a high-cost plant, an old plant, and might have to close some day. 'Accordingly', I said, 'I would like to read you a letter from the company which has been mailed this morning to the home of each employee of the Baker plant, both salaried and hourly, and which will be posted on the bulletin boards in the plant by noon today.'

"Then I read them the letter. It took about two minutes to read it. When I was done, no one said a thing. I looked at them. Some of them were stony-faced, others pale, others just looked like it hadn't registered at all. These men were all in their forties and fifties, and a few lucky ones in their early sixties.

"I said: 'I know this brings up a multitude of questions. All I can ask you is not to ask any questions now. There will be more meetings with individuals as well as groups. The company will keep you informed.'

"I paused. They just stared at me. I said: 'While this is a shock to you and me, All I can say is: now we know. This gives us time to prepare ourselves. I, for one, am going to do the best job I know how. I know as a Baker man myself I can count on you. I don't know whether we'll succeed or fail with this closing but I know for me, I intend to walk out of this plant with my head up.'"

It was a line he would use again and again and which in the end would come home to haunt him.

"I stood up and Howard Green stood up and we left. Behind us was a silence, no comments, caustic or otherwise. But as they went down the hall outside my office I heard one man—Bob Lewis, the stock control manager, give a nervous laugh and say: 'Well, now we know.'"

The meeting with the top supervisory staff had lasted all of ten minutes. Howard Green left for Pittsburgh almost immediately. He and Robertson shook hands silently. There wasn't much to say. Before he got in a cab to go to his motel and then to the airport, Green repeated Harrah's advice about not doing anymore than reading the letter to the union committee at 10 A.M.

Before the 10 o'clock meeting with the union, however, Robertson had two more meetings. One at 9:15 was with the lower echelon salary people—foremen, clerks, technicians, and chemists. He said essentially the same things here that he'd said earlier. A few minutes later he met with the last of the salaried people—the ones he was in closest physical proximity to—the office group: cost accountants, computer operators, secretaries. The majority were women and he expected some tears and got them—though, as he later reflected, almost all the women were married and their husbands had jobs.

After this third and last meeting with the salaried people he had about 20 minutes to prepare himself for the meeting with the union.

This one, he knew, would not be a ten-minute meeting. He could ask them till he was blue in the face not to ask questions, but they would. His plan was to have Lee Jones read the letter to them.

He went to his office to wait. At 9:45 he heard the outercall ring for Ned Rockwell and he knew it was the guard announcing the arrival of Perry DeMoss, the union rep.

They would all go right to the cafeteria and speculate on what it could be about. He wondered how the letter would hit Perry DeMoss. How much of a fight the union would put up. How much of a fight could they put up? He re-read the letter. It was a good letter, honest and vague. It left a door open that wasn't really open. It was, he decided, not a good letter because it was honest but because it was vague.

His phone rang. It was Lee Jones. The union committee was on its way over for the meeting.

Robertson picked up his copy of the letter and went downstairs.

The Letter

11/13/63

Dear Fellow Employees:

I have for some time been aware of rumors circulating concerning the future of Baker. Rumors, as we all know, are often conflicting and confusing. Therefore I feel it is important to inform you now of the considerations the company has in regard to Baker.

The paint industry, as we all know, has much in common with other industries. Markets change, customers move, plants become obsolete, and there are the other normal changes which happen over periods of time that make imperative the study of current industry practices and facilities. Thus the Pennsylvania Corporation has for some time been studying this plant, as well as others, and at this moment is considering plans that, if put into effect, may result in closing the Baker plant sometime during the next year or so.

None of this will perhaps come as a surprise to those of us who have worked at Baker for a long time. The company knows, as we do, that it costs more to produce a gallon of paint here at Baker than it does at any of the other company plants. Baker's costs are high because we are using old machinery spread out in a number of buildings. At the same time we must compete with plants containing the latest in modern machinery in new, well-designed buildings. As we also all know, in our industry the markup on a gallon of automotive finish is quite low. If one is to compete, he has to have the highest possible production at the lowest possible cost. Extensive studies have taken place to determine whether Baker's production would be increased enough if the company installed the latest in modern equipment to justify the costs of these new installations. These studies have pointed out that even if extensive remodeling took place Baker would continue to be a high-cost plant because of the type and arrangement of the buildings that would house the new equipment and facilities.

To get a truly modern efficient plant here the company would have to tear down all our buildings and machinery and build an entirely new plant on this spot. Baker would of course be unable to manufacture automotive finish during this process. Other plants could possibly take up the slack, but they could not keep producing for the two or possibly three years that the construction of a new plant would require. If Baker was forced to drop out of the automotive finishes business during the construction of a new plant on this spot, we could find it impossible to get our old customers back.

I would add this: the considerations the company has for our plant are part of a larger picture involving several of the company's other plants. Similar situations exist in other plants in the division, and because of this and the fact that some of our customer's plants have relocated and there have been changes in their requirements, the corporation is considering a total realignment of its manufacturing operations in the Coatings and Resins Division. Involved in this realignment would be the transfer of manufacturing operations among plants as well as the building of a new automated plant which would produce several of the products now being manufactured at other plants including Baker. This new plant would not then replace Baker for it would not be manufacturing all of the products presently being produced at Baker. What the company is considering is a plant that would manufacture industrial finishes as well as some of the automotive finishes currently being manufactured here. At this time, these industrial finishes are being manufactured at other plants in the division. Southern Michigan would not be the appropriate geographical location for this kind of facility.

Let me emphasize that if the company decides to put these considerations into effect, this would not result in the closing of this plant for many months to come.

This has not been an easy letter for me to write. I have served at this plant for 37 years and I bear a deep affection for all of the people with whom I've worked. I regret with all my heart that we might be confronted with the possibility of having to close this plant, but as we all know, this is a very competitive industry, and one in which Baker has been finding it increasingly difficult to compete in the marketplace.

I assure you there will be conferences and meetings with the union shop committee during which we will explore whatever suggestions the committee may put forward with regard to these contemplated moves. As I indicated above, there have been no contracts let but I thought it was only fair to present to you all the facts that I have at the earliest possible time, rather than leave you at the mercy of confusing and conflicting rumors. Whatever proposals are made either by the union shop committee or any other employees in regard to whether the company should move along these contemplated lines will be given full consideration by me as well as the company in Pittsburgh. I would have preferred to have given you more definite information than this letter contains, but unfortunately I have none. As matters develop, however, it is my firm purpose to keep you fully informed.

Yours truly,

Frank R. Robertson,
Plant Manager

Union Rep

Name: Perry DeMoss
Age: 44
Married: Ruby Martinson, 6/29/46
Children: Steve, 22; Angela, 17; Roy, 15; Ruthie, 9; Esther, 3
Religion: Protestant
Employment: 1937–42, various jobs: janitor, painter, handyman
1942–43, U.S. Army, medical discharge
1943–63, Baker Color Company:
lye tank, shipping and receiving, lab technician, kettle operator—resin dept., maintenance dept.
1963–   , union representative, West Side Local
Residence: 18340 Rosedale, Detroit, Michigan
Health: generally good; diabetes discovered while at Baker, now under
control.

Warren Avenue in Detroit is a wide, treeless street with the traffic lights staggered to accommodate a pace of 35 miles per hour. Small stores, machine tool shops, and large factories line both sides of the street. Occasional large supermarkets, set back from the street, remind the visitor that on the sidestreets off the thoroughfare, be-hind the gas stations, the body shops, the factories, the abandoned stores, live people in little frame houses with gardens and porches and tire swings that hang from leafless maples.

Two blocks off the intersection of Warren and Livernois is West Side Local ——— of the United Automobile Workers of America. It is Walter Reuther's old local—the local from which the whole auto-mobile industry in America was organized back in the mid-thirties.

Today West Side Local ——— is housed in a modern cement block building with a neatly kept lawn in front. Inside are conference rooms, a 200-seat auditorium, a large modern kitchen in which sandwiches, soup, and coffee can be prepared for men on the picket lines.

Large glass doors separate the headquarters section of the building from the meeting rooms. In the headquarters area are some half a dozen small offices with beige or light blue paint over the cement blocks. The floors are brown linoleum. On the walls of the offices hang pictures of Walter Reuther, of President John F. Kennedy, of President Franklin Delano Roosevelt. Pictures of President Lyndon B. Johnson are noticeably absent. There are many family pictures.

West Side Local —— is an amalgamated local, meaning it represents many plants—96 in all—that either make cars or provide materials for car manufacturers. Altogether there are some 25,000 members of West Side Local with seven union staff members (union reps) to represent them in collective bargaining, grievance procedures, unfair labor practice claims. Perry DeMoss, one of the union reps, is personally responsible for close to 3,000 workers, 300 of whom, until the plant closed on December 10, 1965, were Baker employees.

DeMoss is a chunky, well-built, distinguished-looking man in his mid-forties. His hair is graying. He wears a short gray mustache, dresses conservatively in a dark gray-flecked suit. He is a Negro. Most of the time his face registers no emotion as he listens or speaks. He is careful, cautious, circumspect.

He is interested to learn that after the plant closing Frank Robertson went down to Arkansas. He nods when told that Robertson today is a sick man.

"He's suffering too," DeMoss says softly, "he's paying too. I don't feel sorry for him. A lot of them are sick. He didn't have to take that job—burying the plant. You say he says he wanted to make it as painless as possible for the men. I'm not so sure. The plant was a personal thing to Robertson. He promoted incompetent people on the basis of personal loyalty to him. He ran that plant like a politician. He was devious. Maybe he had to be. They put incompetent people over him. Merritt, who was plant manager before him, was one. Robertson really ran it then too. In the end, though, he got to the top. They used him to close it. Maybe they knew what he'd be best at."

Like Frank Robertson, Perry DeMoss started at the bottom, as a laborer. Unlike Robertson, he never got to the top, never made it to a salaried position. By necessity, he was forced to take a parallel track upwards in union politics.

When DeMoss went to work at Baker after his medical discharge from the Army in 1943, there were two kinds of jobs available to Negroes. One was work in salvage disposal—in the lye tank, a hot water tank in which you cleaned out cans and buckets, all equipment that had to be reused. It was dirty and sometimes dangerous work. The second kind of job open to blacks was working on the "bull gang"—unloading box cars and transporting stock from one building to another.

DeMoss worked in the lye tank for a little over a year, then applied for a vacant stock clerk's position in Shipping and Receiving that paid ten cents more an hour than the lye tank. He was ambitious, alert, intelligent. Whenever a vacancy was posted on the company bulletin boards, he bid for it by taking a test.

It was about 1946 that DeMoss first bumped heads with Howard Green, then plant manager at Baker. "It was new to them," DeMoss says, "someone putting in so boldly for advancement. Green tried to talk me out of it. He tried to talk me into leaving Baker. He said there was no real avenue of advancement for a man like me. He told me he thought I'd be better off going elsewhere. I told him I'd stay there from now on."

Sixteen years later in 1962, when DeMoss was chairman of the plant's union bargaining committee and Green had moved from Detroit to Pittsburgh where he was running industrial relations for the whole resins and coatings division, they found themselves on opposite sides of the table negotiating for a new contract. The union rep then, Hank Bassem, wasn't much, and DeMoss did most of the bargaining. It was a long and hard negotiation and when it was over and the contract was drawn up, Green, right in front of everyone, DeMoss says, right at the table, took out his business card and wrote down his home phone number and told DeMoss that if he ever wanted a job to call him. "Here's my home phone number, Perry," Green said, "not many people have it."

"And this," DeMoss says, "from the guy who had tried to talk me out of staying at Baker sixteen years before." He returns to his story. "Well, in '46 I did stay, though, and I got the job and it opened doors for everyone."

Baker was a good place to work, he says. Green was a tough, cold antagonist but always honest. A real man. According to DeMoss, Green made Baker a good place to work. So did Matt Gargan, Tom Morgan, and Lloyd Shearer.

"Baker was years ahead of itself in relation to togetherness among the employees. Ten percent of the employees were Negroes. On the whole a man was treated as a man, and things got to be the same for promotions."

After his early encounter with Green, DeMoss applied for and got a position in the research and development lab as a technician.

In 1947 he got interested in union politics. He ran for recording secretary on the plant bargaining committee and won. It was the first time a Negro had a position like that at Baker.

DeMoss worked in the lab for five years and then moved to the resin department where he earned top pay—$2.80 an hour. He was a kettle operator, in charge of four 2,000 gallon electric kettles in which resins were mixed for paints.

During this time he was also moving up the ladder of union politics. After two years of recording secretary he became chairman of the bargaining unit, a job he relinquished 15 years later in the spring of 1963 when he gave up 20 years of seniority to go into full-time union work as a union rep at West Side Local ———. Ned Rockwell, a committeeman who worked in shipping and receiving, took over as chairman.

DeMoss remembers Rockwell telephoning him on the morning of November 11 and saying that the company wanted a meeting with the committee and the union rep at 10 A.M. on the 13th.

"What about?" DeMoss asked.

"They won't say," Rockwell said.

Right then and there, DeMoss remembers, he knew it was pretty severe. He thought maybe it could be about the Lee Mays case which they'd finally settled the week before. One morning Mays, a stake truck driver with 18 years' seniority, had cussed out his supervisor and stormed off the job. He was gone for ten days and no one could locate him. The company fired him then. DeMoss got a call from Mays' sister. She said Lee was taken off a bus in Virginia, unconscious. After checking with various doctors and his famly, DeMoss found the condition was diagnosed as a tumor on the brain.

DeMoss immediately requested a meeting with Lee Jones, the industrial relations manager, and told him this put a different slant on things. Jones said Mays had quit and they weren't willing to reinstate him based on the medical evidence.

As far as the union was concerned, this was a genuine grievance. DeMoss wanted medical leave for Mays, as there was no doubt he was sick when he cussed out his supervisor and stormed off. He wanted Mays' seniority, Blue Cross, Sickness and Accident insurance retained, and he wanted Mays subject to reinstatement if and when his doctors said he was ready to come back to work.

He and Jones went back and forth on it for several weeks as doctors' reports continued to come in. Finally on Friday, November 1, Jones gave in and the threat of going to arbitration ended.

It had been an expensive settlement for the company and Perry DeMoss thought that conceivably the meeting on the 13th could be more about the Mays grievance.

He took the Mays file along, just in case.

We Laughed at the Time

For Ned Rockwell, the stocky, blunt-faced, blunt-talking chairman of the plant's union bargaining committee, that Tuesday started as any day. He punched in at shipping and receiving at 7 A.M. and went over to the tank house. He and Mitch Sims—whom everyone called "the old man" and of whom it was said "they built the goddamn tankhouse around him"—put a hose in a tank car of resin, adjusted the safety collars and opened the valves.

From 7:05 to 7:45 they emptied the tank car. At 7:45 Rockwell went over to the cafeteria for some coffee and a gander at the office girls' legs. While he was there a young fellow from the lab stopped at his table to complain about the kind of rubber gloves they were issuing him. Rockwell told him to talk to his supervisor about it, and when the man said he had and the supervisor told him to quit bitching, Rockwell wrote down his name and said he'd look into it. This was the kind of thing, a small safety measure, that could get out of hand quickly and turn into a larger grievance. It was Rockwell's job to take care of the men in the plant, to protect them, to make them aware of the power of their union shield.

The grievance procedure was a four-step plan for airing a complaint between the employee and the foreman. If the employee wasn't satisfied, a member of the union committee came in and spoke to the foreman. If satisfaction still wasn't received, the parties concerned, including now the chairman of the bargaining unit, took the grievance to the industrial relations manager sometimes with the union rep coming in from the outside. The last step of the grievance procedure was arbitration, often long and costly, involving top management of the plant and company and the union rep and possibly even a lawyer from the headquarters of the international union. If satisfaction still wasn't obtained then strike authorization would be sought from the international. All along the road written clauses specified how much time might elapse between steps, how notification of other parties was to be effected—everything in the procedure was designed to prevent grievances from escalating without just cause. Ninety percent of the grievances were stopped at Steps 1 or 2.

Rockwell made a note to talk to the lab man's supervisor. After that he drank coffee till 8:15 and gabbed with a girl he knew who worked in the main office and lived near him in Redford township. Then he went back to the tank house. The old man was reading the paper. Together they took some resin samples from a tank truck. Then he read the old man's paper till 9:15, at which time he returned to the cafeteria for the morning pinochle game.

The pinochle game, which had become a ritual more than ten years ago, was scheduled from 9:30 to 9:45. They had worked to an earlier starting time gradually through the years. This day, Rockwell remembers, it started early and ended a little later, and so he didn't get back to the tankhouse till almost ten. The old man was grumbling about his absence when the bell sounded. It was his outercall, #41. As chairman of the bargining committee Rockwell had an outercall along with supervisory personnel which sounded throughout the plant. He picked up the phone.

"Ned, this is Lee Jones," said the officious voice of the industrial relations manager, "can you get over to my office right away?"

"What's up?" Rockwell demanded.

He didn't like to move for any man. Especially this Army-type son of a bitch. As chairman of the committee, Rockwell believed that one of his most important jobs was to uphold the dignity of the working man, and that meant never taking any shit from management. In his capacity as a living symbol of the union Rockwell had, for instance, from time to time sworn publicly at every superintendent in the place. He believed it was always a bad thing for the men when they saw their shop chairman acting like a sheep before management.

"Come over and I'll tell you," Lee Jones said, and hung up on him.

You son of a bitch, Rockwell thought. Like everyone else in the plant, he hated Jones the ex-Army colonel and Pittsburgh's latest attempt to cut some of the fat they associated with Baker. Jones, of course, got nowhere. Not only did the men hate him, but Robertson and the rest of the old guard—Tom Morgan, Matt Gargan, Lloyd Shearer—all disliked him. Jones wasn't a Baker man and never would be. They all, hourly and salaried alike, referred to him as "the colonel."

Rockwell put on his jacket. "Where you going now?" the old man asked him.

"Union business," Rockwell said and grinned. "Have another cup of coffee, Mitch. I'll bring you back a doughnut."

The old man swore at him and Rockwell, laughing, left the tankhouse and went over to the receiving dock. He went inside and into Matt Gargan's office. The big supervisor was hunched over his desk toting up some figures.

"Hello, Ned," he said, without looking up.

"Matt, I got to take Dick Tyner along with me on some union business to the Colonel's office."

Matt waved his hand. "Go ahead."

There never was any trouble with Gargan. He'd been a union man himself before he moved into management. They always bought off the good union men with salary jobs. Then they usually changed and became sons of bitches. Not Gargan though. He was all right. Maybe a little tricky at times. You had to keep a double eye on Matt because he knew so much about union thinking and procedure.

Rockwell found Tyner, his recording secretary, helping load a pallet onto a fork truck. He told him to drop it and come along with him.

"I don't know what this is about, but I want my recording secretary with me," Rockwell said.

Tyner signed out and the two of them set out across the yard to the main office building. There are five men on the Baker union committee. The chairman, his recording secretary, and three committeemen. They, along with the union rep at the local, do the bargaining on grievances and contract matters. They can call on legal help from the international at Solidarity House in downtown Detroit whenever they feel they need it.

Crossing the yard with Dick Tyner, Rockwell was wondering if the matter of the rubber gloves for the lab technician had got to Jones but he rejected that; it was too small an item and could be settled between the shop steward in Building 5 and the supervisor. It shouldn't even be necessary for him as chairman to get involved.

Jones was dictating a letter when they arrived. He didn't interrupt it; he didn't ask them to sit down. When he was done he turned to them and said:

"Ned, we want to have a meeting tomorrow morning at 10 A.M. with the committee and DeMoss."

"Who's 'we'?" Rockwell asked.

"Me, Charley Burns, and Mr. Robertson."

Charley Burns was his assistant. A do-nothing college boy.

"What's it about?"

"I can't tell you now. Could you make it at ten?"

Ten was usually when they had the meetings that involved Perry DeMoss. Perry didn't have to come to work at the local till nine o'clock.

"Why not?" Rockwell said.

Once outside the office he told Tyner to round up the other members of the committee, making sure they signed out with their supervisors, and tell them to meet in the cafeteria. Meanwhile he was going to call up DeMoss.

He called DeMoss at the local and told him what Jones had told him. No, Jones wouldn't tell him what it was about. Perry said he'd be there at ten the next day.

Rockwell remembers that as he walked to the cafeteria to meet with the other members of the committee he rejected the idea that it would have something to do with the contract. The contract had just been signed a year ago July. It was a good contract. For the company too. He didn't see why they'd want to renegotiate it.

When he got to the cafeteria Rockwell told the other members of the committee the rep was coming in tomorrow morning at 10 for a meeting. They were all to be in on it. They sat around the rest of the morning and most of the afternoon too speculating on what it could be about. Guys floated in on them from time to time, wondering why the bargaining committee was meeting. Rockwell remembers that he didn't like telling them that "they want a meeting with us tomorrow but won't tell us what it's about. The rep is coming."

He does remember at one point one of the committeemen, he doesn't remember whether it was Jimmy Bailey or Wayne Bender saying: "I bet they want to close the son of a bitch up."

"We all laughed at that," Rockwell remembers.

A House'll Stand Up
if It's Got Love in It

Name: Ned Rockwell
Age: 41
Married: Mary Chambers
Children: Ned Jr, 18; Mary, 17; Ruth Ann, 14; Joseph, 12; Evelyn, 10;
    Rose, 7; Bobby, 5; Jefferson, 4
Religion: none formally, born Catholic; wife and children Presbyterians
Employment: 1945–65, Baker Color Company:
                                lab technician, utilityman, lacquer mixer,
                                shipping and receiving, tankhouse attendant,
                                shop steward—1950–53, recording secre-
                                tary—1953–63, Chairman of bargaining
                                committee—1963–65
          1966,   laborer, Beaver Machine Tool Company
Residence: 14043 Gorton, Redford Township, Michigan
Health: poor. Suffers from arthritis, ulcers, hypoglycemia, low blood
    pressure; has occasional dizziness and blackouts; absent from
    work month of January, 1967—"just couldn't get enough strength
    to go."; physician has recommended psychiatric consultation;
    Rockwell refuses to consider it; in 1966, laid up six weeks with
    pneumonia.

Ned and Mary Rockwell and their eight children live in a small brick and frame house in a subdivision just outside the city limits of Detroit. The two oldest children sleep in the basement that Rockwell finished last year; the other six share two bedrooms. They are all well behaved.

"When you got eight kids living with you in a five-room house," Rockwell says, eyeing them fondly as they study and watch TV in the small living room, "they better be well behaved."

The Rockwells live just a few blocks from Grand River Boulevard, which, in other times, Ned used to take down to Baker. The governmental unit is the township and twice since being terminated at Baker Rockwell has run for the position of township supervisor and has twice been defeated—the second time in the Democratic party primary. Rockwell ascribes this second defeat to the fact that he was laid up in the hospital with an ulcer during much of the campaign.

This, however, did not prevent his punching his Democratic colleague in the nose election night. Oddly enough, the other man's name was Rockwell too, but there the similarity ends. "He's got more friends in Hanoi than he's got in Detroit," Rockwell says flatly.

Apart from that one-punch victory, life, Rockwell admits, has been a series of defeats for him since Baker closed. He has a job as a laborer in a machine tool company. Most of the time he operates a crane lifting heavy equipment around the plant. It is a dangerous and confining job and Rockwell hates it. He misses the freedom he had at Baker, he misses the importance of his role as Chairman of the union bargaining committee, he misses those days, especially during the closing, when he could roam the plant at will, tending to his men's wants and needs. At the machine tool shop where he now works, he is at the bottom of the barrel; he has only 18 months seniority.

"The funny thing is," he says, sipping a cup of tea, "I could have had a good job before Baker closed, but I stayed till the very end. I wanted to take care of my men. I wanted to ease the pain for them."

Mrs. Rockwell, a slight attractive woman with a quiet, intelligent face, listens to her husband, hushes the children so he won't have to, responds with her eyes, anticipates his wants, smiles with faint apology when he swears. She nods as he talks about his feelings for the old plant.

"It's true, they were a family at Baker," she says. "I never resented it except at the end. Then it took too much of his time. It wasn't fair."

Towards the end Rockwell stayed over each day into the second shift to see that things were going right with the men on the afternoon shift.

"That son of a bitch Jones told me I was taking up too much time on union matters. I told him to go see Frank Robertson.

Frank came to me one day and said: 'Ned, I want you to take as much time as you want on union matters. I want you to make it as easy as possible for the men.'

"I'll be frank: I hated Robertson's guts until the closing. Sure he was the genius behind the place. Tom Morgan was a nice guy but he was spineless. Howard Green was nothing but a drunk. Merritt and Ed Connor, who were plant managers before Robertson, didn't know a thing. It was Robertson's genius that made it go all right, but I hated him. He was a sneak.

"One day the boys were rolling bones in receiving storage. I'd dropped five bucks and was out of the game. Just standing there watching. Some brownie must've tipped off Robertson because all of a sudden the door opens and there he is, the little guy, smiling, and saying: 'Can I join your game?'

"That's what he says. Next thing he's sent for the seven guys throwing dice. He wants to fire them, and he can. It's strictly legal, in the contract. He can fire anyone caught gambling. I go along with them since I'm a committeeman then, and I was in the game just before he caught them. I went along and told him how he ought not to fire them, that more guys were in it before he broke it up, me among them, that it wouldn't happen again. Anyway, I talked him out of it and he gave us a seven-day vacation without pay. But it was the way he did it, his grinning when he caught us.

"A few years later, during the closing, and I'm chairman, I'm sitting in the tank house with my feet on the table when there's a knock on the door and it's Robertson and he asks me if he can come in.

" 'Hell,' I say, 'it's your plant. Come on in.'

"He comes in, looks at me direct but blank. Robertson never let you know what he was thinking. And he asks me why I don't like him.

"So I say to him: 'I don't like you cause you're a goddamn weasel. Always grinning when you're firing people. Grinning like that with all your teeth. Like a weasel in the corn crib. You're a weasel and a weasel's worse than a rat.'

"He stands there a second. Then he puts his hat back on his head and says: "Thank *you*,' and leaves.

"I never liked him till the closing. The closing was something else. He wanted to make it as painless as possible for the men. I

honestly believe that. We both worked for the men. He told me
to spend as much time on union matters as I wanted. I did. I never
left that cafeteria. The last week of the plant, in December of '65,
he comes over to my table in the cafeteria and asks me how it's
going and I tell him, 'Boy, I can't wait till Friday.' Friday's the last
day.

"He blinks and asks: 'Why not?'

"Because Friday I'm going to cuss you out and this goddamn
place, that's why.' And I laughed like hell. I laughed all over him.

"Robertson doesn't say anything for a second and then he says:
'Do you think there's anything I can do for the men now?'

"Later I find out through my girl friend in the office he's scared
stiff the men are going to wreck the plant the last day.

" 'Sure,' I say to him, 'you can give them a half-day off Friday
with pay.'

" 'You think they'd like that?' he asks.

" 'Sure they would.'

" 'I'll do that then,' he says.

" 'And there's one more thing,' I say. 'Friday at noon we're going
to go across the street and get drunk. I want you to come over there
and have a drink with us.'

"He's surprised for a second and then he says quietly: 'I'll be
there.'

"He came. I bought him a drink and he bought me a drink and
everyone drinks. It cost him thirty or forty bucks, I bet."

Rockwell is silent. Mrs. Rockwell, at the sink, watches him
closely. "Do I miss Baker? Sure I miss it. I loved it there. A house'll
stand up if there's love in it. A company too. I cursed it and cussed
it. But I loved it. I loved the company. Nineteen years I worked
there. Honest to God, I never did anything to hurt the Baker
company."

He chokes off the sob that comes into his voice.

"Have some more tea, Ned," Mrs. Rockwell says calmly, and
turns on the burner. In the living room some of the older children
are still watching the television. The oldest boy is in the basement
working with a saw. Every now and then a child comes in to kiss
Rockwell good night. He is gruff and affectionate with each one.

Failure is written all over this man, etched in his words. But it
will be years, if ever, before his children perceive this.

You're Flying Blind
Most of the Time

If you didn't count Frank Robertson's office, there were two meeting rooms at Baker—the big fancy color conference room upstairs with the plush seats, and what Rockwell calls the "flunkeys' conference room" in the basement near the industrial relations manager's office.

The first meeting between the full union committee and the management on the subject of the closing was held in the flunkeys' conference room in the basement at 10 A.M. on Wednesday, November 13, 1963.

By prior arrangement the union committee assembled early, at 8 A.M. in the cafeteria, had doughnuts, coffee, and smoked. The cafeteria, one of the few places in the plant where smoking was permitted, had traditionally been the union headquarters in the plant. The five members of the union committee: Rockwell, Dick Tyner, Jimmy Bailey, Wayne Bender, and Rudolph Bimmler sat there waiting for word from the main gate that Perry DeMoss had arrived. At 9:45 Rockwell got a call from the guard at the main gate telling him that DeMoss was there. The committee left the cafeteria as a unit, met Perry at the gate and escorted the union rep down to the conference room.

They all had great respect for DeMoss, especially Rockwell. "It took a long time for the bosses to realize how smart Perry was, Rockwell says. "He was a Negro and they didn't figure it out for a while. I always liked and respected Perry. It's true he was out for himself most of the time, the way he got me to run interference for him when he got the job as a union rep. And deep down he's not really a union man. He voted for Nixon in 1960. I know that for a fact. Perry's a Republican by instinct. Careful, conservative but . . . he was a good rep, a lot better than Hank Bassem, and Perry was a Baker man through and through. He knew the plant, the men, and he knew the company too. We couldn't have asked for a better rep at the time."

The committee plus Perry DeMoss went inside the conference room, a plain, green-painted room with two tables put end to end, and about twenty straightback wooden chairs around them.

The men lighted cigarettes and gassed with DeMoss about his soft job at the local.

Finally DeMoss asked them what they thought it was about.

There was the same flurry of speculation with Jimmy Baily again saying: "I bet they're going to close the son of a bitch down." And again they laughed, DeMoss too.

At precisely 10 A.M., the management team entered. Lee Jones, Charley Burns, his assistant, and Robertson, unobtrusive and faintly smiling, as always, bringing up the rear.

DeMoss remembers thinking that if Burns was here that was bad news. Burns was always the guy they used to hand out the bad news.

There was a round of handshaking, jokes, chit-chat with Perry about how he was doing, about how many workers he was representing now.

Rockwell who always refused to shake hands with anyone from management finally slammed his hand down on the table. "OK, what the hell is this meeting called for?"

Lee Jones then handed each man a copy of the letter dated that same day and asked them to read it. Jones said a copy of the letter was being mailed to everyone who worked for the Baker company.

The union committee and the rep sat there and slowly read the long two-page single-spaced letter that announced the Pennsylvania Corporation was considering closing the Baker Color Company. When they were done, Perry DeMoss said: "What's it mean in plain English, Mr. Robertson?"

Frank Robertson said softly: "It means, Perry, that the company is now considering a move. There's a probability that this plant will be shut down."

"You sons of bitches," Rockwell exploded, but no one paid any attention. DeMoss played it cool. Any union-management confrontation is complicated, and most of the time the rep is flying blind about management's true intentions.

"I think we get that from the letter, Frank," Perry DeMoss said. "Do you mean it?"

"I think there's a probability that they do," Robertson replied, answering DeMoss's "you" with "they."

"You realize we have a contract that doesn't run out till December of '65. The company can't follow this course of action. It would be in violation of the contract."

Robertson looked down at the letter. "Perry, I'm just here to inform you of the plans the company has under consideration. Howard Green, who's in charge of the team, is willing to meet with you to discuss it further."

"Discuss it, shit," Rockwell said, "we won't let you bastards get away with this."

The other members of the union committee sat there, half-stunned, beginning to realize the implications of the letter. The meeting went on for an hour and a half with DeMoss probing over and over, asking the same questions: Do you mean it? What's wrong with the operation? Is it contractual relief the company is looking for? Do they realize the contract here still has two years to run?

Over and over it went until Rockwell stood up and said flatly: "I've had enough."

Perry DeMoss hesitated and then he too rose. "You'll be hearing from us, Frank." He shook hands with the management people. The committee and Rockwell did not. They just started to walk out.

Lee Jones said: "A copy will be mailed to everyone's home address."

"Don't bother mailing me one," Rockwell snapped. "My wife's got orders—any letter that says Baker or Pennsylvania Corporation on it she gives back to the mailman. I don't let any company propaganda in my house."

Robertson shook his head, smiling faintly: "It's not exactly propaganda, Ned."

"That's what you say," Rockwell snorted, and left, followed by his committee.

Although that's what he said, Rockwell didn't mean it to have the implication it had. "I swear," says Rockwell, four years later, "from the moment I read that letter I knew it wasn't propaganda. I knew the company wasn't bluffing. I knew they meant it."

Perry DeMoss recalls it differently. "As we left that meeting everyone on the committee, including Ned Rockwell and me, believed it could be a bluff. Ned most of all. He kept calling it propaganda and deep down I thought he was right. Everytime you go up against a company they threaten you with a plant closing. Companies always make that threat when they feel you're pushing them too hard at the bargaining table. At Baker we'd made a contract for three years in 1962, and I can remember Howard Green then, and for years before that, saying how we were going to put them out of business. It was standard operating procedure for management to talk like that to unions. Even this stuff about the big corporate picture was standard talk. I sat there at that table and like everyone else, Ned Rockwell too—because he didn't believe they were going to close till six weeks before they did, no matter what he says now —like everyone else, I thought they were bluffing, that they probably wanted some kind of contract relief. I guess when you get down to it, just like everyone else, I couldn't picture a world without the Baker Color Company."

None of the union committeemen was to return to their jobs that day. When the meeting ended it was about 11:30, close to lunch break. Perry DeMoss accompanied the shop committee back to the cafeteria. Rockwell got extra copies of the letter to post around on various bulletin boards, especially the bulletin board in the cafeteria.

The maintenance crew was the first to come in to lunch. They came trooping over when they saw Perry DeMoss. It was always an occasion when the rep was in the plant and besides Perry was one of them. His last job at Baker had been in maintenance, which was the crackerjack department at the plant and the highest paid.

But they were also aware that an out-of-the-ordinary meeting had been called for this morning. Rockwell believed in communication. He believed in letting everyone know what was going on, and the whole plant had been aware of the meeting. Now the maintenance boys wanted to know what had happened, and DeMoss told them exactly what had happened at the meeting. He gave them his copy of the letter to read.

There was discussion right away. Perry was asked his opinion. He was careful. A union rep doesn't have any personal opinion, he believes. The rep can't say: "I don't know, but this is what I personally think . . ." because it gets transmitted as "The rep says it's this . . ." So he was, in fact, as non-committal as Frank Robertson had been, referring the men to the letter.

The consensus was that the company was bluffing. "They're trying to soften us up for contract relief," was an opinion voiced over and over.

"I told them," DeMoss says, four years later, "that if the company was trying to engage in contract relief it would be no dice. I never said I thought the company was bluffing. I didn't know. Just last weekend I was getting a haircut and the barber tells me that a federal mediator who gets his haircuts there and runs his mouth says that the week before DeMoss could've got six cents out of a company I got four cents out of. I ate my heart out all weekend. But how was I supposed to know? You don't know. You never know. You're flying blind most of the time. You want to close up and move? 'Go ahead, close up and move,' you say to the company. But you don't know yet whether it's a bluff or not. You got to play it cool. You can break your neck if they're bluffing. I never said the Pennsylvania Corporation was bluffing. I may have said it was a possibility because it was, goddamn it. But I just didn't know."

DeMoss remembers Ned Rockwell saying he was certain the bastards were bluffing. Ned was chairman of the committee inside the plant and his opinions carried a certain amount of weight— "depending on what the men wanted to believe. Like little Jimmy Jackson," DeMoss says, "he worked in the resin department. He comes back to the table in the cafeteria after reading the letter on the bulletin board and he says: 'They're faking. They'll never close up Baker!' "

Little Jimmy Jackson, DeMoss remembers, was to believe that for the next eighteen months. He was to believe that until three days before he was permanently laid off.

All day long the committee stayed in the cafeteria and answered questions. They didn't go back to work for three days. Rockwell held court there and, to Mrs. Rockwell's despair, his sessions spilled over into the second shift.

Perry DeMoss returned to the local after lunch. On his way to his desk he spoke to several people, including some of the other reps, about the meeting and the letter. He wasn't sure how to pro-

ceed now. This was the first real closing threat he'd come in contact
with as a rep. Peter Thompson, president of the local, wasn't in at
the moment; Cal Koonz, head of Region 1A of the UAW of which
the West Side Local was a part, was not at his telephone. DeMoss
left messages for both officials to call back.

On his own desk were several call-back messages. One was
about a man at American Metals who'd had three garnishments
in the past 12 months. Another was about a man applying for
emergency welfare aid. There had been four or five calls about
guys being discharged, a call about a membership meeting at the
local. An important call about a contract he was negotiating at
McIntosh Stamping. DeMoss was trying to get four cents on that
contract and the company was holding out for two. They were
screaming that the union was forcing them out of business. DeMoss
was convinced he could get the four cents. Probably he'd settle for
three and learn indirectly the following week the company would
have given five. And he'd eat his heart out. But how was he to
know? If he screwed up he'd hear about it. If he didn't, no one
would say a thing.

He put the Baker letter off to one side and went to work on
his call-back messages—little yellow slips that fairly shrieked out
the words: WHILE YOU WERE GONE _____ CALLED.

All in all, the simple truth was that Perry DeMoss represented
more than 2,500 workers, only 300 of whom worked at Baker.

Perry's Baby

11/13/63–12/26/63

Busy as he was, Perry DeMoss had the Baker Color Company very much on his mind the rest of that November.

He talked the November 13th letter over with his office mate, John Matchet, who had once been the local rep for Baker; he also talked at length with Peter Thompson, president of the West Side Local.

Thompson's office is just down the hall from DeMoss's. It is a larger version of the same office but no plushier. The same brown linoleum floor, the beige cement block walls, pictures of Walter Reuther, JFK, FDR, and many family pictures. Thompson, in his early fifties, has a frank and open face; he sits in his shirtsleeves, collar unbutttoned and tie pulled down comfortably, and he likes to talk. He is one of those long-winded, shrewd people who make judgments of people while talking rather than listening. His first words are blunt.

"This isn't going to be an anti-union book, is it? Because we did everything we could. The Baker closing was something that just couldn't be stopped."

Although it was the fall of 1967 when Thompson talked with me, two years after the closing, he can recall quite clearly when DeMoss first came to him in 1963 with news of the possible closing of the Baker plant.

"My first job," Thompson says, "was to get a profile of the company's financial position from Perry. It's the only way to find out if they're bluffing or not. Do they mean it? Are they toying? If they're not toying, what can we salvage out of it? Perry and I talked about it. As far as I was concerned it was a damn sad state of affairs. I was the servicing rep for Baker from 1947 to 1950 before I moved up to secretary-treasurer in the local here. I knew a lot of the men personally. I knew what happens when a plant closes up."

Thompson leans back in his chair. He prefers to talk about closings in general rather than Baker specifically.

"The first closing I had when I was a rep was the old Wayne Steel Casting Company. It was an old family-operated concern

75

and they decided to sell out right while we were in the process of negotiating a contract. Well, they sold it to a man from New York named Ebersole, or something like that. He flew in and said if it didn't show a profit in three months he was going to liquidate it. Melt down the machinery into ingots and sell it. I thought it was just a threat, but damned if he didn't do just that. The plant didn't show the profit he wanted in three months and he sold what machinery he could and melted the rest down into ingots. My only regret is I didn't buy some when he offered them to me for sale. This was during the war and there was a real steel shortage right after that.

"The point I'm making is, for every Ebersole who really means it, there are five or six who're bluffing, who're pleading poverty to get contract relief. Perry's job was to decide what the score was and act accordingly. We at the local, the regional director, the people at Solidarity House were around to give him advice and counsel, but basically Baker was Perry's Baby."

As contrasted with the Pennsylvania Corporation which is a monolithic organization whose main office in Pittsburgh dictated every move of the management side of the Baker negotiations in Detroit, the UAW or the International Union, United Automobile, Aerospace and Agricultural Implement Workers of America—to give it its long and exact title—is a decentralized organization, and Perry DeMoss, although at times accompanied by an attorney and an actuary from the international union, was, in fact, in charge of the union side of the Baker closing negotiations. He had come a long way from his first days in the lye tank some twenty years ago.

After discussing the November 13th letter with his fellow union reps and with Peter Thompson, president of the local, DeMoss felt his next step was to talk with his regional director—Cal Koonz.

The headquarters of Region 1A of the UAW is, like the West Side Local, a low, modern red brick building on the west side of Detroit. It is slightly smaller than the local, contains an auditorium with a movie screen, folding chairs, and a television set, and many small offices. Out of these offices operate union reps who, like West Side Local reps, represent the workers of individual plants on day-to-day problems, contract negotiations, and so forth. The

West Side Local is unusual in that it is a large amalgamated local handling many different plants and having its own staff of reps. Most local unions are one to a plant and their reps are supplied by the regional headquarters.

There are nineteen regions in the UAW, and the job of each regional director is to oversee the operations of various locals in his region, provide service and counsel, approve and sign all contracts on behalf of the international union, authorize strikes, and act as a liaison between the locals and the international headquarters at Solidarity House. Each regional director sits on the executive board of the UAW.

Cal Koonz, director of Region 1A, has his office at the end of a long L-shaped corridor. The room is large and well appointed. It is furnished with beige wall-to-wall carpeting, four black leather armchairs, a yellow leather sofa and panelled in walnut. Green venetian blinds are adjusted to let in a discreet amount of sunlight. Many pictures, including a sketch of FDR and JFK, hang on the walls; none are of family. There is a photograph of former congressman Weston Vivian who from 1964 to 1966 represented the 2nd Congressional District of Michigan in Washington, and a picture of Senator Edward Kennedy arm in arm with Cal Koonz. On the wall over the sofa there is a large, colored picture of Solidarity House and next to it an enlarged photo-copy of the first UAW-General Motors agreement dated February 11, 1937, in which the union is appointed sole bargaining agent for the hourly workers. On the back of a side door is a copy of President John F. Kennedy's inaugural address. There are small gold-tinted statuettes of President and Mrs. Kennedy, and between them a set of red bound volumes of Labor Arbitration Reports. Copies of *Business Week* are on an end table.

The room's atmosphere of power and well-being is reinforced at once by the appearance of the regional director himself. Cal Koonz is a powerful, well-built man who seems to flow immensely out of a blue sharkskin suit. He is in his late fifties. Big-jawed and with a broken nose, he gives the impression of a fight manager rather than a fighter. He wears a thin gray mustache, more visible than Rockwell's mustache, less visible than Perry DeMoss's. A little UAW stickpin that catches the light from the window pierces his silk tie. Koonz's large hands are in constant motion, either turning to the phone to make calls of a political nature—he was, at the moment, seeking to get a candidate nominated to the Wayne County Road Commission to replace a union member of the commission who had just died—or he was turning the pages of his Baker file, seeking to recall the facts of the closing. His secretary kept putting calls through to him.

Finally he pushed a button and told her to hold all calls. He smiled apologetically at me. "You can see I've got too many jobs. Just leaving out politics, I've got 268 separate contracts in Region 1A. This file seems to go back only to 1965 and that won't be much of a help to us about the Baker plant. Negotiations there started in 1964."

He closes the file reluctantly. Perry DeMoss's file on the Baker closing was thin: Cal Koonz's is even thinner.

"You ask how did it happen? When did I come into it?" He leans back in his chair, steepling his fingers, aware of his self. "I suppose I got a call from DeMoss. He'd have to call me about something like this right away, wouldn't he? Every agreement a local signs with a company is a tripartite agreement: the company, the local, and the international union. As regional director, I represent the international union. We approve and cosign all contracts. We approve and sign strike authorizations. In the case of a closing like Baker's, Perry would certainly start the ball rolling by calling me."

Although his recollections of the Baker closing are not many, Koonz does recall going to at least two meetings with management. His total impression about the Baker closing was that there was no real bitterness or vindictiveness. The corporation gave plenty of notice, unlike many other companies—Baer Wire, for instance, which told the union they were closing their plant only two days before they shut down. The Pennsylvania Corporation said their decision was irrevocable and they indicated early that they were prepared to negotiate on the impact of change on the employees. They were not trying to muscle the union. They were making money in Detroit, but not enough money. They were looking to a long-term future. They wanted to consolidate operations in a new automated plant.

"I can understand it," Koonz says, ignoring a light flashing on his phone. "A company's in business to make money. Plants relocate because they think they can make more money elsewhere, usually in a lower wage area, but this wasn't the case at Baker. Baker was part of a big corporate changeover. I believed them when they said that. The Baker closing wasn't like Daisy Air Rifle when they moved from Plymouth down to Arkansas. In my opinion that was an immoral move. They moved out of a high wage area— incidentally, we didn't have a contract with them, though they blamed us for the high wages in the area which they had to compete with—down to a low wage area in Arkansas. And now because there's no money down there, they ship their products up north to sell where there's high wages and consumer money. That, in my opinion, was an immoral move; Baker's wasn't.

"In England if you want to move a plant you have to apply to the government for permission. You've got to prove your present location is really hurting you. Then the government determines whether your employees can be readily absorbed elsewhere in the area. They study what the impact of your move will be on the area you're moving out of and the area you're moving into. In other words, as far as English law is concerned, a company has a responsibility to a community as well as to its stockholders.

"If we had had that law over here—and I hope to God someday we will—a company like Daisy Air Rifle, in my opinion, would never have been allowed to move, but Baker probably would have. They were not pleading poverty or yelling about high wages. They had to go, and I can see it from their point of view."

He is silent, waits for a question.

"If the union couldn't prevent the company's move, how well do you think you prepared the employees for the termination?"

It is a sore point, a sticker in the craw of many a worker's throat. Today, a surprisingly high proportion of the Baker employees are not mad at the company. The faraway corporation somehow managed to sell its case to the workers: the case being the larger corporate picture, a return on investment. But the union is close by; Cal Koonz, Perry DeMoss are accessible, tangible, and vulnerable. Essentially without a case, the union sold nothing to its people.

Koonz shrugs. "I know a lot of Baker people thought the company was bluffing about leaving Detroit and they refused to believe the plant was going to close down." He hesitates, smiles ruefully. "And that big explosion they had there didn't help. When part of that plant blew up I thought they'd close her all the way down right away, but damned if they didn't rebuild the damaged parts. Well, my friend, if you were a worker at the Baker plant and saw them rebuilding the plant, would you still believe they were planning to close it down within a year or so?"

"But they did."

"Yes, they did. That's right, they did. And some of our people were not ready. OK, maybe our communications weren't too good. I know that Ned Rockwell and the shop committee thought it was a bluff right till the very end. I blame Perry DeMoss for that. Perry is a smart rep and a good bargainer but he likes to be one of the boys. He came out of Baker himself. He still likes to wear a rank and file suit, if you know what I mean."

Koonz swivels slowly behind his huge mahogany desk. Behind him the gold-tinted statuettes of John and Jackie Kennedy glitter in the afternoon light that seeps through the green venetian blinds.

Perry DeMoss's next move after contacting Cal Koonz was to get legal help from Solidarity House—headquarters of the International union. Koonz gave him permission to seek the services of one of the UAW's six Detroit-based attorneys. DeMoss chose to contact attorney Arthur Phelan, having worked with him briefly on one aspect of a contract negotiation a few weeks before and been impressed by his sharpness.

Almost everyone who came into contact with Phelan seems to have been impressed by his incisive mind and his youthful vigor. In Arkansas, Frank Robertson remembers him clearly.

"He was young and tough and sharp. I thought he was going to go after Green and Harrah. In those early meetings I hoped he was going to take them apart. The union could have got so much more than they did. The Pennsylvania Corporation was running scared. They couldn't afford a break in their Chrysler production. But for some reason Phelan didn't fight. He started out strong and then he just accepted everything the company offered. He didn't fight. He and the union bought the whole ball of wax, just the way the company offered it to them. I never understood that. I never understood why the union didn't fight. They could have hurt the company badly."

There is something pathetic about the plant manager rooting

for the union, wishing the union would pay the company back for killing his plant.

Another man present at all the management-union meetings on the closing of the plant was less impressed by Phelan.

"Phony Phelan," Ned Rockwell snorts today, "he sure talked tough. He fooled everyone but them. 'We won't let you get away with this move,' he says to them. 'We're going to do this and that. I got this law and that law on my side. I've won this case and that case already. I prevented this plant and that plant from moving. We're going to clamp down on you and keep you here and if you move, we'll make you pay through the nose for it.'

"Phony Phelan," Rockwell snarls. "He didn't fool them one bit. They just sat there and grinned at him. Their little Perry Mason knew all about Phony Phelan's so-called legal victories. No, he didn't fool *them*, Phony Phelan just fooled me and the committee. Us poor bastards believed every word he said. He made fools out of us, and out of me personally."

Perry DeMoss's appointment with Arthur Phelan was for December 26, almost six weeks after the November 13th letter. "Arthur Phelan's a busy man," Perry DeMoss explains, "and so am I."

On December 14, for example, he chaired the regular Baker membership meeting at the West Side Local. By union law, membership meetings are to be held once a month for the purpose of keeping members informed of union activities. At this meeting, one month after the letter, Perry DeMoss talked to the men about the possibility of Baker closing.

"There was a good turnout, for once. They asked a lot of questions about the November 13th letter. To a man, they were sure the company was bluffing. I told them I wasn't so sure."

"He didn't tell us anything of the sort," Ned Rockwell says. "He stood up there, Perry did, and said there was always the possibility the company was bluffing. And Christ if you'd worked at Baker all your life and your father maybe worked there too, wouldn't you grab at that possibility?"

"I told them they had to look at the situation realistically," De-Moss says today. "The plant was an old one. The rumors had been going around for years. A week later we had our annual Christmas party. The wives come to this one too. I usually use the Christmas party as a forum to get to the men's wives and urge them to get their men to attend regular union meetings. This time, though, I talked to them and told them there was a definite possibility that Baker was going to close. But I told them the union was going to do all it could to prevent this from happening. I told them they had a big powerful union going for them. I believed it too."

The day after Christmas, Wednesday the 26th, DeMoss drove downtown to Solidarity House to talk with Arthur Phelan.

Union Lawyer

Name: Arthur Phelan
Age: 37
Married: Jean Edwards, 8/23/56
Children: Pam, 10; Susan, 8
Religion: Protestant
Education: Beloit College, B.A., 1952; University of Wisconsin Law
     School, 1956
Occupation: Ass't. General Counsel, UAW 1957–67
Residence: 15692 Geddes, Grosse Pointe Woods, Michigan

Solidarity House rises, white, gleaming and modern, over the Detroit River on the east side of the city. It is a simple and eloquent testimonial to the single most powerful union in the United States. Any factory worker arriving here for a meeting, for advice on retirement, to see a film on Social Security, is certain to be impressed with his union's headquarters. They are as solid, as big, as modern as anything General Motors, Chrysler, or Ford could throw up. Of course if the union doesn't do justice by him on his contract, or if he has a grievance his union rep hasn't settled satisfactorily, then it will be "the union's lost touch with the ordinary worker; they live in their fancy penthouse down on Jefferson." But the odds are that the building, which is designed to house the working staff of the international, plus conference rooms, auditoriums, film amphitheatres, impresses even the most dour factory hand favorably.

Inside the lobby the decor is tasteful, quiet and muted, modern chairs, a few leather sofas. The only difference between this building and a corporation headquarters is the people working in it: a good many Negro women, Negro men, and both white men and black men work with open tieless shirts. Almost everyone says hello to a visitor. The guard, stocky, hard-faced, and wearing civilian clothes is a quiet but firm reminder that Walter Reuther, President of the UAW, was once the target of an assasination attempt.

Arthur Phelan's office is on the second floor. Large, spacious, with a table and chairs for meetings. Phelan, young, clean-cut, wearing tweeds and smoking a pipe, looks more like a junior professor at Harvard than a union lawyer. It is somehow difficult to picture Perry DeMoss sitting here, bringing the news that Baker might close down. It is difficult to imagine Phelan's reaction, and none of this is made any easier by Phelan who has few specific recollections about the details of the Baker closing. He has even less of a file than Cal Koonz has. It is clear that the higher one goes in the union hierarchy the fewer the recollections and the less immediate the concern that often keeps the past alive.

In the absence of correspondence, memos, and other papers, Phelan, thoughtful, articulate, drawing on his pipe, says he prefers to keep our discussion academic. How the closing, from his point of view, must have gone in principle.

"Since a company doesn't ordinarily announce too far ahead of time that it's going to relocate, my first job would be to determine if it was a bluff. If they were trying to get contract relief. My recollection is that the union committee led by . . . what's his name?"

"Ned Rockwell," I say.

"Yes, Rockwell. How's he doing now, by the way?"

"Poorly."

"Oh. I'm sorry to hear that. My recollection is that Rockwell, and Perry DeMoss felt that the company was bluffing."

"Did you think that?"

"Not after the first few meetings. I could tell right away that the corporation had gone into this thoroughly; that the termination of the Baker plant and the building of a new one was part of a larger corporate restructuring, just as they said.

"Having found that out," he continues, speaking crisply, clearly, "my next job was to determine what rights we had there. In labor law there are two sources of rights. The first is a clause in the contract prohibiting plant relocation. If it, the contract, contains such a provision and there's no arbitration clause, then the union can go to court to see that the contract is enforced. Unfortunately, we've succeeded in writing very few contracts with relocation clauses in them."

He taps his pipe.

"Our second source of rights is the National Labor Relations Act.

We can seek to get relief under that act. Under its terms, if an employer makes a large change in operations that entails possible loss of employment for workers, he has got to give the union advance notice and give the union an opportunity to engage in collective bargaining. Since the Pennsylvania Corporation gave advance notice, a union lawyer's first job is to try to get them to change their minds. Failing that, he would turn over the bargaining to the union committee—in this case led by DeMoss and Rockwell. So in these first meetings my job was to try to talk the company out of moving. And so I tried to ascertain first why they were moving. Did it have anything to do with the union? Would a wage cut help? What were the ways, in short, that the union could help the company keep this plant in Detroit? Do you follow me?"

"Yes."

"It was quite clear, as I've just indicated, that there was nothing the union could do in the way of contract relief that would help the company keep this plant going. This move, they made quite clear, was part of a larger reorganization. So I came to point number two, the second stage of my legal strategy: I would claim that this move was a violation of the 1962 contract. Although the contract contained no specific relocation clause, my claim was that the very nature of a three-year contract implied that the plant would be there for three years. Do you follow me?"

"Yes."

"My argument was that the existence of a contract was an implied provision against relocation."

Phelan smiles ruefully. "I do remember that I talked pretty tough at those first few meetings. I was riding high on a couple of other cases. One was a company that had shut down in the suburbs here and went down to Tennessee. We were suing them for damages in the move, under the argument of an implied provision, that the existence of a contract precluded relocation. The company had filed a motion to dismiss the suit, and the judge in the district court here had denied the motion to dismiss. The case was down in Cincinnati on appeal and I felt good about its chances. Mike Harrah, Pennsylvania's lawyer, had done his homework. He was very sharp. He knew this case was up for appeal. He knew too I'd settled other cases for severance pay rather than a change of mind on the company's part. I suspect he even knew how much severance pay I'd

settled for. I didn't give up, of course. I talked tough." He shakes
his head. "Maybe too tough."

"How do you mean?" I ask.

"I didn't fool Harrah or—Green, I think the other fellow's name
was—but I fooled my own people, the union bargaining committee.
DeMoss and Rockwell wanted me to go to court right away. Well,
it was about this time that I lost in the Circuit Court of Appeals in
Cincinnati and my suit was thrown out. The implied clause was
finished. I tried to explain that to Rockwell but he either couldn't
or wouldn't understand it. The only thing left to do now was to
bargain on the impact of the change on the employees. I knew the
company would be willing to bargain on that. In my opinion, it was
a decent company. They'd given notice, bargained, and there was
nothing we could do to make them change their minds. Now our
job was to make it as easy as possible for the men and to see that
those men who wanted to transfer to the new location could—and
could take their seniority with them—and that those that didn't
want to transfer would get severance pay."

Phelan is silent. "We didn't get the transfer rights, but we got
the severance pay. The company offered it right away. It wasn't in
the contract. They didn't have to. They came right up with it."

"Maybe they stole your thunder."

He shrugs. "You might say that. I like to think they were determined to do the decent thing all along."

"But you didn't get transfer rights."

"No. Transfer rights are a difficult thing. Who would have
gone anyway? These were all long-term people, Detroit people,
their fathers had probably worked at Baker, their cousins, brothers-
in-law were working there. There was a good proportion of Negroes.
How many of them would have gone to live in a small town in
southern Ohio?"

"Rockwell says it would have been nice to have been asked."

"No doubt about that."

"Nor did you get what you were asking for in severance pay."

"Do you happen to know what we got? I forget."

"Thirty dollars a year for every year of seniority."

He purses his lips. "That's a little less than we're getting now.
The average is about fifty dollars. The highest we ever got was
$100. Of course we wanted more."

"Why didn't you strike? Frank Robertson, the plant manager, do you remember him?"

"Yes. Very well. Quiet, mild-mannered little man."

—"He says you bought their whole ball of wax. He says you could have really got more from the company. They couldn't afford a strike or a work stoppage. They couldn't afford to lose a single customer in the transfer of operations. He says the union didn't fight."

Phelan is silent. "A strike would have been illegal. They could have sued the international for as much as they lost—and for more to cover future losses."

He pauses, trying to mask his irritation. "Look, the union had no legal weapons once my implied theory was shot down in appellate court. We could have been sued. Furthermore it was a decent company, an enlightened company willing to bargain. Only the men would have suffered from a strike. You say there's bitterness on the part of some of them, Rockwell in particular. Well, perhaps there was a breakdown in communication between me and the committee. I probably oversold them, bluffed my own side but not the company. That's always bad, if that's what actually happened. But as far as the overall picture is concerned, until some new legislation gets written to protect the working man there is nothing else I could have done. I went into those meetings determined to do my best. And I think I did. I have no regrets."

The Negotiators

Arthur Phelan actively entered the Baker closing on January 10 when he attended a meeting with the company representatives at the Baker plant. On January 6, Peter Thompson, President of West Side Local answered the November 13th letter of Frank Robertson in which the shutting down and partial removal of the Baker plant was contemplated. Thompson wrote:

> We wish to inform you that if the company insists on pursuing this course of action during the term of the present collective bargaining contract it will be in violation of that contract and the union shall immediately take necessary and proper legal steps to protect its rights.
>
> It is our belief that this matter requires immediate discussion and I ask you to arrange a time and place for a meeting.
>
> Yours truly,
>
> Peter Thompson
> President
> West Side Local ——— UAW

The time and place was set by the company on January 8, when Lee Jones, the personnel officer, telephoned Ned Rockwell and told him Howard Green and Mike Harrah would be coming in from Pittsburgh for this meeting.

Rockwell immediately got in touch with Perry DeMoss and told him the big brass were coming down on the 10th from Pittsburgh and "we'd better get some brass of our own."

"Our brass," Rockwell says contemptuously, "consisted of Phony Phelan, that big fat phony regional supervisor Cal Koonz, Perry DeMoss, and me and my committee."

The meeting was to be held upstairs in the fancy color conference room. Rockwell got permission from Robertson for the committee to meet with the union rep and Phelan for a few minutes before the larger meeting began.

"We met by ourselves at 8:30 and this was when Phony Phelan first told us not to worry; he wasn't going to let them move; he'd make it financially impossible for those bastards. We were going to sue Pennsylvania for damages, sue for rights to go with the plant, sue for $125 a year severance pay and we were going to win.

"You know how he talks? Clean as a whistle, smart, tough, blue eyes going right through you. An educated guy—our lawyer from the international. Well, we believed him. Hook, line and sinker, we swallowed every word of it like it was the gospel truth.

"And then in they come, management. That drunk, Green, Harrah wearing his suspenders and looking like a taxi dancer, and little Robertson tiptoeing along in the rear, smiling his little weasel smile at everyone. Robertson opened the meeting and passed out copies of a letter and then he read it out loud.

January 10, 1964

Dear Fellow Employees:

On November 13, 1963, I notified you that the Pennsylvania Company was considering plans that if carried through would result in the eventual closing of manufacturing operations here at Baker.

I have now been informed that a decision has been made to purchase land in Ohio to construct a plant which will manufacture industrial finishes. These finishes are at present being produced at various plants in the coatings and resin division, including our own. The company will also soon begin to make experimental shipments of automotive finishes from other plants to see whether these finishes can be satisfactorily manufactured at these plants.

These moves will not have an immediate effect upon the Baker personnel. However, the long range picture is no longer an optimistic one for us here. Our assumption is that while the new plant in Ohio will not be in operation for a year at least, the transfer of original automotive finish production will undoubtedly occur before then.

The Company conferred with your union representatives in November and we agreed then to meet again and discuss with them all problems which might concern Baker employees should the company decide to eventually close its operations here. The Company is ready to fulfill this pledge as soon as arrangements can be made.

"And then he says," says Rockwell, "Very sincerely yours, Frank R. Robertson.' "

"*Christ*, I think, and I slam my hand down on the table. 'This means you lousy bastards have decided to close us down.'

"Robertson, he never stops grinning he's so goddamn embarrassed. He looks over at Green but that big drunk never looks at him once. It's Green's meeting. They flew him down from Pittsburgh for it, and he takes over. I know his style. Talk soft, talk slow, let you fill the empty pauses, hang yourself, swallow air. Green's an engineer but he should have been a lawyer.

"He looks at me and says: 'Ned, I don't think that kind of language is going to make negotiating any easier.'

" 'Let's negotiate about this move then,' Perry DeMoss speaks up, and just as quiet as Howard Green. 'What'll it take to keep you here, Howard?'

" 'Nothing,' Green says. 'It's got nothing to do with the union, with wages. As Mr. Robertson pointed out in his November 13th letter, all this is part of an industrywide reorganization.'

"Green then goes on and tells us about the history of this move, how back in 1958 they made a nationwide study of production and markets. He carefully says there are six other paint plants involved beside Baker: there's Torrance in California, Cleveland plant, Milwaukee, Atlanta, Newark, Springdale. They're all being reorganized and different kinds of work are being transferred out between them. Baker, he admits, is the only plant being shut down.

"Perry DeMoss says softly: 'Howard, you just told Ned you didn't like his language. You said, quote, it wouldn't make negotiating any easier, end quote. When I ask you to negotiate about this move, then you go on and say there's no negotiating possible. How many ways do you want it?'

"Green looks at DeMoss. What's he thinking? This nigger started in the lye tank twenty years ago and he's crowding him now at the bargaining table?

" 'Perry, you received a letter from us on November 13th. That's about two months ago. In that letter we told you we were contemplating a move and that we invited counterproposals from the union. That was two months ago. In that time we received no counterproposals. Accordingly the company went ahead with its plans. The negotiating I'm speaking of now has to do with the impact of the move on employees, not the fact of the move itself. The company realizes it has an obligation to soften this blow in whatever ways it can, accordingly—'

" 'Hold on,' I say. 'I got that November 13th letter right here and you can't tell me from reading that you really wanted a counterproposal. You say, quote: There will be conferences and meetings with the union shop committee during which we will explore whatever suggestions the committee may put forward with regard to these contemplated moves. End quote. OK, we're having that conference meeting right now. So it's seven weeks after the letter? So what? Have you bought that land already?'

" 'No,' Green says, 'we haven't.'

" 'Then we can still negotiate about the move. What do you guys want to say?'

"Green's face doesn't change. He hates me and I hate him. How they can take a drunk like that and put him in charge of industrial relations for all their paint plants is beyond me.

" 'I just told you, Ned, we're not after contractual relief, wage cuts or anything like that. This is part of an overall plan.'

" 'So what kind of counterproposal could the union have given you?' Perry DeMoss asks.

"And Green is silent. Even Phony Phelan who's sitting there taking notes looks up for the first time. Finally Green says: 'I don't know, Perry. I really don't know.'

" 'Well, I got a counter proposal for you bastards,' I say, 'and that's a law suit. We're going to sue the hell out of you.'

"Green looks at me and hands me that phony pitying smile of his that says 'that poor slob Rockwell, they oughtn't to let him at these meetings.'

"Finally Phony Phelan speaks up clear as a bell. 'I'm not so sure Ned Rockwell isn't speaking the truth. The union will consider any movement prior to the termination date of the contract, December 15, 1965, as illegal. We will also consider it a violation of the contract if all or any part of the work is taken away from this plant prior to termination date.'

"That wakes up Mike Harrah, the company lawyer. 'Art,' he says—they know each other you can tell that right away, maybe from conventions, other negotiations—'we've been transferring work and machinery between plants for a number of years.' And then Harrah begins to cite from a paper the kinds of operations that have been transferred back and forth between plants during contracts. He's sharp as a tack. He's come prepared.

" 'I don't think you'll have much of a case there, Art, telling us it's illegal to move property out of one plant and into another.'

"Score one for Perry Mason.

" 'Furthermore, Art, I'd like the specific language that would let you go to court to prevent our moving to another location.'

" 'The very fact of a three year contract,' Phelan says, 'implies recognition that this plant is going to be here for three years. The seniority clause, preamble and classification of the contract imply that there will be a Baker plant until termination date. Until the contract expires there can be no move, and no preparations for a move. We will take any such preparations as an illegal act and seek redress in court.'

"Harrah grins. 'That's pretty tough talk, Art. That theory about recognition. That's not law yet, is it?'

"Phelan replies, 'I've won in another case here in Michigan similar to this. We've gone to court to sue for damages and the court has turned down a company motion to dismiss. This case is similar to the one that confronts us now, except that I think we've got a better case here. I think we both know about the Glidden case back east, Mike, and we know what the rulings there have been. The union will sue and sue for plenty if the company proceeds to carry out this illegal move.'

" 'I appreciate the frankness of your position, Art,' Harrah says. He grins at me. 'And your frankness too, Mr. Rockwell. But the fact remains that the company waited two months for a counterproposal about its desire to make the move and heard nothing. In the meantime it is our position that such a move is entirely legal, the preparation for such a move is also entirely legal. We've been transferring both work and machinery out of Baker for years without a dispute.

" 'Our position is that this move is not an anti-union move. We are moving to stay competitive over the long haul. This move involves a move in every one of our plants. We appreciate the difficulties the move will entail for the people here at Baker and thus we think the union would more profitably spend its time negotiating the best deal for its men on the impact of the move rather than trying to fight the move itself. This, in the long run, would cause even more hardship, for the company would find itself having to spend its money fighting a law suit rather than giving severance pay to the men.'

"Phelan shuffled his papers. 'We appreciate your looking out for the men, Mike. I can only repeat what I just said: the union is going to fight this move on the basis of court cases I now have pending. We will fight the preparation of this move. And we will win our fight too.'

"And that was it. There was nothing more to say. Silence. Impasse.

"Perry DeMoss then said we'd contact them when we desired another meeting. In the meantime there had better not be any work shipped out of the Baker plant. The meeting ended on that note.

"I must say I was impressed with Phelan. I didn't understand a lot of the stuff he and Harrah were saying to each other. They knew each other; they knew each other's work. They were a couple of lawyers. They had more in common with each other than we had with Phelan. I see that now; I didn't then. Then I believed every goddamn word Phelan said. Harrah knew better. He knew it was a lot of hot air—that great case of Phelan's in Michigan, the case back east.

"That meeting lasted about two hours. It was getting toward lunch time. Phony Phelan went back to Solidarity House and Perry drove him, the two of them figuring the grand strategy.

"Me, Dick Tyner, Wayne Bender, and the other members of the committee went over to the Skyway and had a couple of beers and congratulated ourselves on having this tiger Art Phelan on our side. Then we went back to the cafeteria and everyone came buzzing around and we showed them that second letter and how it was going to be mailed to them and we told them not to worry because if the company insisted on this move, Phelan was going to make a bundle of loot for us. He'd sue them for a couple of million bucks and we'd be rich the rest of our lives.

"We decided to call a special membership meeting. This was Friday. You have to give seven days notice when you call a special meeting, so that meant Saturday, January 18th. Dick Tyner and I put the notice up. I got the chief steward on the afternoon shift to notify the second shift. I stayed myself till after five talking to guys from the second shift. Perry was back at his desk that afternoon and he agreed with me that a special membership meeting was a good idea. The plant was just buzzing that whole day about the second letter. The fat was in the fire.

"I guess production went down the following week. I know mine did. I spent a lot of time in the cafeteria answering questions. I didn't have any answers but I know it reassured the men seeing me there.

"Saturday more than two hundred guys showed up for the special membership meeting. More than we'd ever had. Almost half of our people. Two hundred guys, and they filled that room to overflowing.

"And that's when I made an ass of myself. I got up and reread the company's letter. And I told them Phelan was going to sue the company. And we were going to make a bundle. And I told them if they did move and paid us off, we were also going to get transfer rights, seniority rights to go to the new plant. I talked for about twenty minutes and I told them that Phelan was taking care of us. Solidarity House was taking care of us.

"Then Perry got up and he talked too. And he said the same thing. Solidarity House was behind us. If Baker was going to move they were going to have to pay plenty for that move. And he said what I said—I guess I said it, I know I thought it—that there was always a chance of the plant staying. We could make it too tough for them to move. Phelan had said that. He had said we could make it too much of a hardship for them to move.

"Afterwards some guys come up and asked me if I didn't think the company was bluffing about the whole thing, and I said, I didn't know, but it didn't make any difference because we weren't going to let the bastards get away with one thing.

"Monday we went back to work. But I never made it back to the tank house and I don't think I spent two hours in the tankhouse all that week. We took up battle stations in the cafeteria and the men kept coming around. Some of them wanted to strike. 'No,' I said, 'if we strike we lose everything. The company'd laugh at us. A strike'll just hurt us.'

"I still believe that. I know now they were going to close us no matter what. Maybe we couldn't have done anything. But that's not the point. The point is that Phony Phelan fooled us. That's what I resent. He led us to expect something more and I got up and promised the men something more and we got nothing. The company outsmarted us all the way. Sure, I'm bitter about the company because they didn't have to close; they just wanted to make more money. But I'm more bitter about our own people—the union. Not Walter Reuther—he's next to God as far as I'm concerned—but Phony Phelan. He took me down the primrose path and I'll never forgive him for that."

If Arthur Phelan was leading Ned Rockwell down a primrose path, he was not aware of it.

"I really thought we could prevent that move," Phelan says today. "I thought we had them legally. I was making new law with my implied recognition clause. On January 10th, I'd have bet money we could prevent Baker from closing."

In addition to the confrontations with the company officials, Phelan hoped to arrange a concerted multi-union attack on the Baker problem. And so on January 10, the afternoon of the meeting, he dispatched a letter to Mr. Jack Conway, executive assistant to the president of the I.U.D.—the Industrial Union Department of the AFL-CIO—and formerly an officer of the UAW asking him for help on the Baker problem. Since operations were to be moved from various Pennsylvania Corporation plants to the new plant in Ohio and since these plants were under contract with unions other than the UAW, Phelan wished to explore the possibility of a coordinated legal attack on the problem and wished Conway's help in determining which unions had contracts with which Pennsylvania Corporation plants.

Conway replied within a few days giving Phelan the information he desired.

Phelan promptly got in touch with the various unions concerned, including the Teamsters, Chemical Workers, and Electrical Workers, but he received no cooperation. The fact was that none of the other plants were being hurt by Baker's closing. Indeed, several would be taking on more work. As for the principle of transferring work between plants, this, as Mike Harrah had indeed pointed out, had never been questioned before.

And so by mid-January, Phelan had to drop the idea of a coordinated legal attack on the Baker problem.

On January 10, the day of the meeting and the date of his letter to Conway, Phelan also wrote another letter, which was to be sent out under the signature of Peter Thompson, President of West Side Local.

The letter stated for the record the union's position on the proposed termination and relocation of the Baker plant—that the union regarded moving of the plant or any of its operations during the current collective bargaining contract as illegal. It also stated for the record that the union did not believe the company was bargaining in good faith. "We asked that you take additional time to consider the union's legal position," it said, "but we were informed by you that this would not be necessary since your decision had already been made."

In the letter Phelan went on to state that although the union believed it had the contractual right now to prevent the company from moving and would look to the courts for the enforcement of that right, it still wished to try to talk the company out of its decision to move and requested that another meeting be set up to bargain on whether or not the company will move.

This demand for bargaining, Phelan emphasized, in no way acknowledged that the company had the right to move, only that the union was "willing . . . to try to bargain the company out of doing something it [had] no right to do." The union was prepared to enforce its rights in court if bargaining failed.

If Rockwell in hindsight thought it was a primrose path he was being led down, at least Phelan knew it was a desperate and delicately balanced line he was treading—threatening legal action angrily with one hand and extending the olive branch of collective bargaining with the other.

Mike Harrah, the company lawyer, had nothing but sympathy for Phelan's predicament.

"A man always talks tough when his client is around," Harrah says. "I knew or had a good idea Phelan's legal theory was going to be pulled out from under him. I think he knew it too. But his client, the union committee, was there, and so he talked tough. He didn't fool me, though. I'd done my homework." Harrah grins. "I've been a labor lawyer since 1956 . . . representing the great capitalistic company. I know when a union's got a case and when they're bluffing."

He laughs. "I respect Art Phelan; he's intelligent and a real gentleman. Unlike a lot of union lawyers. He wears tweeds, and, well, with that pipe of his you'd think he'd be representing the company. Me? To look at me with my loud shirts and suspenders, you'd think I'd be representing the union. As a matter of fact, that's what I wanted to do when I got out of law school. I wanted to represent a labor union. Honest. But I couldn't get a job with one. So I took up the cudgels on behalf of the great capitalistic company. Isn't that something?"

I'm the Only Democrat
Around Here

Name: Mike Harrah
Age: 42
Birthplace: Chicago, Illinois
Education: parochial schools; St. Ambrose College, B.A., 1944; North-
    western University Law School, J.D., 1950
Emlpoyment: 1944–46, Lieutenant j.g., USNR
            1950–55, counsel for NLRB
            1956–67, Ass't. General Counsel, Pennsylvania Corpora-
            tion
Married: Louise Holmes, 1955, deceased in 1958. Harrah with help of
    his mother-in-law raised 16-month-old son, Grant. In 1963 he
    remarried: Patricia Fruhling. They have two children of their own:
    Gary, 4; and Anne, 2
Religion: Catholic
Politics: Democrat

Rockwell calls him Perry Mason; Phelan says he is sharp; Frank
Robertson remembers him vividly in his "yellow shirts and red suspenders—my, oh my." All agree he was an extremely able lawyer for
the company. No one is mad at him, and Harrah, too, is hugely,
pleased with himself. He grins a lot, slightly self-deprecatingly, but
he enjoys his position in the company.

"I'm the only Democrat in a high level position here," he says.
"I'm labor oriented and I like the money."

He chuckles and a beam of sunlight sparkles in the huge red
signet ring he wears on the pinky of his right hand. There is something flashy and cheap and bright about the man. He has red hair,
thinning, freckles, and blue eyes that have a humorous evasiveness
in them. His face is flat, his body small, chunky, tending to pudgi-
ness. He looks as if he eats well, drinks well, his fleshly appetites

are taken care of. Yet when he talks of his first wife, who died of a brain hemorrhage when their son was 16 months old, and of how he brought the boy up alone with the help of his mother-in-law, the effect is startling. Perhaps there is a deep inner strength in this man. That he is clever and bright and wry is apparent. That he has, in his own mind, "sold out" is also apparent, and he himself seems amused by this.

"Ever since I studied under Willard Wirtz at Northwestern," he repeats, "I've wanted to be a labor lawyer." So after five years with the NLRB I tried again for a union job—with the United Steelworkers. That was in 1955, and they weren't hiring then, so I got this job here. And I like it.

"I write most of the anti-union propaganda here, but I'm not anti-union. None of us here are. We have to work too closely with unions to be against them. I do think a working man should have a choice between being unionized and not. So when an election comes up, I tell him the advantages of not being unionized—and there are plenty."

Harrah shuffles through his file on the Baker closing. Unlike Phelan, he has an extensive file. He has also brought along his expense account vouchers for the years 1964-65 for these can tell him exactly when he made trips to Detroit and how long he stayed.

"That's something else I'm going to miss," he says with a laugh. "I liked going to Detroit. Green and I used to stay at the Dearborn Inn, and you don't find hotel or motel rooms like that elsewhere. High ceilings, fireplaces . . . the motels in York, Ohio are nothing. We've got paint or glass plants and distributors in almost every state in this country and I've travelled to just about all of them on some arbitration case and I can tell you the Dearborn Inn has the best accommodations."

Harrah estimates that in the ten years he's worked for the Pennsylvania Corporation, he's worked between 500 and 600 arbitration cases and won almost all of them.

"I love it," he says, grinning, "and I love winning. In 1966 I won 18 and lost none. We couldn't lose with Baker. We carefully stayed within the law. We gave early notification—my God, more than two years notice. (Our sales people thought we were out of our minds; they thought production would fall apart. But I didn't think so. We had a good man running that plant—Mr. Robertson—and

I knew he could hold it together.) When manufacturing made its decision to close Baker down and told us to find out what our legal obligations were, I knew exactly what they were. We had to give the union a chance to bargain; we had to stay loose.

"That letter of November 13th, that first letter, I wrote that, except for a few sentences from Frank Robertson about what the plant meant to him—that was pure Frank Robertson. But I wrote that first letter and I worked hard on it, and we left the door open for a counterproposal. I couldn't for the life of me see what kind of counterproposal the union could make. The plant was obsolete. It was a monstrosity; for an automotive refinish business it was poorly situated geographically. Inefficient work habits were entrenched there. The plant was giving a poor return on the dollar and it had to go. But first we gave the union a chance to bargain. They didn't; they threatened. I didn't think they'd strike. We could have sued them for millions. Right at the beginning I assured Wysse Allen there'd be no strike. You see, our big task was to create the right image. To let the union and the men know we were aware of their problems. If they struck, the longer they struck the less of a club they'd have over our heads. We were going to move anyway. Instead of threatening and striking, it would be in their own interest to help us soften the impact of the move on the employees.

"So I told them: 'If you guys want a lawsuit for twenty-three months, OK with me. But meanwhile you could be helping your men, bargaining about severance pay.'

"Now I knew they weren't ready to do this. Phelan had his clients with him. The UAW spends a lot of money convincing the rank and file that the union will take care of them. So he threatened us and perhaps he sincerely believed he could prevent us from moving. He cited the recognition clause in the contract—the clause which states that the company recognizes the union as the sole bargaining agent for the men. All of which meant, according to Art Phelan, that the company had no right to close down the plant during the life of the union contract."

Harrah grins. "Arthur was riding high on the Glidden case. Glidden was a paint company that closed out a plant quickly in Elmhurst, Long Island, and moved to Allentown, Pa. practically overnight . . . with two years to go on their contract. They moved without negotiating with the union; they took their old equipment with them. The court held that the people were entitled to their lost wages for the rest of the contract period. It may have been a fair decision humanly, but it was bad law and it was later overruled. A contract collectively bargained does not limit a company's right to relocate or to close down a plant. In those days, though, Glidden was on everyone's mind and Art Phelan held it over my head during that first meeting. But Glidden hadn't negotiated, and we were ready to—a fact I pointed out to him.

"Arthur also talked about another court case he was winning against a Michigan company that had relocated, which he was suing for damages. I didn't know at that January 10th meeting what company it was, but I checked up on UAW suits through the Commerce Clearing House in Chicago which reports on interesting labor cases—so does the Bureau of National Affairs—and I found out the UAW was suing the Atlas company. Atlas makes automotive locks and they had shut down in suburban Detroit and gone down to Tennessee to make their locks. The union had a suit against the company. The company had filed a motion to dismiss the suit. The judge had denied the motion to dismiss, and the company was appealing.

"I contacted the lawyers representing the Atlas company and they briefed me on what was happening and to sum it up I was pretty certain that the UAW was going to lose out in the appeals court."

Harrah sits back, looking up from his file, humble and pleased. "All in all, by the January 23rd meeting I knew pretty well what Art Phelan had up his sleeve and what he didn't have. And he knew I knew it, too. But his own people didn't know it. They were still buffaloed, and they wanted to stampede all over us." Harrah grins. "We took some pretty good cussing from old Ned Rockwell in that meeting of the 23rd."

Nothing Beats Experience

—Howard Green in the meeting of 1/23/64

The meeting of January 23 was set up by Peter Thompson's letter of January 10 in which Arthur Phelan, under Thompson's signature, put the union's position in writing and requested that the company "set a time and place for collective bargaining on the basic question of whether or not the company would move."

Howard Green, through Frank Robertson, set January 23 as the date for the meeting. Present for the company were Green, Mike Harrah, Lee Jones—the plant's industrial relations manager—and Frank Robertson. Present for the union were Thompson, president of West Side Local ———— Arthur Phelan, Perry DeMoss, Ned Rockwell, and the other members of the plant committee.

Green opened the meeting by reviewing past events starting with the letter of November 13 in which, he stated, the company asked the union for any suggestions it might have which would help keep the plant in Detroit. Since no suggestions were forthcoming from the union, the company went ahead with its plans to move. Not till almost two months later did the union ask for a meeting. Nor at that meeting were there any positive suggestions from the union, just threats of lawsuits, NLRB injunctions, etc.

"Indeed," said Green, "the only thing the union has said up to now is that if the company moves it will be liable to a lawsuit."

On the other hand, he went on, the company had conscientiously and sincerely taken the union into its confidence with an early warning to its employees and with the solicitation of suggestions; without any feedback from the union, the company was forced to go ahead with its plans which called for a two-year phasing out of the Baker plant and the construction of a new plant in York, Ohio.

"And I must make it clear again," Art Phelan interrupted, "the union will consider such a move illegal and we will seek redress in the courts."

"Art," Mike Harrah said mildly, "it's our position that the move is entirely legal."

"Ah shit," Rockwell said, "we've been through all this before."

"You're damn right we have," said Peter Thompson, president of the local, "it's right there in my letter of January 10th. We want to know what else you've got to say. Something new. Not the same old tired things we've been hearing already."

"I think our position is perfectly clear, Mr. Thompson," Green said. "In two letters the company has stated its intention to move. Now we'd like to discuss with the union ways of softening the impact of this move on the employees."

"To hell with that," Thompson said. "Are you willing to bargain on the question of the move itself? That's what we're here for."

"We're certainly willing to listen to anything you have to say."

"I'm glad of that," Arthur Phelan said, "because we are willing to bargain you out of the move. You don't want a long court fight and neither do we. We are successfully prosecuting a case against a Michigan company that moved out on us illegally, and it looks like we're going to collect quite a lot in damages. But that's not what we want. We want the Baker plant to stay in Detroit and men who've worked there all their lives to keep on working there. We're willing to talk you out of this illegal move. And I take it that it is still possible now to bargain on this basic question of moving the plant."

According to Frank Robertson, who sat on Howard Green's left, watching Phelan and Harrah eye each other like tiger cats across the table, you could have heard a pin drop at this point. Howard Green began tapping his file of papers softly. He was a good man in a situation like this, Robertson thought reluctantly. He slowed things up. But if only they knew—Phelan, DeMoss, the others— how scared to death the company was of a work stoppage, what unsure ground they were on. . . .

"Let's put it this way:" Green said slowly, "an overall decision has been made to move and, indeed, to realign all operations of the company's paint and brush division. We want to talk with you; we want to bargain with you, but only about matters that are relevant—namely, the impact of the move, not the move itself. A law suit, you understand, would tie our hands to bargain on these other things. Isn't that right, Mike?"

"I think that's fairly stated," Harrah said. "We're willing to listen to any suggestions you may have, but in my opinion, gentlemen, the company will not change its basic position on the move. We consider the time you had between November 13th and January 10th to have been ample to discuss this move. You didn't discuss it.

We were forced to go ahead."

"Balls," Rockwell said. "You didn't want an answer and you know it. I've read that November 13th letter a dozen times. It's so vague you couldn't make any counteroffer to it."

"Have you bought the land down in York?" Perry DeMoss asked.

"No," Harrah said, "we have not."

"Then," Thompson said, "the decision hasn't gone too far?"

"We are always willing to listen," Howard Green said. "But the overall picture—the industrial realignment, our fulfillment of obligations to our stockholders—indicates to me that the larger corporate picture will not change. Baker is a tiny speck in this picture. I myself feel that any change will have to be made on a corporate basis."

"Is there anything in contract relief that would help keep this plant here?"

"No," Green said. "At no time have we said that wages were too high or production too low. I don't know what it would take to keep the plant here but I don't think the union has anything to give that would keep us in this location. We're not pleading poverty. We need to have a basic industrial realignment to stay competitive over the long haul."

"In other words," Harrah added, "you'd have to convince us that our five-year study undertaken in 1958 is all wrong. You'd have to convince us that geographically it's important for us to remain when our study tells us now that geographically Detroit is a poor place for the automotive finish business."

The study was wrong there, Robertson thought. The automotive finish business was a day-by-day pressure business. It could only be helped by being down the block from Chrysler when they ran into a problem, a shortage. Being 300 miles away could only hurt. Maybe a lawyer like Harrah who never made a can of paint in his life could talk like that but he, Frank Robertson, knew better, and he knew that Howard Green knew better. In fact, Howard was carefully looking down at his papers right now. And by God, Rockwell and DeMoss who were Baker men knew better, too. Why didn't they speak up? Why didn't Phelan speak up? He could hurt the company that was killing the Baker plant if he threw the lie back at Harrah.

But none of them spoke up. And Harrah had gone smoothly on,

talking about the obsoleteness of the plant which nobody could deny. He talked about customers for refinish being located all over the country and how much easier it was to service them from York, Ohio, than from Detroit, and he repeated the argument that the reshuffle would in some measure affect all the paint plants, though, he conceded, Baker was affected the most and the company wanted to do the right thing by the men, which was what they ought to get down to talking about.

Phelan spoke up: "Mike, would contractual relief in all the plants help?"

It was a weak try. They all knew that Phelan had no chance of getting contract relief in all the plants with the Teamsters and other unions in the pictures there.

Green treated it as a serious query, though, and replied that a re-shuffle would still have to be made and every paint plant east of the Rockies would be affected—Houston, Atlanta, Springdale, Milwau-kee, Detroit, Cleveland, Newark. Only part of Baker's work would be going to Ohio. The rest would be divided up among the other plants and some work from other plants would be sent to the new plant.

Robertson watched Phelan and Ned Rockwell—one the man of reason, the other the man of passion. The man of reason was silent. He was giving up. And well he might, Robertson thought, for there wasn't anything on God's green earth that would prevent the com-pany from closing down Baker, although Phelan could get a lot for the men. He could punish the bastards in the company badly for this move.

While Phelan was silent Ned Rockwell exploded. "You goddamn bastards act as though this plant was being carried by the company. Did we or did we not make money for you guys?"

Green glanced at him. "Ned, in the last ten years this has not been an *efficient* operation."

"You mean we didn't make *enough* money, is that it?"

Green shrugged.

Perry DeMoss asked quietly: "You say you haven't yet purchased land in York, Ohio?"

"No, we haven't."

And that was a lie too, Robertson thought wearily. Purchase was a funny word. They had signed options to buy. The land was as

good as purchased. Signs were already up on the land. Why didn't
the union send someone down to Ohio to see if the land was bought
or not? The union wasn't fighting back; they were just sitting there
asking pathetic questions.

Phelan cleared his throat. Everyone looked at him. "Let me ask
this: Does the company think it would be beneficial to take people
from Baker who have experience working in a paint plant to the
new location?"

No one said anything. With that question, a change had taken
place, and everyone knew it.

Green said: "The new plant is being automated, Mr. Phelan. It
will naturally not have as many people working in it. But,"—he gave
a half-amused glance at Rockwell, who was smouldering—"nothing
beats experience."

"You'll screw us all right," Ned said, "but we'll make you pay for
it, won't we?"

Arthur Phelan, annoyed, closed his file and put his papers in his
attaché case. Perry DeMoss took the cue and said there was obviously no point in meeting any further now. The union would make
its decision on what course to follow and get back in touch with the
company.

The meeting adjourned at 11:20 A.M.

From the Recollections of Frank R. Robertson

1/23/64

Thursday. An exhausting day at the plant. The meeting with
the union took more out of me than I expected. And then
Green wanted to stay around the plant. For all his tough talk
about moving, he's going to feel almost as badly as I do. Harrah went right back to Pittsburgh, but Howard is staying an
extra day in Detroit. I was tempted to ask him what he really
thought when Harrah said Detroit was a poor geographic location for an automotive finish and refinish plant, but I didn't
have the heart to. He feels as bad as I do about this thing. He
says he only feels good when he's around here and watches the

plant clicking and smells all the old smells. He claims it does him good to get back to a production atmosphere. "You never get the feeling you've accomplished anything at the desk in Pittsburgh, Frank," he said to me, and I smiled at him to say I understood but I was thinking: *You've accomplished plenty at those desks in Pittsburgh. You're killing us off from those desks.*

Home at 8 P.M. and Doris had a drink and dinner ready and wanted to know how it went. I didn't want to talk about it but she wanted to hear about it. What Phelan said, and what Mike Harrah said, what Ned Rockwell, whom she calls "the animal," said and so forth. She wanted to know if Phelan could prevent the move and I tell her "No, Doris, nothing on God's green earth will prevent this move. All Phelan can do is make the company pay the full price for murdering the factory and I'm sure they'll do that." And she didn't care about that. Just as long as Phelan didn't prevent the move. She should have been sitting with Green and Harrah. She'd have been tough on the union. I felt very sorry for her.

Friday. I walked through the plant before going to my office. The men greeted me cheerfully, the old ones calling me "Frank" or "Robbie." They're all working hard. No bottlenecks. Two letters have gone out about the plant closing and not one person with more than two years' seniority has left. A few transients have taken off, but that's all. There's been no sabotage. It's true, for two weeks after that November 13th letter, production was down about 11 percent while they sat around the cafeteria and worried the thing to death. But it bounced back. The men are working harder than I've ever seen them. Even Dave Masiak, for whom we made a job a year ago when he strained his back, is sweeping up instead of leaning on his broom.

I walked through the resin plant and a Negro worker named Wallace Moore, who has been here almost as long as I have, said hello to me. "Frank," he said, "is it true they're gonna close us up?"

My God, I thought, I haven't heard right. Hasn't the union told them? Haven't they read the two letters? I answered: "It sure looks like it, Wallace."

He shook his head. "I heard people saying it, but I don't believe it. Why we working harder than we ever work before.
We got more orders than we ever got before. They can't close
us up, Frank."

I stood there for a second. It's not my job to make them face
facts. It's my job to keep the plant running. Already some
other men had come around us. Already production was stopping, slowing down because of a discussion about the future
of Baker—a future they should have been aware of. A future
that it isn't my job to make them aware of.

"Well, Wallace," I said, "the company can do whatever they
want with us. And if they say they mean to close us up, well
then I think that's what they mean to do."

Wallace won't let me go. "But do *you*, Frank? Do you think
they gonna close us up?"

"Yes, I do, Wallace, I think they're going to close us up."

He stood there, unconvinced. "*I* don't think so," he said.

Over in Building 10, the refinish department, I was surrounded
the moment I came in. Milt Maulbetsch, a 24-year seniority
man came over, wiping his hands on his apron. Milt's a tinter.
A skilled trade. $3.05 an hour. He'll have no trouble finding
a new job.

"Hey, Robbie," Milt asked, "what's the score on them closing
us?"

The union had done a poor job convincing their people the
plant was going to close. This wasn't my task. I was quite
aware that the men who were listening to me now are skilled
workers and important to production.

"What's the score?" I repeated, "well, they say they're going
to close us up."

"They say," someone said, "but do they mean it?"

"The company usually means what it says," I replied.

"I think they're bluffing, Robbie," Milt said. "They won't close us up."

"Well, suppose they do," someone else said. A fella named Cowie, eight years' seniority. "What do we do? Take off and look for work? What're you gonna do, Mr. Robertson?"

His question came at me so unexpectedly, for a moment I didn't know what to say. And then I said what I shouldn't have said. I said again the phrase that haunts me today. I said: "I don't know what I'm going to do yet, friend, but I know one thing. I've put a long time in here and I'm going to go out with my head up."

"That's right," someone said.

"Me too," Milt Maultbesch said. "I been a Baker man 24 years and I'll go you one on that, Robbie."

Somehow I got out of that, but the full meaning of what I'd said and how they'd take it hit me later. But I did know one thing. I hadn't lied to them. I hadn't fed their delusions about the company's bluffing. It would have been easy to do, General office would have wanted me to, but I would never do that.

I was at my office at 9 A.M. and the desk was loaded with mail and advertisements and telephone notes. I was to call back Newark and Springdale about paint shipments. Cleveland was having trouble in matching our original finish. I had to send someone from the lab down there. There was a call from our distributor in Spokane. He couldn't get hold of Harold Peterson and he'd had complaints about some refinish for a 1961 Ford Galaxie. I told my secretary to get hold of Harold and she told me in turn that Louie Arnot wanted to see me.

Louie's a stout, short, energetic French-Canadian. He's a spanky dresser, a good host and he and his wife like to give lots of parties. He's responsible for all the Chrysler plants in the U.S. I found out about six years after we hired him that he had a history of nervous care, but since it didn't seem to interfere with his work, it didn't matter to me. Perhaps it went along with being a salesman.

Today Louie looked upset. "I don't know whether you know this or not, Robbie, but they've transferred me to Cleveland."

I didn't know it, and it came as a surprise to me. It was a logical thing to do. We were moving original finish to Cleveland. He was our main salesman for original finish, but I would have liked to have been told.

"The thing is I've got to stay here in Detroit and report to Kahane in Cleveland. Harold's upset about it. I don't mind it yet. It means driving to Cleveland three times a week, but it's OK with me."

There wasn't anything I could do for him. Ultimately, when this plant closed down completely he would be transferred to Cleveland. We talked about it and I told him that it would be hard on him for a while, but when the transfer was completed, then he'd be operating out of Cleveland.

"And then driving to Detroit three times a week," Louie laughed without any humour.

And I thought: so much for Baker's being in a poor geographic position.

I don't mention this visit from Louis Arnot, our chief original finish salesman just to show you how wrong General Office was in their thinking. I mention this because Louie was one of three salesmen who passed away during the two-year period of this closing. We had seven Detroit-based salesmen in all, and three of them died during the closing. Louie had a fatal heart attack almost five months to the day after he first came into my office worried about his transfer to Cleveland. Will Calloway, a refinish salesman, had a heart attack right in the plant and died. That was in September. And Harold Peterson, he just died. As far as I know, he died and that's all. Harold, Will, Louie Arnot were all nervous excitable men. Perhaps this goes with being good salesmen. Perhaps it would have happened to them anyway. I don't know. But three of them died during the period of closing.

After Arnot's visit, my day settled down. The plant was running smoothly. Howard Green came by at noon and we had lunch together at a small restaurant on Grand River. I asked him about transfer rights. How many old-timers would be taken along?

"None from the hourly people," Howard said. "Frank, you know as well as I do, it's going to be easier to start from scratch in a new, automated plant."

Sadly he was right. He wanted to know if I could picture Ned Rockwell moving down to Ohio and telling everyone down there how he used to play pinochle every morning from 8:45 to 9:15. And I smiled, and we changed the subject.

Howard did congratulate me on the rise in production. "It's amazing," he said "They don't know what to make of it in Pittsburgh."

I said, "Tell them the men are loyal. They're Baker men, and they always will be."

Howard agreed. He said there never would be another plant like this one. Tell people they're going to be terminated in a year or so time, and not only do they not walk out, break machinery and windows—they work harder.

I guess by mutual silent agreement we both changed the subject again. We were old friends and knew each other and our lives too well and we were just fast running out of things to talk about that wouldn't embarrass us. But that's not fair either. We were both doing our jobs. I was burying the plant, and he was watching me.

I got home early and Doris and I went out to eat. We try to eat out at least twice a week. Cooking's hard on her. We went to Karl's and Doris talked about a letter she got from her brother Dick who's opened a gift shop down in Arkansas. They wanted us to come down and stay a few weeks. Doris had written them about the plant closing and my early retirement. They said there were plenty of places down there to rent while we made up our minds about buying. I would love the lakes, the fishing, the walking; I would love this and that. It seemed her family wanted me down there in the worst way.

Could they be a little hard up? I wondered. It made Doris happy, though, to chatter on about moving, so I sat there and smiled and we talked about Arkansas: I owed her that at least.

Saturday. This morning I went in to talk with the two college boys who come in Saturday mornings to try to computerize our operation and see what's going wrong. I listened to their complaints about this and that and told them not to worry, we're producing more paint these days than we ever did before. Before 1963 our average was nine gallons of paint per man-hour. In the spring of 1963 when I had taken over, I had it up to 12 gallons per man-hour. Last month it was 17. In the old days we used to congratulate ourselves when we turned out 25,000 gallons of paint a day; this past month we were past 40,000. In our so-called obsolete plant that the company has written off. The men are sticking and working harder. So it turns out loyalty is a one-way street running from Detroit to Pittsburgh. The college boys looked a little embarrassed at my speeches and busied themselves with their punch cards.

Home at noon. Doris saw me picking up the *Free Press* and she said, "Frank, what are you going to do today?"

"Why, I don't know," I said. "Read the paper to start with."

"Let's go shopping together, Frank. We haven't gone shopping together for years."

"What do we need?"

"Let's go shopping, Frank."

There was a little girl plea in her voice so I put down the paper and we went shopping. We went out to Northland shopping center, the J. L. Hudson out there, and we walked through it. And I mean walked through. She went to look at some blouses and I followed her and for a moment it was like old times when we weren't so well off. But she didn't buy any blouses and then she started going from one counter to another, looking at things, holding them up, no buying.

Blouses, skirts, stockings, shoes, kerchiefs, jackets, coats, hats, jewelry—she moved like the wind, never staying at one counter more than two minutes and I followed her until finally she was through at a notions counter, going through a hundred things and chattering like a magpie and starting to move toward the perfume counter. I stopped her, took her by the arm and made her look at me square in the face. "Doris," I said, "what the devil is the matter?"

Tears came into her eyes. "Frank," she said. "Frank," she said.

"What is it?" I demanded.

She only shook her head and said: "If you don't know by now you never will."

I knew. I'd always known. You know, it's a terrible thing not to need anything, and it's a terrible thing not to be needed yourself. It's no good, being childless. It separates you from other people, and it separates you from each other. It wasn't the kind of thing I dwelled on because I had my baby—the plant; but I could see the time was soon coming when there might be nothing for me to do but wander through counters like her, not needing anything. I swore then and there that I wouldn't let that happen to me; and I swore I'd pay Doris the debt I owed her. I'd pay her back for all the happiness the plant had given me and all the unhappiness it had somehow caused her.

Sunday. Drove into the country. Plymouth, Ann Arbor, Howell . . . looking for miniatures.

Monday. The plant is humming as it has never hummed before. Men are more certain than ever the plant will not close. At least that is their outward demeanor. Sometime during midmorning I ran into Ned Rockwell sitting with a group in the cafeteria. When I came back through a few minutes later he was alone. He looked up at me.

"And I aim to stay right here too, Mr. Robertson," he says with that tough voice of his.

I smiled. "Can I join you for a cup of coffee, Ned?" I asked him.

He was flabbergasted. "It's a free country," he finally said.

I got a cup of coffee and I could see the whole place looking at us. Rockwell eyes me suspiciously and I could see him wondering whether or not he ought to send out for the rest of his committee so it didn't look as if he was being friendly with management or running a chance of being taken in by management.

"No, Ned," I said. "This isn't business or anything. I just want to say: these are going to be difficult times ahead for us all. For me, for you, for the plant. Above all, for the men. I want to tell you to take as much time as you want looking after the men. I'll put someone else in the tankhouse with Mitch Sims if you want. You take as much time as you like on union business."

I guess nothing I could have said would have astonished him more. He stared at me and he could see I meant it. He swallowed and said: "I'll do my best to take care of the men."

"I know you will," I said quietly, "and if there's anything I can do to help you. Let me know."

He didn't say anything more. We talked about other things. I finished my coffee and left and I could feel his eyes on my back as I left. And I knew what he was thinking. He was thinking that he wasn't the only one that cared. From that time on Ned Rockwell and I were partners. I guess you might say I used him to keep the plant going. I did. It paid us more to have him in the cafeteria keeping the men content than it did to have him working in the tankhouse. Later Howard Green congratulated me on having used Rockwell so effectively, but at the time, at that moment in the cafeteria, I know, I swear, I was just thinking of the men. I was thinking of how they felt, their sanity, their health. Some of them, I knew they knew what was happening. Like Duane Paddleford, a lab technician. He had eighteen years with Baker. One day he assured me the plant wasn't going to close. The company was bluffing, the union would make sure anyway that the plant stayed open. But the day after I talked to Rockwell in the cafeteria, I saw Paddleford in the lab and I was astonished. He was a young man, in his forties, a good-looking man with a full head of hair last week, and now he looked just terrible. His skin had broken into rashes and his hair was falling out in huge patches. It was the damnest thing I ever saw. I said to him: "Duane, what the devil's the matter?"

He smiled sickly and said: "I don't know, Mr. Robertson. The doctor tells me it's a nervous condition, but I don't even know when it started or why. I'd like to keep a hat on but it gets so hot in here."

And on he blabbed about how he got up one morning and his hair was falling out and he didn't know why, and he was one of those who supposedly believed the company was bluffing. I wondered how many other walking wounded we had around there. And then I thought: *But what does it matter? Production is up; the plant is performing miracles, and if the insides of Duane Paddleford and a few hundred other poor fellows are churning up and down in fear and confusion, what does it matter as long as they do their jobs? It's Duane Paddleford's production figures that show up on a desk in Pittsburgh, not his hideous scalp or his nervous condition.*

What did it matter, indeed? Well, I found out later how much it mattered—to my own insides.

I put Paddleford out of my mind and went back to my office and tended to my own affairs. That day and other days too.

Phase One Ends

There was every reason for the hourly-rated men at Baker to believe either (1) that the company was bluffing about the closing or (2) that the union could prevent the move even if they were not bluffing. Nothing in the union negotiations with management had indicated otherwise.

The union was still seeking to bargain on whether or not the company would move when, early in February of that year, Arthur Phelan settled with the Atlas Company out of court. He settled because the judge in the Circuit Court of Appeals in Cincinnati informed him that he would be ruling against his argument that the existence of a contract restricted a company's right to relocate from one town or one state to another.

The judge would cite the NLRB ruling in the Brown Transportation case of 1953 which stated that if a company moved from one town to another, even if the towns were only five miles apart, the contract did not follow, although in the California Footwear Case of October, 1955, the NLRB had declared that if a company relocated a plant within a metropolitan area the union and the contract followed the work. Even if the company moved twenty miles within the metropolitan area.

In short, Arthur Phelan's attempt to make new law had failed and he settled out of court with the Atlas Company and also with another company the UAW was suing—the Lincoln Tube Company.

Lincoln Tube had moved from Detroit to Arkansas without giving prior notice to the union and without engaging in collective bargaining. The UAW had been seeking damages of $12 million— $60,000 for each of the 200 employees affected by the move, plus $75 a year in severance pay for every year of seniority.

Because of the ruling against the UAW in the Atlas case, the UAW settled with Lincoln Tube for $50 per year of seniority in severance pay. A suit against another company, an automotive parts company, was also settled about this time for $30 a year in severance pay. The Atlas settlement amounted to $54 a year for every year of seniority.

The settlement with Atlas took longer than the others because the union rep there claimed that the plant manager at the time of contract negotiations three years before had agreed verbally that the company would not relocate. The company denied such a verbal commitment. There was no proof and this hassle delayed, but did not prevent, the union's settling out of court.

Mike Harrah was aware of all these out-of-court settlements, aware of the "complication"—the alleged verbal commitment—in the Atlas case, and, most importantly, aware that Arthur Phelan's attempt to make new law had failed.

He was therefore not at all surprised when on February 18 Howard Green called him into his office to read a letter from Peter Thompson, President of West Side Local, which said, in part:

February 18, 1964

Howard H. Green
Divisional Director, Industrial Relations
Paint and Brush Division
The Pennsylvania Corporation
1 City Center
Pittsburgh 22, Pennsylvania

Dear Mr. Green:

At the January 23, 1964, meeting of the company and union representatives, the company's position as stated by you was that viewing the situation realistically, you felt there was no counter-proposal the union could produce which would influence the company to change its decision to close and relocate the Baker plant.

Therefore, considering these circumstances, it seems appropriate to us that the company and the union now discuss the matter of the impact of said move upon the employees. We request, therefore, that the company set a time and place for a meeting so that collective bargaining on this point can take place.

By proceeding to the matter of collective bargaining the union does not in any way acknowledge that the company has fulfilled its statutory duty to bargain on the basic issue of whether or not to move. Nor do we acknowledge that, under the present collective bargaining contract, the company has the legal right to move. I repeat what I stated in my letter of January 10, 1964— the union reserves its right to enforce its contractual rights should these matters not be settled satisfactorily through collective bargaining.

Yours truly,

Peter Thompson
President
West Side Local ———— UAW

Carbon copies had been sent to F. R. Robertson, C. Koonz, A. Phelan, and N. Rockwell.

Arthur Phelan was throwing in the sponge, Harrah thought, and well he might.

"What's your schedule look like, Mike?" Green asked him.

"Pretty much the same as yours," Harrah replied. The two of them were arbitrating grievances in Springdale, Pennsylvania, and Newark, and the only clear dates they had in the near future were March 10 and March 12.

"Do you want me to draft an answer?" Green asked him.

"No, I'll do it," Harrah said. "I'll offer them a choice of March 10th or 12th and also respond to the last paragraph where they're still threatening to sue us if we move." He grinned. "They don't go down easy, do they?"

"No," Green said, "and I can't say that I blame them."

Harrah drafted a reply to Thompson to go out under Green's signature. After offering the union a choice of the two March dates, he went on to state:

I sincerely regret the union feels the company has failed to fulfill its statutory obligations to bargain on the basic decision whether or not to close the manufacturing facilities at the Baker plant. We advised you on November 13, 1963, that such a possibility was in the offering and stated at that time our willingness to consider any proposals the union would have which might permit the Baker operations to continue in Detroit.

The union, however, failed to reply to our request until January 6, 1964, at which time the Company was advised by the union that it regarded a shutdown of the plant during the term of the present contract as a violation of said contract and asked for a meeting to discuss this whole matter. At the meeting, held on January 10, 1964, the union again failed to propose any alternatives to the company but again repeated that the company had no legal right to close the Baker operation during the term of the present collective bargaining contract. Indeed, it was not until January 23, 1964, after the decision to close the facility had already been made, that the union finally expressed any willingness to discuss this matter.

Accordingly, the company feels it has satisfied its statutory duty to bargain since the union failed to respond within a reasonable period to the company's invitation of November 13, 1963.

Yours truly,

Howard H. Green
Divisional Director of Industrial Relations
Coatings & Resins Division

Carbon copies were sent to F. R. Robertson, C. Koonz, A. Phelan, N. Rockwell, and M. Harrah.

And there it was, Harrah thought, both sides stating it officially for the record once more as they moved out of Phase One and into Phase Two, for it was a delicate business and who knew at what point one might have to backtrack. The important thing was to have a clean record. To show good faith, even though it was obvious to the union and to everyone else, for that matter, that the decision to close Baker had been made a long time ago and nothing could really change it. Still one had to play the game for the record, for the NLRB or the courts, should Phelan take it there. And Phelan had to play the game for the NLRB and for the courts also, and— most importantly—for his own people.

Actually, everything was proceeding satisfactorily. The plant's production was satisfactory; Frank Robertson had proven the right choice to close the plant; they would probably not lose a single customer and they would be doing, in Harrah's view, the decent thing by Baker's workingmen.

On March 1 Howard Green received a letter from Thompson stating that the union would like to meet on Thursday, March 12, at 10 A.M. Green immediately responded, accepting the date and the time. The battle to save the plant from closing, now just about over, was entering phase two—how best to soften the impact of defeat on the men.

The Doctors Say It
Must Have Been Nerves

```
Name: Duane Paddleford
Age: 44
Married: Norma May Carter, 1947
Children: Barry, 18; Stuart, 17; Susie, 3
Religion: Protestant
Education: high school in West Virginia
Occupations: 1941–42, hardware store clerk
             1942–47, paper mill
             1947–65, Baker Color Company:
                        stock clerk—1947–49, refinish dept.—
                        1949–59, lab ass't.—1959–65
             1965–    Ford Motor Company, inspector on line
Residence: 14320 Elder, Livonia, Michigan
Health: history of allopecia areata—or partial hair loss.
```

Anyone who had predicted that Duane Paddleford would get a good job after Baker closed would have been hooted at by the men and even by Paddleford himself. Paddleford, low in self-esteem, was sure that his world was going to fall apart when the Baker plant closed.

Of course during the two-year period of the closing Paddleford, like many of the men, didn't put much stock in the company's threat to move. The plant covered twelve acres and included eighteen separate buildings. No one, to Duane Paddleford's way of thinking, was going to move this plant anyway.

Like the others, he was aware that the union was meeting with the company and discussing things, but then they were always meeting together and discussing things. Paddleford didn't put much stock in the union, and not much more in management. He just hoped things could stay the same. He liked Baker; it was a big family. And he liked going home each night to his own family. The work at Baker was never so strenuous that he couldn't throw a ball with Barry and Stuart in the late afternoon when the weather was good. Every Monday night he ran a meeting of Troop 408 of the Boy Scouts and he wasn't too tired for that. Paddleford loved being a scoutmaster. He liked bringing the boys along, helping them on their advancement, the older scouts on their merit badges. He taught them to box compasses, read maps, apply first aid; they were a church troop and he was pleased when the boys greeted him at Sunday morning services. Many of them were sons of professional people—engineers, lawyers, dentists. He liked camping with them —whether on a quick overnight to Kensington or a weekend to Point Pelee, Ontario, or a two-week rugged hiking tour of Isle Royale. Barry, his older boy, was an Eagle Scout now and a real help with the troop. Barry was a fine athlete also, and so was Stuart. Paddleford was proud of his boys, who had an easy confidence that somehow he always lacked. He was crazy about little Susie. Everyone made jokes when they heard that he had boys 18 and 17 years old and a girl of three. The fact of the matter was that he and Norma had half-kidded for years about trying once more for a girl, and then had sort of given up when, well it was one of those things, you know how those things are. He took a little kidding at work when they found out, and Norma was half-annoyed and half-frightened at her age to be having another kid, but when it turned out to be a girl, well they always wanted a girl and they were happy. They were spoiling her, he knew that, but well, there weren't going to be any other kids and she was such a cute little thing.

"I paint," Paddleford says. "That's my hobby. Painting pictures. Nothing fancy. I mean, to tell the truth, I can't paint at all. I paint by the numbers, but you see those pictures?—Well Norma insisted on framing them, but I know they're no good. Still I get a kick out of painting. Little Susie sits and watches me paint. I painted the whole house inside last winter. Not by the numbers, no. Ha . . . that's a good one. No, I painted it with good old Baker paint. I've still got quite a bit. They never minded us taking paint out. Of course they never said we could, but just about everyone walked out of that plant with a quart or two of paint under his shirt at one time or other.

"My last job at the plant was in the lab. I helped them analyze paint. I'd spray the paint to get the right color and then the chemist would break it down. I'd have liked to have had his job, but I wasn't smart enough to get to college. My boys, I hope they'll go to college. They're a lot smarter than I am. So's my wife. I just try to keep busy with painting and scouting and throwing a ball with the boys and watching out for Susie. I like my new job. I make more money now than I did at Baker but it's a lot different. Less personal. You don't know the guys the way you knew guys at Baker. There's a Baker man working the same shift with me and he tells me that Whitey Stinsik who used to work in shipping is over at Ford now and I looked him up and Whitey and I talk about old times when we can. He says there's two more guys from Baker working at Ford on the afternoon shift but he's lost track of most of the guys.

"I missed Baker at first, but I was lucky to get this job. I don't even know how I got it. I was sure I wasn't going to get a job. I'd been at Baker all my life. I thought I'd stay there till I retired. I just couldn't picture working anywhere else. I got movies of the old place. In September of '65, a month before they terminated me, I took movies of the guys leaving the morning shift. You weren't supposed to do that, but I did it. Norma gave me an 8 millimeter movie camera for my birthday and I got up on the roof of maintenance and took pictures. Ned Rockwell, Steve Toucek, Matt Gargan, Big Dave Masiak, Ben Harrison—hourly guys and supervisors, all,— they waved up at me as they left the plant. I never knew they'd mean so much to me.

"At Ford, it's an assembly line and I'm an inspector. I work hard. Harder than I ever worked at Baker. None of us worked hard there and that's why they closed us up. We didn't deserve that plant. All the goof-offs and goldbrickers. It was a regular old folks' home. I was sure none of us would get new jobs. I really didn't know I was thinking this. I found out my subconscious was. I guess I had what they call an emotional breakdown. I didn't know what it was. You won't believe this—a couple of months after we first heard that the company was thinking about closing us down, my hair began to fall out. Overnight like. In big clumps. I was embarrassed all right. I don't remember much about it now; the doctors said it must have been nerves, so I guess I was pretty worried and didn't even know it. I can hardly remember it at all now, can you, Norma?"

Norma Paddleford is a pretty, plump, gentle-faced woman in her early forties. She and Paddleford come from the same town— Wilton, West Virginia—but she didn't know him till much later. Paddleford's parents had gone up north in 1935 when he was twelve to look for work and Paddleford had grown up in Detroit. But he always remembered Wilton, and when he was sixteen he began taking summer trips back there to visit relatives. It was on one of these trips to Wilton that he met Norma May Carter. He saw her every summer till they both finished high school, she in Wilton and he in Detroit. Then he went down and married her, and for three years during World War II they lived in Wilton while he worked in a hardware store and the paper mill. In 1944, they moved up to Detroit and he got a job at Baker.

"It didn't matter much where Duane worked as far as I was concerned," Norma Paddleford says, "Baker was as good as anywhere. He never complained about it."

"Why'd I complain?" Paddleford says with a laugh. "It was an old folks' home, like I said. But tell'm about my hair falling out. Norma saw it before I did."

Mrs. Paddleford blushes. It's not really the kind of thing one talks about or one wants to remember, and she's annoyed at her husband for being either so innocent or so stupid or so proud—or all three— about it, but she does remember the first time it happened quite clearly. It was a weekday morning and the alarm had gone off at its usual time: 6 A.M. Duane had to be at work at 7:30, the boys at school by 8, and so she woke up at 6 and then woke Duane at 6:30.

It was a cold, dark, March morning and a rain was falling, and she remembers thinking how nice it would be if after she got Duane and the boys off Susie would sleep for another hour and maybe she could get a little nap in and then she remembered she was going to the market that day anyway.

Mrs. Paddleford put on her bathrobe, putting on the closet light to find it. She remembers looking back at Duane sleeping and it struck her there was something funny about him, but she didn't know what. The way his hair lay was funny, but it could have been because he'd slept on it. She went downstairs, turned up the heat, set the coffee on, made orange juice and turned on the radio. It was supposed to rain all day. She set the table for breakfast.

It was close to 6:30 when she went upstairs to wake Duane. Ordinarily he was a light sleeper. She was about to touch his shoulder when she saw clumps of matted hairs on the sheet, on the pillow. She reached out and touched his head and a clump of hair came off in her fingers.

"Duane," she gasped, "Duane."

He woke instantly and looked at her. "What's the matter?" he asked.

She bit her lip, pointed to the hairs lying on the sheet. "Your head —your hair—"

"What's the matter with it?"

He felt the top of his head. "What the devil is going on?" He got out of bed and went to the bathroom mirror. He stared. His hair was falling—had fallen—out in clumps. Patches of bare skin shone in the overhead light. "My God, Norma, I'm sick."

He felt faint, a sudden rushing in his stomach. "I'm sick, Norma. I can't go to work."

She was at his side. "It's probably nothing, Duane. It's something Ralph can fix." Ralph was their doctor. He was also a fishing buddy. He had a boy in the scout troop. That was how they'd come to know him. Ralph was on Paddleford's troop committee. He could call Ralph up at any time of the day or night. He could call Ralph up right now. But he'd never been sick in his life. Not a single day. He'd never been inside a hospital except to visit.

"I'll get the boys up, Duane," Norma said. "You go back to bed and rest. You don't have to go in to work. Try to get some more sleep."

But that was foolish and they both knew it. He lay in bed and stared at the ceiling and every once in a while he'd pass his hand over his scalp and feel the skin and once another clump of hair came off in his hand and he was scared and frightened, because he knew he was sick now, real sick. He was sure he was going to die.

"We saw Ralph at nine o'clock that morning. His office is around the block. I wore a hat. I never felt more embarrassed in my life. But I'll say this much for Ralph. He acted like he always expected me to walk half-bald into his office.

"He examined my head under the light and a clump of hair came off in his hands. He made me strip to the waist and then he gave me a thorough exam, checking my skin all over and then my heart and lungs. He asked me if I ever had ringworm, and I said no. He said he couldn't see any signs of it and he guessed this condition of mine might be caused by some emotional problems, and I said I didn't have any emotional problems that I knew of and Norma who was there said: 'Baker's closing.'

"Ralph says, 'Oh.'

"And I say: 'Naw, they're just bluffing about that. That's what I think.'

"And Ralph shakes his head and says: 'You may think you think that, but deep down you're probably thinking something else.'

"He gave me some pills to take. Tranquilizers, I guess, and told me to stay home for a couple of days and take it easy and that I could go back to work when I felt like it. He'd write me a letter for the company. I guess I got upset and told Norma I couldn't ever go back to work, looking like the way I did. They'd kid the pants off me. I could hear them already and Norma says that they'll do nothing of the sort and if I felt funny about it I could wear a hat. She was sure lots of guys wore hats in labs because of the paint spraying sometime, and I said no one in our lab wore a hat but I'd think about it and what I thought was, 'You got to go back to work no matter how embarrassed you feel and one way or another your hat has got to come off during the course of a day, so if I'm going to go back to work I'll go without a hat.'

"I went back to work two days later and I didn't wear a hat and everyone stared at it OK and asked me what was the matter and I told them honestly: 'My hair's falling out because I got emotional problems.' And no one kidded me. Not a soul. Not even the kidders.

"I took the tranquilizers and kept on working. The kids at scouts didn't say anything. I wear a scout cap there anyway, but I told them I had an illness, but I'd be all right and not to worry.

"I kept doing everything I'd been doing, and I guess the pills helped. Because about a month later Norma looks at me across the table and she says: 'Duane, your hair's starting to grow back.'

"And I look in the mirror and by God, sure enough, I can see little hairs growing back. And Susie she kisses me. I almost cried then for real. This was in March of '64. By December all my hair was back and I was almost ready to go to the barber's again. And by September of '65, I'd pretty much forgot the whole thing. I was off the pills too.

"And then do you know what happened? The next month? October of 1965—it started all over again. I woke up one morning and my hair was falling out again. I couldn't believe it. Not again. It was awful, even worse the second time. I felt like crying. You didn't think it could happen again. Not twice. But it did. Of course, in one way I knew it wasn't so bad. I knew I wasn't going to die; I knew it was my nerves and I knew what it was making me so nervous— Baker. Just the week before I had got the letter telling me I was to be terminated the following Friday. And I guess that did it. Started it all up again. I guess I was more worried about finding a new job than I knew.

"I went back to Ralph and he put me on the pills again. Three days after I was laid off at Baker I signed on at Ford, and I haven't missed a day's work since. I've even been promoted to inspector— and look at my head! It started growing back two weeks after I started in at Ford, and now I go to the barber's twice a month. He's got his work cut out for him too. Isn't it something how you can be worried about a thing and never know it till your hair falls out?"

Throw the Sponge Slowly

The meeting of March 12 was the first of a series of meetings designed to find ways to soften the impact of the move on the men. The battle had moved to Phase Two. Officially, however, Perry DeMoss would state that Phase One wasn't really over, the union merely agreed to expand the discussions to include the impact of the move.

When the UAW threw in the sponge, Mike Harrah thought, they threw it in very slowly. He could sympathize with Arthur Phelan and with Perry DeMoss too. They were bargaining under the noses of their clients—Rockwell, Tyner, Bimmler, Glazko, Bender, and other members of the shop committee.

Harrah had flown into Detroit the night before and stayed at the Dearborn Inn. Green stayed with friends in Detroit. This morning Harrah, Green, and Lee Jones, the industrial relations man at Baker, met in Robertson's office at 10 A.M. The three of them discussed what might happen in the meeting while Robertson sat behind his big manager's desk with all its coats of varnish and said nothing. Harrah glanced at him curiously now and then. It was strange, to say the least, to see a plant manager so detached, so remote from the battle raging between the company and the union. He looked almost in some emotional no-man's land, but, Harrah guessed, he might have production problems on his mind. He was doing a remarkable job with the plant, shipping original finish to Cleveland—six truckloads weekly—keeping production higher than it had ever been before, getting ready to dismantle the plant. The managerial genius that dwelled within Frank Robertson's small-school-teachery-looking exterior Harrah could not see, but he would be pleased to testify to it in any court of the land.

Green predicted that the union would move very slowly this morning and that they would start bargaining high. It turned out that he was quite right.

They went into the color conference room, two doors down from Robertson's office, at 10:45 A.M. The meeting convened at 10:50 with Harrah, Green, Lee Jones, and Robertson on one side, and Perry DeMoss looking grim, Arthur Phelan shuffling his papers—

looking confident, just as a smart lawyer fresh from a series of defeats should look, Harrah thought—Rockwell and the rest of the union committee looking as if they'd just been briefed not to talk too much, seated on the other side.

Everyone shook hands except for Ned Rockwell who announced for the umpteenth time he wasn't shaking hands with any company sons of bitches. Howard Green whose hand had been mechanically extended for the umpteenth time was caught again. His face turned red. Robertson smiled and turned away. Phelan pretended to study his papers, and Mike Harrah laughed. Ned Rockwell always took him back to the south side of Chicago where he'd been born. Harrah had an idea that he and Rockwell could have a fine time emptying a bottle together.

Since the meeting was officially called by the union, Perry De-Moss began talking first.

"We asked for this meeting in order to try to begin another phase of our talks regarding the proposed relocation of the Baker plant," Perry said. He looked across the table at Green. "But before we get into that, I want to take issue with the letter you sent to President Thompson. This letter suggests that it was the union's inaction which was responsible for the company's decision to relocate the plant. I find this an incredible idea. I know of no other case where a company has approached a union and said it was considering a relocation and the union went out and took the initiative to bargain. It would be suicide for a union to initiate negotiations and offer relief. We feel the company has not satisfied its legal duties and we will not take the rap for your decision to move the plant."

Harrah nodded. Everything was going as it should. Talking for the record DeMoss was countering the company's position. This would be important if the whole thing ended up in court.

Green replied: "I'm sorry you feel this way, Perry. You should be aware—as I'm sure your counsel, Mr. Phelan, is aware—we had no legal obligation whatsoever to get in touch with you last November. We did that, however, because we didn't want to hurt any of our people unnecessarily."

And that made two of them talking for the record. Harrah mentally applauded Green's statement as a bid to wrest away some of the shop committee's confidence in their union rep and legal counsel.

Phelan spoke up: "Let me interject here for a moment. I think we're all of us aware that both sides have a paramount interest in making as good a record as we can. I think your attitude about the November meeting is a falsely based one. Just because you didn't act as badly as some other plants have in the past, this doesn't mean you have fulfilled your legal obligations. The union is entitled to the opportunity to bargain the company out of his decision to close down the plant and move, and they are, most importantly, entitled to do this bargaining far ahead of the decision. There would be no point to it all otherwise."

Green smiled. "I'll go along with you, Mr. Phelan, when you say that each party is interested in protecting its position. Again, I say we have fulfilled our legal and moral obligations."

There was a pause. That, after all, was that.

Perry DeMoss changed the tack slightly. "A couple of weeks ago I met with the plant committee. I've been part of this committee for a long time, and I'll say now that the company in the past has always treated the Baker workingman decently. The committee continues to be hopeful that the company will go on giving us good and fair treatment. As a result of this meeting two weeks ago, we called Mr. Phelan and asked him *not* to proceed with the lawsuit—"

Perry paused, waiting for the implication of his words to sink in. Harrah did not dare grin. He looked down at his papers. Poor Arthur Phelan. Did he squirm at a time like this? Or did he think the company wasn't aware of his reverses in court? Or perhaps it was merely that Phelan hadn't informed DeMoss (and if not DeMoss, certainly not the others) that his attempt to make new labor law had been shot down. *I'm not going to inform them either,* Harrah thought, *unless he forces me too.* And he didn't think Phelan would do that.

Perry DeMoss went on. "Let me at this point remind you that at our last contract negotiations in 1962 we asked for severance pay. Because you assured us at the time that no plans for closing the plant existed, we dropped that demand."

Harrah heard Green sit up. *We should have gone over this,* he thought. He knew what Perry DeMoss was doing. The settlement with Atlas had taken longer because the union rep there claimed there had been a verbal agreement by the plant manager at the time of contract negotiations not to close the plant during the term

of the contract. Atlas denied this. It was loose, vague, a stumbling
block, a threat, but it would not stand up in court, as Arthur Phelan
well knew.

Harrah looked at Green to see if his colleague wanted help field-
ing this one. If he did, then Harrah would officially inform Phelan—
and thus might also be informing Rockwell and his committee—
that the company was aware that all of Phelan's cases had been defeated in court.

But Green responded magnificently on his own.

"Perry, but you know and I know that no such assurance was given
you. No such assurance could have been given. I had no knowledge
of this plant's closing. I would have been an idiot to try to predict
the future of any plant over a period of two or three years. I couldn't
give that assurance here or any other place. You know as well as I
know the background for what has happened here. For too many
years Baker put all its eggs in one basket with the Chrysler Corporation. I can remember, not so long ago, when I was plant manager I'd lie awake nights wondering what kind of future a plant
like this could have. Everything was wrong about it. Its facilities,
its operations, its sales. It's true we had good years, years of great
prosperity; for every one of those years, we had a bad year, years of
great jeopardy. I can state for a fact, Perry, if Baker hadn't been a
part of the Pennsylvania Corporation, we would have gone down
the drain a long time ago."

Perry DeMoss shook his head. "Howard, I find this difficult to
believe. I know this is not an up-to-date plant, but with all its problems, this plant has been making money for the company."

And this was old hat and no one wanted to go back over it. They'd
covered this ground in the last meeting.

"If I may interrupt," Arthur Phelan said. "I wish to point out,
Mr. Green, that while the union has stated its willingness to bargain
on the impact of the move on the employees, it does not waive its
other claims. I think Mr. Thompson's letter to you pointed this out,
Mr. Green."

Harrah smiled. *Arthur Phelan writes Thompson's letters. I write
Howard Green's.*

"So can we now talk about the impact of the move?" Perry De-
Moss asked. "There are about 300 employees here who will be
totally affected by the shutdown and relocation of this plant. I

understand that the new plant in Ohio is going to employ about 200 people."

Howard Green shook his head. "Perry, if you understand that, you understand more than I do. I haven't got the slightest idea how many people will be employed at the new plant, and I would like to restate something I've said before, we are not exchanging one plant for another. Baker isn't the only plant affected in this move. In all probability, in time it will not even be the only plant totally affected—though right now it's the first. I have no way of knowing, of course, but it's quite possible that in one, two, or five or even ten years from now, some of our other facilities will follow this same route."

"If that's the case," DeMoss said, "we'd like a standard clause added to contracts. . . ." He paused and leaned to one side and began whispering to Phelan. They were, Harrah thought, deciding on a standard clause about relocations to be added to a contract which by December of 1965 would no longer exist. DeMoss had a poor sense of the relevant. Howard gave him a glance and Harrah noddded. They would speed things up a little.

"Perry," Howard said quietly, "rather then try to get too specific at this time, why don't you just indicate to me generally what you want? I've got no specific proposals to make today. I came here to listen."

Phelan nodded and DeMoss began: "To start with, we want employment rights for our people—we want them to be able to transfer their seniority to the new location; secondly, for anybody who doesn't want to go or is unable to go, we want severance pay."

And there it was, out on the table. In time, they'd also bargain about the pension fund, retirement benefits, health insurance, but these two—transfer rights and severance pay—were the key issues. The company's position was set; it had been set for some time now. They knew what the UAW had settled for in severance pay with Atlas and Lincoln Tube, and as for transfer rights, Wysse Allen had been very specific about that.

Now that the subject of bargaining on the impact had been broached, it was time to go slowly again.

Howard Green pointed out that the company had had no formal plan about severance pay until a month ago when they negotiated a severance pay plan in their new fiberglass division—although various situations in fiberglass were not comparable to this one. The employees there had life-term seniority. Since bad times had fallen on the glass division, several thousand employees were laid off. Some for years. Neither company nor union knew where some of them were now located or whether indeed they were interested in returning to work. As a result, a severance pay plan had been established and those employees who stepped forward and claimed severance pay would be irrevocably removed from the seniority list.

Here at Baker, although the company was willing to discuss severance pay, it had no legal obligation to discuss it.

"We haven't drawn up any severance plan offer," Green said, which was not exactly true, Harrah thought, "but we're prepared to talk about this with you."

"What about transfer rights?" Perry asked.

Green sighed. "I can't give you a clear-cut answer, Perry. We will accept job applications from here or anywhere else."

"That's damned white of you," Ned Rockwell sneered.

Green went on, ignoring Rockwell, "We'd be very happy to accept applications, but as far as seniority goes and transferring it, this, as you know, is a very complex problem."

"Not to us, it isn't," Rockwell said. "It's damned simple. You're taking away our jobs."

"These are layoffs of considerable magnitude," Green said. "I can assure you the company will have skilled personnel experts who will aid Baker people in this situation. We will send these experts from our home office to help Frank Robertson and Lee Jones in getting Baker people jobs in other industries in Michigan; we will, in fact, be establishing a free professional job-hunting service."

"We're not interested in a free job-hunting service," Rockwell said. "We've got jobs. We're interested in keeping them."

"That's right," said another member of the committee.

"What about other jobs with the company?"

"I'd be less than candid with you, Mr. Phelan, if I didn't say that this is a very remote possibility. All our other plants have long seniority lists, and there are no gaps in employment. I'd be very surprised if there would be job openings for more than eight or nine people presently in the whole division."

"What's wrong with Baker people going with the new plant in Ohio?" Rockwell asked.

Phelan nodded. "We'd like to discuss some of the problems you
see in letting our Detroit people here go down to Ohio with the
new plant, so we can take appropriate action."

"All right," Green said. "One problem is that we're going to have
the Ohio plant in full operation before this plant is shut down. Your
long seniority people have the right to work on here longer than the
short seniority people, yet you will argue that these are the people,
the senior people, who should get preferential employment rights
in the new plant. A situation like this, you'll agree, is impossible."

"They're going to weasel out again," Rockwell said.

"We might be able to work out something with our high seniority
people here," Phelan said.

"I've been around industrial relations quite a bit," Howard Green
said, "and it is my view that most older employees have little desire
to move anyway. They usually have deep roots in the place they are,
and would rather remain."

"You made the big move to Pittsburgh all right," Rockwell said.

Arthur Phelan gave Rockwell an irritated glance. Then he said:
"Mr. Green, I've been told by the shop committee that there are
quite a few people who would like to move with the plant to Ohio.
After all, this isn't like leaving the United States. Ohio's right next
door to Michigan."

Green was silent. Then he said: "What else do you want?"

Perry DeMoss said: "Besides severance pay and transfer rights,
we want to know more about the pension plan we've been part of all
these years. As I understand it, the plan calls for it to be funded
in thirty years, but some time ago the company told us they would
be doing it in ten years."

"I'd like to point out," Green said, "it was at the insistence of the
President of the union before Mr. Thompson—Mr. Boland—Mr.
Boland felt that too much wage money was being diverted into the
pension fund and it was he who insisted that the Baker plan be
funded over a thirty-year period. Fortunately for you, the company
did not give in. Right now it's my understanding that the pension
fund is completely funded. I should have the exact figures on the
status of the pension plan when we meet next."

The pension fund and health insurance were minor issues. Severance pay and transfer rights were the major ones. Perry DeMoss
returned to severance pay. That, at least, they knew they could get.

"One other thing, Howard," DeMoss said. "I think any severance pay plan we draw up ought to cover everybody. Since the company notified us of their intention to move, some of our people have been able to find jobs and they'll be leaving. It seems only fair to me that these people ought to be covered too."

Harrah smiled. Perry DeMoss was starting his bargaining high, all right. He was starting beyond the philosophy of severance pay, the aim of which was to keep people at their jobs until the company terminated them.

But this had to be handled tactfully. Severance pay worked as a tool for the company, it was also a sop to a defeated union—something they could save face with, with their members.

Howard was good at talking around it. "What you're suggesting, Perry," he replied, "seems to defeat the purpose of the plan."

Harrah glanced at him warningly. Green went on. "Let's face this thing as it is. Any severance plan we agree on isn't going to be a permanent umbrella for an employee the rest of his life." Harrah relaxed. "A severance pay plan, any severance pay plan, is merely designed to bridge the gap between jobs. In my opinion it's unreasonable and unfair to take money out of the kitty and give it to employees who already have jobs at the expense of employees who don't."

Arthur Phelan spoke up. "If we're going to work out a severance pay plan that is in any way comparable to other UAW plans any decisions about how a fund is to be divided will probably be made by the union. The company would establish such a fund and the union will decide how it should be split up since the company doesn't really care."

Green nodded. "What you say has some validity. I would remind you, though, that the melon is only so big, and whether you cut it up into squares or balls or whatever kinds of chunks you want, those parts of the melon you give to those people who already have jobs will have to come out of the others' shares."

Dick Tyner spoke up for the first time in his reedy voice. "You make it sound like some of the guys working are going into good deals. We've got people here with lots of seniority. Maybe they're making two-eighty an hour here. They go out and get another job and it only pays them a dollar-eighty."

"My advice is that if they're offered a job at a dollar-eighty and can't get a higher paying one, then they ought to take it," Green said.

"Sure," Dick Tyner said bitterly. "But we're talking about guys who've spent almost their whole working lives here. Twenty, twenty-one years. Don't you think they deserve something for all these years they put in for the company?"

"Besides a kick in the ass," Rockwell said.

Howard Green shrugged. "I'll only repeat: the melon is so big and how you divide it will be your affair. But I would point out that even if a man is earning a dollar-eighty an hour, that's still more than thirty-five hundred a year."

"And with a pack of kids to feed," Ned Rockwell snorted, "that thirty-five hundred is going to take him a long way."

"Let's make sure we understand each other, Howard," Perry De-Moss said to Green and to Harrah. "What we want for the Baker employees is transfer rights to the Ohio plant based strictly on seniority and qualifications of the employees who want to go. Secondly, for any employee who doesn't want to go, we want severance pay in the amount of 125 dollars for each year of service with the company."

Harrah grinned. The UAW had been settling for severance pay ranging from $30 to $75 a year.

Howard Green responded softly, with a faint smile, "You'll never have to worry about starting the ball rolling too low, Perry. You know that anything like that is just out of the ball park."

Perry's mouth twisted in a knowing look. "You're the same old Howard Green I've known for twenty years."

"You haven't changed much either, Perry. You'll never have to worry about starting too low."

"We could have begun at 250 dollars and worked our way down to 125, but 125 is where we want to end and where we will end. And you know as well as I do, Howard, it's a small enough amount for people who've worked here an average of eighteen years. That kind of time put in is no joke."

"I'll go along with you that it's no joke. The company feels it has an obligation to its people and intends to meet that obligation fairly. We will study your proposals carefully, but I would warn you that what you're asking for is liable to run close to a couple of million dollars."

"A drop in your paint bucket," Rockwell said.

Perry DeMoss said: "I guess we've gone long enough today. You know what our demands are. The next move is up to you. Will you get in touch with us when you're ready to have another meeting?"

Green said: "We will do that."

The meeting was adjourned at 11:57 A.M.

Severance Pay
But no Seniority

Ralph Muzetti, vice-president in charge of industrial relations for all of the Pennsylvania Corporation's plants is *not* anti-union.

"Let me make it clear from the first," says Muzetti, a sharp-faced, stocky executive with a blotchy skin, "unions are part of our management lives. Like the weather, like sunlight and moonlight. It behooves us to understand them and for them to understand us."

Muzetti talks with a raspy voice. Flanked by Mike Harrah and Howard Green, who was once his boss but who now works under him, Muzetti makes a speech. And in his speech he tells how he emerged from Washington in the 1930's as a New Deal lawyer, and how he took a job with the company and how it was when he engaged in his first contract negotiations with a union, which was in 1936 in West Virginia, and how up till that time, though a labor lawyer, he had never met any union leaders, and how shocked he was.

"We entered the room, and I and my boss and the plant manager sat down across a table from the union committeeman. A tall, raw-boned hillbilly. I don't remember his name. And we had hardly said hello and emptied out our briefcases when this union leader plunged in and said: 'You goddamn bastards want to fuck us and I can tell you right now we're going to make you bleed. We're going to make you bleed if it's the last thing we do.'

"And that contract negotiation, that bargaining session, went out the window right then and there. There was a strike, of course. On the train ride back to Pittsburgh, I was going on about the brutishness of the union leader, the kind of language he used, his closed mind, and my boss who was then vice-president in charge of industrial relations—only there was no such thing as industrial relations then, he was just a vice-president—an older man, a lawyer, he just sat there and when I was done all he said was:

" 'I wonder what's wrong with us, Ralph, that that man hates us so violently? Somewhere along the line we've failed with that man and his union.'

"It was a very old-fashioned way to think, to talk, but he was right. A week later he called me into his office and said: 'Ralph, we're going to have a retreat at one of the company's hunting lodges. A no-holds-barred weekend. I want to invite that man and others like him; I want to know why they hate us.'

"Well, we had that retreat, and for three days we holed up in the mountains with some good food and good whisky and a big fire, and there were about thirty of us, half management, half union leaders, and we talked. We talked carefully at first, but under the wise guidance of my boss, we opened up. Frank talk. About who we were, who our fathers and mothers were, what kinds of families we had, what we hoped for from our sons, from life. The union people talked and we talked and something wonderful happened as we were doing this—differences blurred. We were men together.

"The next year, we had another contract negotiation and it was with another plant in West Virginia and that same man who'd been so foul-mouthed the year before and then been to the retreat was representing the plant, and before we opened our talks, he came up to us and he said he was sure we could get together on this thing. He didn't see the need for a strike. He understood our problems just as he was sure we understood his. We were men together.

"Why do I relate this? To say again that neither I nor any member of this big, capitalistic company is anti-union. We can't afford to be. The union is part of our lives; we have to live with them, and they have to live with us.

"But this doesn't mean we like our plants unionized. Frankly, we don't. If we in the Pennsylvania Corporation can do business without a union we're so much the better-off. If we get the union in one of our plants we do our best to work with it honorably, but I'd be less than candid if I said we liked having unions. At one time there was a real need for unions. Unions were a correct antidote to a real abuse. But it's gone way past that today. Today unions throw up real barriers to expanding business, to turning to new lines. Today in our unionized plants only an electrician can screw in a light bulb. So we wait while an electrician is hunted up. We can't change product lines because lines of seniority are so set. We can't bring in new men who could make new products. Seniority prevents us from hiring them and paying them what they're worth. Seniority makes it impossible for a competent young man to be paid more than an incompetent older man. So you find it cheaper in the end to close down the old plant and terminate it and terminate the incompetent older man. They don't understand this yet, but seniority ends up destroying the older worker.

"We're not unionized in the new plant in York, Ohio. The men don't want a union. They're getting paid over the union scale in the area and their fringe benefits are better too. In a recent election they rejected a bid by the Teamsters to represent them. Now over in Newtonville where we built the new resin plant—a plant with only 18 employees—they're unionized and rightfully so. We had lousy management down there and they committed a dreadful series of mistakes and the men voted the union in as a matter of self-protection, and I, personally, don't blame them one bit.

"The fact is we don't always have the right management people in the right spot at the right time. At Baker when we were closing it we had the right man. He was compassionate, he could keep the place together till the very end. You know, he had a nervous break-down when it was all over. What was his name again?"

"Frank Robertson," Howard Green says softly.

"That's right. Robertson. He took that plant closing harder than anyone. He was the right manager at the right time, but down in Newtonville we had the wrong man and so we lost control of the men and the union took over. But in York we're doing all right. Just the threat of the union is keeping us on our toes in York. Our argument there is that we can take care of you better than any union can, and we'll still keep open lines of progress, stay flexible to meet industrial changes. Seniority is an industrial glue. It hardens, and in time things stagnate. We never considered, even for a second, letting the Baker men have seniority transfer rights."

Down in Arkansas, far removed from the gleaming steel and glass towers of Pittsburgh, and the automated plant in York, Ohio, and the dark, dead series of buildings that was once the Baker plant, Frank R. Robertson looks out at the hills and talks about seniority. He too is unhappy about it, but not from the point of view of industrial progress—more from the point of view of the human condition, as he sees it.

"You give a man seniority," Robertson says, "and you take the man out of him. You give him a vested interest in the past, not the future. You make him afraid to make a change, afraid to take a new job, afraid to take his family and move to a new city, a new state. You make him a scared animal. You turn his job into a rut and soon enough into a grave. If some of those men in Dr. Cobb's study are ill because the Baker plant closed, it's because they were led to believe they had jobs for life, led to believe they never had to worry anymore because they had seniority. Seniority destroys men; it doesn't help them."

"But you're sick now yourself and you didn't have seniority."

He smiles. "Maybe I should have moved off earlier too."

Seated behind his desk in Detroit, under the picture of Walter Reuther and four pictures of his own wife and children, Perry De-Moss also has a picture of seniority and it is different from the ones that Muzetti, and Frank Robertson have.

"Seniority has freed the American workingman," says DeMoss with quiet conviction. "Before seniority, a workingman couldn't get a loan from a bank. What was he? A poor stiff that could be fired the next day at the whim of the company. Now on the basis of that little white card stating his years of seniority, a man can buy a home, a car, he can plan his life in a way he never could before. Seniority has given the individual workingman security, stability, and dignity—and I'll take that before industrial progress any day. Christ," he says, leaning forward, "what in hell is industrial progress for anyway?"

He sits back and then because he is smart and tough and honest and can sense the question coming even before it's uttered, he says with an ironic glance at the wall above him: "No, as a union official I don't have seniority. Mr. Reuther doesn't believe in it for us."

In his office in downtown Pittsburgh, sixteen stories above the ground, overlooking the confluence of the Allegheny and Monangahela Rivers and the hills of Millvale and Glenshaw across the Allegheny, Mike Harrah, a lawyer, is not concerned with legalistic answers to the question of transferring seniority rights to the new plant. Nor is he concerned that transferring seniority rights from Baker to York might have meant transferring seniority rights from six or seven different unions, though, he concedes, that was one argument they cited at the bargaining table.

"The real problem, my friend, is that when you take an old, inefficient plant like Baker with people who've been working poorly there for twenty years or more and let these people transfer to a new efficient automated plant—well then you're asking for trouble.

"The Baker people would have brought their bad work habits with them. Past experience tells us that old workers moving to a new plant are always telling the new people in the new plant how it should be done, how they used to do it in the old plant, when the reason we closed the old plant in the first place was because they were doing it badly. Transferred employees create more problems than they solve. They restrict their production to the level they felt was satisfactory at the old plant.

"They also make for discipline problems within the new plant. They're not prone to take orders from newly hired supervisors."

Harrah grins broadly. "And I'll give you this too: they make for problems in community relations. A lot of these guys relocate without their wives. They're trying out the new job and the new town. Three of them will take an apartment together and before you know it they're also trying out the local girls. They find out they don't miss their families as much as they thought they would. They give a few parties, knock up a few of the local belles and the company has got a real public relations problem on its hand in a new community, a community that had welcomed them down there, that in some cases even made tax concessions for them, might have bought them land, and so on. This sort of thing has happened to us twice in towns where we worked hard to get off to a good start. Our image gets considerably dirtied up by these temporary bachelors, half of whom will quit the job anyway within three months."

"Yet at the contract negotiations of March 12th, Howard Green said that 'nothing beats experience.'"

"In a general way that's true," Harrah concedes, "but not with a new automated paint plant. Who needs skilled workers in a new paint plant? Do you know who we've got working for us in Ohio? Farmers. In a paint plant only the maintenance people and maybe the resin kettle operator are legitimately skilled workers. Tinting used to be a skilled trade but down in York we've got electronic tinting. There's no need for experience, and that's a fact."

Harrah stands up and looks out the window. "I'm making us out to be a heartless corporation. We're not. But we exist to make money. There's no other reason for our existence. We're in business. If we don't show a good return on the dollar we go out of business. Baker was showing a poor return. And it had to go. Sure, we felt sorry for the people, the men. We gave them severance pay which we didn't have to, but we weren't going to let them take their seniority into the new plant. That, my friend, would have been poor business."

Seniority Doesn't Mean Security

or

I Wasn't Going to Let It Happen a Second Time

Name: Jerry McNerney
Age: 45
Married: Elizabeth Beggs, 1953
Children: Jerry, Jr., 13; Mary, 12; Tom, 10; John, 9; Gary, 7; Susie, 2
Religion: Catholic
Education: high school in Port Huron
Occupation: Baker Color Company:
        shipping and receiving—1947, resin plant—1950, resin
        plant kettle operator—1951–65
        United Paint Co.—shipping and receiving, one month
        Detroit House of Correction—guard, 1965–
Residence: 12099 Huebler, Detroit, Michigan
Health: pneumonia during period of closing; periods of depression since
    taking present job; wife in poor health since new job.

The difference between Jerry McNerney's present job and his old job at Baker is that no one likes him where he works now and everyone liked him at Baker.

"He was a good worker," Otto Mueller, the last superintendant of the resin plant says, "the best resin kettle operator we had. What is he doing now?"

"He's a prison guard in Detroit."

"McNerney? I don't believe it. He wouldn't take that kind of job."

"But I would, McNerney says with a bitter unhappy smile, "I did."

He is a tall good-looking Irishman with pale blue eyes. A weak, genial face, now morose and unhappy. His eyes light up when he talks about his kids, about baseball—he was once a fine high school ballplayer—but his face clouds over when he talks about his present job, and he tries to be philosophical, detached, "expert" on how he came to his present impasse.

"It was a stupid thing, I know, and I'm a genuinely stupid man, and that I know too. But I thought at the time I was being bright. You know how those things go, don't you? You sit down and figure it out logically and you end up holding the bag. Well, I did just that. I was determined not to let it happen a second time, getting terminated like that. I read up on automation. I heard lots of plants were going to be automated. And if they could close up Baker, just like that, Baker that had been in Detroit for more than half a century, why what could happen to the fly-by-night factories? No, sir, I was determined not to let it happen a second time. My next job would have security. Not seniority. I had the seniority all right. At Baker I had eighteen years and it didn't get me anything. Seniority doesn't mean security, no matter what the union tells you. So I told Elizabeth and swore to myself the next job I took was one where I'd never get laid off.

"I pride myself on being a hard-headed Irishman. I never thought the company was bluffing. For years there'd been rumors about us being obsolete. We were making money, but not enough to suit a big corporation. When that first letter came out I was worried sick. I didn't sleep nights. Elizabeth asked me about it and I told her not to worry, the company was probably bluffing. Why almost everyone thought that. The orders were coming in like they never had before. Production was booming. We'd never been so busy. Frank Robertson was a good plant manager. Why, no one believed that first letter. I don't even think Mr. Robertson did. Of course it scared some guys. And they worked a little harder and that didn't hurt production either. But after a while we forgot about the letters. It took so long. Two years. And times were good. Even if they weren't bluffing, it wouldn't be hard to get another job. Not in Detroit.

"It sounds so easy now, and maybe foolish, but I've been think-ing this thick Irish head dizzy about it and I guess it was one of those things. No one wanted Baker to close. And when you don't want something to happen, and it takes almost two years to happen, well, you wish it away. And that's what we did, I guess. It's for sure what I did. When Elizabeth would ask me if I thought I ought to look for work before the plant closed, I told her I wanted the severance pay too. I had eighteen years with that lousy company. I worked for them faithfully and now they were tossing me out like an old dog and I was going to get what was coming to me. Eighteen years. I'd heard the union was angling for 125 dollars a year in severance pay and with eighteen years that would come out to a big chunk. Well, you know what happened, don't you? That 125 dollars ended up as 30 dollars and it wasn't much of a chunk for any of us. I know the boys did their best, but they're just workingmen like the rest of us.

"But at the time I wasn't worried. Besides all that terrific sever-ance pay I was going to collect, the fact was that times were good; I was still young, strong, I was sure I could get the proper job. I had one of the few really skilled jobs in the paint business as resin kettle operator. I wasn't worried. How can a man worry for two years anyway?

"I'd come home at four and the kids would be home from school and if it was good weather I'd get out the bats and balls and gloves. My kids are everything. The family and the church; a man can't go wrong if he's got those two institutions supporting him. Well, I've still got the church, but I don't see much of my family anymore. My wife came and told me the other morning that Tom, our ten-year-old and the one who's best-coordinated, Tom, she says, doesn't want to switch bat anymore. I nearly hit the ceiling. I started that boy hitting from both sides of the plate when he was six. He's got wonderful timing and strength. And desire. He'll make it, the way I never could. I only made it through high school, but Tom will have a chance to get a baseball scholarship to college and even a chance at the pros. He's big, fast, tough, but I can't work with him any longer. Not with this new job. I work afternoons and most weekends too. I have to work when the other guards don't want to work. I'm low man on the totem pole. I haven't seen a Little League game now in close to two years. That's what my life is like.

"I should have planned better. Well, the fact is that most of the

guys didn't plan at all. At least I worked on it. I thought about it.
Of course, there were times during the closing when it was like a
bad dream, and there were times when common sense told you
they weren't going to close. The explosion, August 1, 1964. I heard
it on the radio. It was a Saturday, and I drove down there and
it looked to me like the whole plant was blowing up. This was it. I
went back home and I told Elizabeth it was going to close within a
couple of weeks for sure now and we panicked all over again. Just
like after the first letter in November of '63. But you know what
they did? A week later they started rebuilding the demolished parts.
We couldn't believe our eyes. They were rebuilding a plant they
were supposed to be shutting down in less than a year's time. We
cheered the construction gang, the maintenance crew; we pitched
in, clearing, shoring up, carrying lumber, bricks. It was our plant
we were saving. And we rebuilt it. And even while we were rebuilding it, trucks pulled out carrying original finish to Cleveland, other
parts and machinery to Newark and Milwaukee. We could see
trucks dismantling the plant at the same time the maintenance boys
were rebuilding the boiler room and part of the resin plant. No one
knew what to think. We didn't think. We just worked. We didn't
know anything else to do. I was making close to three dollars an
hour. I worked, too.

"But you know how women are. They get after you. My Elizabeth, bless her soul, is no exception. She badgered me into going to
the church one evening and talking with Father Healy who's our
priest and an old friend. Then I knew the two of them had been
putting their heads together about me and I grumbled, but I went
down, and it was Father Healy who put the idea of a desk job into
my head, the idea of security. It was he that talked about the wisdom, and that was his word, the wisdom of taking a Civil Service
exam and getting a desk job and real security.

"It wasn't a bad idea. There was no reason I couldn't have a desk
job somewhere. In personnel work. I was good with people, I liked
people. Mueller, my old boss in the resin plant and someone, incidentally, who got hurt more than I did by the plant closing—he was
only a year away from retirement and I hear he's driving a school
bus now, him with a college degree in engineering—Mueller once
told me I ought to put in for foreman. But I guess I didn't want

the responsibility. I had enough responsibility with my family. I had enough to do taking care of them. But if he thought I could do a job like that, then I guess I could get a desk job somewhere. I thought it probably wouldn't pay as much as being a resin kettle operator at Baker had, but it would mean security. Real security. And there'd be people around. I guess I pictured a big office and lots of desks and a water cooler and me with a desk and maybe even with a phone, and getting done at four-thirty and taking the bus home to the kids and playing ball. I guess that was the dream I had.

"It was a dream all right. I passed the Civil Service and I got a job, and I got a job with people. You know what I do with people? I guard them. I make sure they stay behind bars. That's my job. work as a guard in the House of Correction. I work from four to midnight and weekends too. And I work with the real dregs of society: drug addicts, rapists, burglars, homosexuals, sodomists— you can't picture my work till you work there yourself.

"The crazy part was, even after I got it, I thought it might be a good deal. I mean, it was different; I could learn things. Looking back now, I know that crazy optimism came from the fact that while I was waiting for the civil service job to come through, I took another job.

"I got terminated at Baker December 5th, right at the very end. I went out, just the way Mr. Robertson did, with my head up. The company could do what they liked with us, but we'd done our best. Well, I spent the rest of that month at home, buying Christmas presents with the severance pay and you know what the big chunk was? For eighteen long years I got all of 540 dollars. Wasn't that something? But at least I had a good Christmas with the family. I figured I'd hear from the Civil Service at least by the first of the year. They told me I would. Well, I didn't. I didn't hear from them until the second week in February. By the second week in January we were into savings, and by the end of that month we were almost out of savings. I knew I'd have to get a job while I waited to hear from the Civil Service.

"Where else does a kettle operator go but to a paint plant? I went down to United. I heard they were looking. Before Baker closed, the company sent us a personnel man from Pittsburgh; he was supposed to help us find jobs. You know what we did? He came to a meeting at the local and got up with a piece of paper and said he was going to read off a list of paint plants in Detroit and there were jobs at each one. That's the kind of personnel expert he was.

"So I went down to United. And you got to understand I had one of the few skilled jobs at Baker. I went down and talked to the personnel people there. They were interested in me all right. Interested in Baker people. And they were interested in the fact that I was a skilled resin kettle operator, but they had a long seniority list of their own, and I could get at the bottom of that list. They could give me a job in shipping and receiving meanwhile and I could work my way up the seniority list.

"Boy, were those tables turned! I had the skill but not the seniority at United, and I knew I'd never have it. It would probably take me at least twelve or fifteen years to get back on top again. I'd be close to sixty. If I lived that long.

"But I had no choice. So I took the job they offered me—unloading drums in shipping and receiving. The same job I started in with at Baker eighteen years ago. Doesn't life play funny tricks? Only then I was in my twenties and strong as a bull and anxious to get ahead. Now I was 43 and worried, and sick too. I got pneumonia in the fall of '65, during the closing, and it took me out of work for a month. I remember the whole family was sick those months. The kids were all the time getting sick: flu, viruses, colds, tonsilitis, one kid would get it and it would spread like fire through the family. That was another reason we went into savings during those days—paying off doctors' bills.

"I made all of a dollar seventy-five an hour at United unloading drums. And that was bad enough, coming down from three dollars an hour at Baker and knowing all I knew about the paint business, but the thing that was worst about it was that I wasn't even earning my dollar seventy-five. I couldn't keep up with the bloody simple work. I was on the loading dock with two colored boys in their twenties, and they were hustling drums too fast for me. They wanted to get ahead. They were like me twenty years ago. Well, I've got pride. I tried to keep up with them. But I couldn't. They laughed, called me "Pops," told me to relax. I couldn't. I came home exhausted each night, aching, sick with a lousy stomach.

"On top of that I was working the afternoon shift, four to midnight. And Saturdays too. That was the beginning of the time when I didn't see my kids. I was sick, tired, and depressed. I hated that loading dock like poison.

"One night I told Elizabeth I couldn't stand it anymore. I was going to quit and look for another kind of job. She's a steady mate, a good wife, the best woman a man could have. She told me she thought it was wise and I ought to look for something else. We could tighten belts a bit more. That was about mid-February. The following Monday my civil service appointment came through. They told me they had an opening for me as a prison guard.

"Prison guard? I couldn't believe my ears. The only prisons I'd ever seen were in the movies. I was in the seabees during World War Two, and we built a stockade for some Jap prisoners and they sat around on their haunches and blinked at us, but I'd never been anywhere near a prison back home. And here I was to be a prison guard.

"Elizabeth had her doubts, but I tell you I was so relieved to get away from those 50- and 100-pound drums of solvents that I jumped at the chance. I'm an optimistic guy by nature, and I thought: 'Well now, McNerney, here's a new twist in your life. A prison guard doesn't have to be some mean guy in a TV movie on the late show. It can be a helper. You like people, always have; maybe here's a heaven-sent opportunity to help people in trouble.'

"Well, McNerney was wrong. He knew in his heart he'd made a mistake the very first day when he took a tour with another guard and a prisoner spat into his face. The prisoner had never seen McNerney before; McNerney'd never seen him. The other guard laughed and said, "I forgot to tell you about Blue-Bells here; he's a spitter.'

"Blue-Bells you could avoid, but there were others you couldn't. They swore at you, cursed you, even when you tried to talk to them. One day two men who were in there for drug addiction—I was talking to one of them through the bars, listening to his story, telling him how I thought he could be helped, telling him about the church, about God, about how to find a good priest, when while I'm talking the other guy grabs me, and then this guy grabs my gun, and they take my keys and unlock the cell door and pull me in.

"They weren't trying to escape. They only wanted to have some fun with me. Well, they had fun. They pistol-whipped me and did some other things which I won't talk about it, and when the other guards finally heard the commotion and came, I was lying on the floor—with no clothes on.

"I never talked to prisoners since. If they've got troubles they can keep them to themselves. I know now that by the time we get those people, they can't be helped. They just got to be guarded. Society has got to be protected against them. When they jab at me through the bars with their hands, they get a billy club right back in their belly and hard too. They got names for me and I got names for them. I hate them, every lousy one of them.

"They've told their families about me. We started getting the calls a few months ago. Threatening calls. Especially at night when I was at work. They'd wake up Elizabeth and call her all kinds of horrible names and tell her they were going to catch our kids on the way home from school and maim them. When I'd get home after midnight Elizabeth would be sitting up in bed, stiff as a board, listening to noises around the house. She's sick now. Got an ulcer, and a crick in her neck she can't get rid of. I don't know what I can do. We have an unlisted phone number now, but she's sure they know where we live. She wants us to move, she says she can't stand it here, but how can we move? We don't have any money to move on. I make less here than I made at Baker. I make less than the Baker guys who got new jobs in factories. Duane Paddleford makes almost twice what I do at Ford. He made a lot less than me at Baker. And then supposing I had the money. And we did move— wouldn't they only find out where we went? If they want to hurt my kids there's nothing I can do. I watch them get released from jail by some crooked lawyer and I find myself calling Elizabeth to see if Tommy got home from Little League practice, if Jerry Jr. is home from his horn lesson, did she see any strange people in the neighborhood while she walked the baby?

"I'm as jumpy as a cat. When I get home it's hard to get to sleep. Hard for us both. I look in at the kids sleeping and they're growing and I don't see them growing. I wake up early in the morning like a cat, wide awake, listening, my nerve ends jangling. Father Healy says it's a trial. He says that every man has some kind of a trial to bear and it's a pale imitation of the trial He had to bear, but, thanks to His example, we can come through our trials and be better men for it. And I guess I believe that. I've got to believe that. There's nothing else I can do."

Jerry McNerney sits back, steadies his hands, looks at them. They are big, strong, capable hands. "I hit .310 my last year in high school," he says. "I want my boys to hit .400."

April–May 1964

There were no formal meetings between union and company from March to the beginning of May. On the union side Arthur Phelan was involved with other arbitration and was still settling some severance pay lawsuits. On the company side, Howard Green recalls, these weeks were spent gathering information on the pension plan funding and writing out a severance pay proposal to present to the union.

At the Baker plant itself things were going smoothly. A few of the hourly people began trying out other jobs during their two or three weeks vacation, but Otto Mueller, superintendent at the resin plant, believes that even at this time the great majority of the hourly did not believe the company was sincere about its plans to relocate.

"The radicals in the union," Mueller says, "tried to stir up trouble, but the men just wouldn't believe the plant would close."

There were tensions, however. Stealing began to pick up at this time. In Mueller's words, "More paint began going over the fence than ever had before." This was to be expected. What was not to be expected was the thieving, especially from the warehouse on Fitzwarren, of larger items: ladders, pallets, dollies—culminating a few months later in the overnight disappearance of a two-ton chainfall from Building T of the main plant. The chainfall was used for hoisting heavy materials; it had been attached to an overhead rail.

"We never solved that one," says Mueller, "and I guess it was about that time that we retained the Pinkertons. Frank Robertson never wanted to believe the men would really steal."

"Of course there was stealing going on," Robertson says. "There always was stealing and always will be in industrial plants. Men were always taking tools out under their shirts, or a gallon of paint or two when spring came round. We could fire men for stealing, and sometimes did; sometimes we looked the other way. Towards the end of the closing I gave lots of little things away—secondhand tools, buckets, funnels, mops, old Stilson wrenches; I tried to set up Ned Rockwell in his janitorial business with stuff from the plant. But there are always some people who'd rather steal than ask for things. It was only at the very end that I think the stealing got out of hand."

What pleased Robertson most during this period was that some of the men who took other jobs during their vacation periods that spring came back to work when their vacations were over.

"I think they saw what a good place Baker really was. They were loyal, and though I told them they were foolish to hang around for severance pay, to a man they told me they were going to stick it through to the very end. They were going out with their heads up."

Production in the spring of 1964 was as high as it had ever been at Baker—25,000 to 30,000 gallons of paint daily. And this with truckloads of raw materials—pigments, solvents, driers, melamines —all being shipped out to Cleveland and other plants.

It was during this time that Robertson began making trips to York, Ohio, to consult with the people down there on the design of their assembly lines.

"They were moving more slowly than the timetable called for. The shells of three buildings were up: There was a tank farm, a one-story building to store solvents; there was an office building, and of course, their pride and joy—a long, low, production building in which raw materials would come in at one end and the finished product would wind up on the shipping docks at the other end. But they were having all sorts of problems, and one line they were designing was absolutely foolish. It took me three trips to straighten them out."

Smoothly as production at Baker was going, Robertson didn't see how it could keep up when the union and the company finally bumped heads on severance pay. And so after one trip to York, Robertson went straight on to Pittsburgh to urge a crash program to speed up construction of the new plant.

"I don't know that I can keep Baker going," he told Ike Kraeger and Tom Frohman. "Production is up and the men, by and large, are loyal, but the whole thing could fall in on us at any moment. You've got to speed things up in Ohio."

Kraeger and Frohman assured him they'd go as fast as they could in York and they congratulated him on Baker's production record. Robertson thought, *You could put some money into Baker right*

now and you'd have a money-making plant for the next fifteen years.
You're murdering Baker—and it's still doing better right now than
any paint plant in Detroit.

But Pittsburgh and Detroit were on different sides of the world
as far as their understanding of his problems were concerned. Howard Green being an old Baker man had some idea but he was power-
less, ineffectual, on his way out at General Office. The tension that
Robertson knew was developing at Baker was brought home to
him and to Green one afternoon while he was sitting in Green's
office in Pittsburgh. The phone rang. Howard picked it up.

"It's for you, Robbie," he said. "It's from Baker."

Robertson picked up the phone reluctantly. It was his sales chief,
Harold Peterson, and he was almost incoherent. Robertson glanced
at Green but his old colleague was tactfully busying himself with
papers on his desk.

"What is it, Harold?" Robertson asked. "I'm not understanding
your problem. You'll have to talk more slowly. We have a poor
connection."

Harold finally calmed down a little, enough for Robertson to
understand what he was saying, and it went like this: 'Frank, you've
got to come back right away. Something terrible has gone wrong in
the southwest area. The refinish manager in Dallas hasn't been
getting his materials. Someone's interfering with our transportation
system. Tell Kraeger, tell Frohman, tell Howard Green. Someone's
been fouling up my shipments to Dallas. Frank, this can only be
cleared up at the home office level; it can't go on; we'll be losing
customers all over the country; I won't be held responsible . . ."
and he started getting incoherent all over again.

Robertson waited patiently till Peterson ran out of breath and
then he told him not to worry; he'd examine the problem himself
in the morning back in Detroit, and right now he should go home
and take a bath. Everything would be all right and he, Robertson,
would take full responsibility for this matter.

He smooth-talked Peterson like that for about three minutes and
then they hung up. He sighed. Howard Green was looking at him,
bemused.

"Harold Peterson?"

"Yes."

"What's going to happen to him, Robbie?"

"I don't know, Howard."

"He's not about to be transferred anywhere. What's bothering him?"

Robertson shrugged. "I'm guessing he can't picture life with a dead plant behind him."

Howard was silent. "He's not going to have it easy," he said. "No matter what they say, you and I know different, Robbie. It's going to be harder for the salesmen with their plant 300 miles away. They can't promise a delivery in an hour, a lab analysis within minutes, they can't make any of the special deals they used to make so easily and which is so important to them."

"Harold knows this. They all do: Will Calloway, Louie Arnot, Conover, Colgrove—but Harold is the only one cracking up about it."

And that they both knew was because Harold was crackable. He walked a paper-thin surface of life anyway. In the case of the hourly people there was a union to protect them, but who protected the managers, the salesmen, the superintendents, the foremen? *I do,* Frank Robertson thought.

When he got back to Detroit that evening he called Harold Peterson at his home. Rhea, Peterson's wife, told him Harold was napping. He'd had a hard day and come home early. Robertson told Rhea to urge Harold to take the next morning off and to tell Harold that he'd take over his job for the morning. She was grateful.

"The next morning I looked into the great foul-up. I made a few calls and found that a shipment of paint intended for Dallas had ended up by mistake in Los Angeles. The jobber in Dallas had called saying he needed one item urgently—a quart of bronze gold for a 1962 Chrysler. That was all it was. I had our inventory man call Los Angeles and had the Los Angeles man put that quart of bronze gold on a bus for Dallas. It got to Dallas the following morning and the crisis was over.

"Harold never referred to it again. But I worried about him; and I worried about Louie Arnot who was driving to Cleveland three times a day. Louie was outwardly cheerful, but I knew the whole business was hard on him. We didn't know yet whether he'd be based in Detroit or Cleveland. His family was in Detroit; his biggest customers were in Detroit, but his office was now in Cleveland. He was on the go all the time, and he was no spring chicken. Louie was

55 years old; he'd been with the company since 1938. A confident ambitious man, he didn't like the change either. I guess staying in one spot a long time isn't much help to a man when someone wants to move him off the spot.

"All of this made me begin worrying more about my salaried people than my hourly people. I thought about the salesmen, people like Peterson, Arnot, Will Calloway—the problems those who stayed in Detroit would have, cut off from the roots of the operation, caught in the middle between the plant in York and the customers in Detroit. They'd been salesmen so long they could see the trouble, the phone bluffing, the frantic calls to Ohio, the pleading calls to General Office. These were men in their fifties. Change didn't come easy to them. And they had no one to protect them anymore. They had no union. They had no one except me—and I was taking early retirement. I was going when the plant went."

Company-union meetings were soon to resume. On April 30 a letter went to Howard Green in Pittsburgh over the signature of Peter Thompson, as President of the West Side Local and Perry DeMoss, as union rep. It read in part:

> At the meeting of March 12, 1964, we suggested certain benefits be given to the employees of the Baker Color Company, benefits which, we felt, would be fair and equitable to those employees. As you may recall, the benefits were these:
> 1. One hundred and twenty-five dollars ($125.00) in severance payment for each year of service for all eligible employees.
> 2. The granting of seniority transfer rights to those employees wishing to relocate to the new plant in York, Ohio.
> At the meeting of March 12, 1964, we also asked for all relevant information on the status of the Baker pension plan.
>
> We now wish to have another meeting with you to resolve these issues and any other issues that confront us. We wish to have this meeting as soon as possible since the membership is putting a good deal of pressure on the plant committee.
>
> Hoping to hear from you very soon in regards to an early meeting date.

The letter had been written by Arthur Phelan. "We had to have all our conversations confirmed in writing," Phelan repeats, "in case we went to court."

According to Perry DeMoss the statement about the union membership bringing pressure to bear on the plant committee was not quite true. Most of the men, he says, still thought the company was bluffing and believed that the company-union meetings were setting up some sort of new contract relief.

However, it was time to come again to the bargaining table. Green answered their letter on May 14, apologizing for the delay, stating that they were still waiting for certain pension information before meeting. He suggested meeting at the Baker plant on Tuesday, May 19, at 9:30 A.M. for the purposes of discussing severance pay, transfer rights, pension information.

The meeting was scheduled as suggested. Representing the union were Peter Thompson, Perry DeMoss, and the plant committee led by Ned Rockwell. Arthur Phelan was not there, a fact immediately noted by Harrah with amusement and sympathy. Between this meeting and the previous one, Phelan had lost still another case—Lincoln Tube. He hadn't even the shadow of a legal position. Harrah wondered whether the others, DeMoss and Rockwell especially, were aware of this. He passed a note to Green saying: "no legal obligation to grant severance pay, recent court cases." Green nodded, crumpled the note into a ball and slipped it into his pocket.

On Green's other side sat little Frank Robertson, quiet and detached as ever, and next to him a man new to Harrah—Tom Morgan who used to be industrial relations manager but was now the super on the second shift. Robertson wanted him at the meeting and Harrah guessed that Robertson wanted to reinstate Morgan in his old job. On the other side of Morgan sat Lee Jones, the present industrial relations manager, a man that Robertson obviously disliked.

"I guess we can begin now," Green said. He gave the union representatives a letter from the company actuary which described the state of the pension plan and projected it through to December 31, 1965. There then ensued some discussion about the pension plan, about amending it to give older workers a bigger break than younger workers. Thompson ended the discussion by stating he would pass the plan on to the union's actuary. Then Howard Green passed around a long, written statement of the company's proposal for severance pay which stated in the fifth paragraph that the company would offer thirty dollars a year for every year of seniority.

"The company," Green said, "has given considerable thought to the matter of severance pay. Our position is that we have no legal obligation to grant severance pay. . . ."

There was no response from the union representatives. They were reading, or pretending to read, the company statement. Harrah decided that Phelan had informed them of his legal defeats.

"Indeed, as you may or may not know," Green went on, "some recent court decisions, decisions rendered since we last met, support this view. However, the company is not unaware of the painful dislocation and distress caused by the closing of a plant. We wish to do what we can to help our people make a transition. It's for this reason that we've prepared the proposal you are now studying. It may be that you will wish to adjourn this meeting in order to refer to your legal department, or perhaps you wish to meet privately with yourselves right now. Please feel free to do so."

Peter Thompson looked up. "I don't need any private meetings to see what this lousy proposal is about. That 30 dollars hits you right away. You just were talking about how bad the company felt about the hardship they were causing the men by closing down the plant, and then you have the nerve to hand this out with that 30-dollar figure. This is the worst proposal I've ever seen in all my years. The Pennsylvania Corporation is supposed to be a high-class outfit. You're nothing but a two-bit outfit, using up labor and throwing them out with a few pennies."

Howard Green's face was expressionless. This was where he was at his best, Harrah thought. Nothing ruffled him. A defeated man learned how to take abuse.

"I'd point out to you, Mr. Thompson, that this proposal adds up to about 125,000 dollars."

"That's a piss hole in the snow for a company your size," Thompson said.

Green smiled. "Well it takes a good deal of paint to make a profit of 125,000 dollars."

"You've got a good deal of paint," Thompson said.

Perry DeMoss said softly: "Howard, this is a very poor offer, and you know it."

"Perry, it's a good deal better than the nothing which legally, we contend, we're entitled to give."

"You don't call this bargaining, do you?" Thompson asked. "We ask you for 125 and you come up with 30."

"That's about par for Baker," Ned Rockwell said.

Harrah wondered whether Rockwell meant that that was about what the company usually spent on Baker, or whether he was just confusing Baker with the company. He decided it was the latter, though he suspected there was truth in the former.

"There's a lot of meat in this offer, if you'll study it, Ned," Howard Green said.

"It may be a lot of meat," Peter Thompson snapped, "but it's lean meat. There's no fat."

Perry DeMoss looked up. "I don't see anything about our request for transfer rights, Howard. Did we lose that when you gave us all of 30 dollars?"

"Perry, the company doesn't want to make any agreement it doesn't feel it can carry out."

"How come people over sixty are left out of this severance pay plan of yours?"

"The company doesn't believe that anyone who is eligible for a pension should get severance pay too."

Rockwell peered across the table. "Did you make up this proposal, Perry Mason?"

Harrah laughed. "Let's call it a joint effort, Ned."

"No wonder they pay you a hundred thousand bucks a year."

"The company has spent considerable time drawing up this plan and as I mentioned before, you might wish to discuss it with your legal department before proceeding any further. If your actuary wishes to discuss it with our actuary that too is certainly possible, and is probably a pretty good idea."

"Howard, your offer is less than 25 percent of what we recently got in another severance pay agreement and we had a hard time selling that one to the membership."

Harrah had to admire the stocky little union rep. Surely DeMoss knew that Green and he knew what they'd settled for in severance pay with other companies. But they fought it out.

Green responded that the pension plan could be altered so that certain younger workers would get less and older workers could get $53 a year, which, along with the $30 a year in severance pay, would give each man a total of $83 for each year of service.

It was also clear to everyone that changing the pension plan would mean a vote by the membership at large and the younger men would put up a real beef.

"Howard," DeMoss began again, "let me ask you this, as an old Baker man yourself: Why is the Pennsylvania Corporation so determined not to let our people transfer their seniority to the new plant?"

There was a silence as they all looked at Green. The pitch was as personal as it was professional. And they all knew that DeMoss and Green liked each other.

"Perry, I can only say what I said before. The company just can't, and I don't think, should, agree to anything it doesn't feel it can carry out. We don't even know right now if this new plant is going to be a success. About ten days ago someone struck oil in a field three miles east of our property. York is so full of people right now you couldn't find room to pitch a tent."

"Let's assume, Howard, oil isn't discovered on the company's property and you decide to manufacture paint in your new paint plant. If that's so, will you take our people?"

Green was silent.

"Howard, in all our history, no plant which left this local has failed to offer relocation rights."

I should have checked on that, Harrah thought.

"What's been the experience when relocations were granted, Perry?"

Peter Thompson answered. "We'll be honest with you, Green. Few of our people have relocated, though most plants that have left our local have left for Mississippi or Arkansas or Arizona. We're talking now about a nearby state."

"Your problem is you're not going far enough," Rockwell jeered.

"And you're not giving us very much to start with," Dick Tyner, the recording secretary of the plant committee said.

"A real joint effort," Rockwell said to Mike Harrah.

"A joint lousy job," Perry DeMoss said with quiet anger. He had taken Phelan's place representing the union. He was the one who'd be talking tough from now on. "We're not going to fall down like sheep for you on this thing." He tapped the proposal with his finger. "We came in asking for 125 dollars and you counter with 30. Don't tell me you've satisfied your legal obligations to bargain collectively."

Green was silent.

Thompson said: "Looking through this severance pay acceptance form of yours, I notice you ask the man signing it to waive his legal rights. You must be scared of something."

"At this time," Green replied, "I'm only asking you to consider our proposal and, if you so wish, to discuss it with your legal counsel and your actuary."

"Well," Perry said, "we've got the minimum and the maximum. And it's a long way from the minimum to the maximum. A helluva long way."

"All I ask you to do is study the proposal, consider it carefully."

Perry DeMoss closed his folder. "If this is all you've got to offer then it's obvious you're unwilling to negotiate. We will have to turn this over to our legal department and you'll be advised by them."

"That's fine," Green said. "I think your legal department should be in on this. Your legal counselor should have been here today. And I would again urge you to present this plan to your actuary. The next time we meet we'll be able to discuss this plan more fully."

"I do have a question before we break up," Mike Harrah said. "There's a difference in the language of the 1962 contract and the language of the pension agreement. In one, the contract, the International is a party; in the pension agreement I see no mention of the International. I take it this latter is an oversight."

Thompson looked at the pension agreement and then removed his glasses. "It probably is, since the International is a party to any agreement the local writes."

"Just so there's no doubt," Perry DeMoss said curtly, "we are still insisting on 125 dollars in severance pay and the right for our men to transfer their seniority."

"In return," said Green, "may I suggest that you study our offer carefully?"

The meeting adjourned at 11:10 A.M.

We Stole Their Thunder, By God

It would take more than eight months to reach final agreement on the company's severance pay proposal, but in the end the union would accept the company's offer of $30 a year for each year of service.

"That offer," says Mike Harrah, a little smugly, "was based on research. In their law suit against Lincoln Tube, the UAW had asked for 75 dollars a year in severance pay and settled for 50 dollars. In their suit against Cornwall Company, an automotive parts company, they settled for as little as 25 dollars a year. The Atlas settlement amounted to 54 dollars a year."

All these settlements, Harrah points out, involved considerable legal expenses for the UAW. The union had gone to court with what it thought was a good case. None of those companies had truly engaged in serious collective bargaining before they relocated. Nevertheless, in each case the union had to settle out of court and for considerably less than they wanted. The Pennsylvania Corporation, says Harrah, had engaged in serious collective bargaining right from the start. Beginning in November, 1963, when they notified the union they were considering moving and asked for counteroffers. There were no counteroffers, a fact Harrah put in writing, and subsequent meetings, such as the one of May 18, focused on trying to soften the impact of the change upon the men.

"Nowhere," says Harrah, " did our contract with the UAW say we had to give severance pay, but we came up with the offer—they didn't. The fact is that we stole their thunder right down the line. We were months ahead of them in planning, and they knew it. Who ever heard of a company telling a union it plans to close the factory in two years? Who ever heard of a company offering severance pay without a threat from the union? We stole their thunder, by God, and they knew it. They were counterpunching, reacting to us; we were ahead of them all the way. They didn't have a complaint coming and they knew it. All the companies they'd dealt with they had to pry out the severance pay. We decided on giving severance pay right from the beginning.

"The fact is we felt we owed these people something. Guys in their late forties, fifties. We knew damn well some of them would have a hard time finding new jobs. After all, how many people do we hire in that age group? It was the decent thing to do.

"But I'd be less than candid if I didn't also say it was also a damn businesslike thing to do too. Our offer of severance pay could forestall a lawsuit that could be troublesome. The UAW didn't have any legal ground to stand on, but the very fact of a lawsuit could be time-consuming and expensive.

"Most importantly, severance pay provided a procedure for phasing out the plant. It helps prevent strikes, walkouts, individual work stoppages that otherwise couldn't be controlled. You understand, no employee could collect severance pay if he left before we terminated him. And most of them stayed. Severance pay worked. It kept the plant together and we didn't lose a single customer during the transfer."

SEVERANCE PAY AGREEMENT

The Baker Color Company, a division of The Pennsylvania Corporation, hereinafter called the "Company," and the International Union, United Automobile, Aerospace and Agricultural Implement Workers of America, AFL-CIO and its West Side Local, hereinafter called (jointly) the "Union," have agreed that:

Inasmuch as both Company and Union are parties to a labor contract of December 14, 1962, hereinafter called the "Labor Agreement," which covered a unit of production, maintenance, and laboratory employees, hereinafter called "employees," who are employed at 6500 West Morton Avenue and 2700 Fitzwarren Street, Detroit, Michigan and

Inasmuch as the Company has advised the Union beforehand of its intention to terminate the production operations of the Baker Color Company at the above mentioned locations and to remove such operations to other Company facilities which are now or will be in operation, and

Inasmuch as the Company and Union have in good faith met and bargained collectively on such matters as whether said operations will be terminated at the Baker Color Company, and

Inasmuch as subsequent to these bargaining sessions the Company has reaffirmed its intention to terminate the production operations of the Baker Color Company, and

Inasmuch as following this the Company and Union have bargained collectively in good faith on the impact a termination of operations will have on the employees,

It is hereby agreed in full satisfaction of all employee and Union rights arising both at law and under the Labor Agreement and any subsequent Labor Agreement that:

1. Severance pay in the amount of $30.00 for each full year of seniority, as determined by the Labor Agreement, will be given to an employee whose last date of hire is before November 13, 1963, provided that such an employee is

   a. actively employed in the bargaining unit after the date of this agreement
   b. continues at his job until permanently released by the Company because of a lack of need for the employee's services resulting from the termination and relocation of production operations
   c. is not discharged for cause before that time
   d. is not employed at any other plant or facility of the Company within six (6) months of his permanent release
   e. is not receiving or eligible to receive upon application a Normal Retirement Pension, an Early Retirement Pension, or a Disability Pension as set forth in the Pension Agreement of December 14, 1962, between Company and Union
   f. executes both Application for Severance Pay and Acceptance of Severance pay in the form attached hereto within thirty (30) days of the date of his permanent release

APPLICATION FOR SEVERANCE PAY

_____   _____   _____   _____
NAME   PLANT   EMPLOYMENT   DATE LAST WORKED
                      DATE

                                          _____
                                          SEX

In accordance with the terms and conditions of the Severance Pay Agreement established by agreement between the Baker

Color Company a division of the Pennsylvania Corporation and the International Union, United Automobile, Aerospace and Agricultural Implement Workers of America, AFL-CIO, and its West Side local, I herewith make application for severance pay.

_____	_____	_____	_____
DATE	WITNESS	SIGNATURE OF EMPLOYEE	APPLICATION DATE

Above application received by Company on _____ by

DATE

_____.

SIGNATURE

SEVERANCE PAY CALCULATION

Years of Service as determined by Labor Agreement: _____ years times $30.00: _____. This amount shall be paid within 30 days after filing of above application, said application deemed filed when received by the Company, and is subject to any with-hold required by law or regulation of Local, State, or Federal Government.

Prepared by _____ _____

SIGNATURE   DATE

Application Approved _____

WORKS MANAGER

Computation checked and payment made by _____

CHIEF ACCOUNTANT

_____

DATE

ACCEPTANCE OF SEVERANCE PAY

I, _____, having been permanently released as an employee of the Baker Color Company, a division of the Pennsylvania Corporation, because the company's operations at 6500 West Morton and 2700 Fitzwarren Street, Detroit, Michigan have now been terminated, hereby accept receipt of my severance pay in the amount of $_____. I acknowledge this payment as a full settlement of any rights I may have, or claim to have, under the Labor Agreement between the Baker Color Company, a division of the Pennsylvania Corporation, and the International Union, United Automobile Aerospace and Agricultural Implement Workers of America, AFL-CIO, and its West Side Local. In addition I accept this payment in settlement of whatever rights I may have or claim to have as a matter of law to my continued employment in the present operations of the Baker Color Company or any other division or operation of the Pennsylvania Corporation. With the acceptance of this payment, I acknowledge that I am no longer employed by The Pennsylvania Corporation.

Executed this _____ day of _____, 196___.

Witness: _____

SIGNATURE

_____

They Can Take Their Severance Pay and Shove It Up Their Asses

---

Name: Stepan Toucek
Age: 48
Married: Mary Wozniak, 1940
Children: Doris, 26, married; Anne Marie, 8
Religion: Catholic
Education: high school, Detroit
Residence: 84300 Grandin, Farmington, Michigan
Occupation:

> 1945, laborer, Baker Color Company
> 1949–65, truck driver, Baker
> 1966, truck unloader, Winston Lithography
> 1966, truck driver, United Paint

When Ned Rockwell, chairman of the shop committee, came up to Stepan Toucek one morning in November of 1965 and urged him to return his application for severance pay to the personnel office, Toucek snapped: "Screw them. They can take their severance pay and shove it up their asses."

"You're crazy, Steve," Rockwell said. "You got 600 bucks coming to you."

"They can shove the 600 bucks up their asses too."

"You're nuts."

"We'll see who's nuts," Toucek said, and walked off.

Stepan Toucek was the only man among Baker's 550 employees who did not accept severance pay and yet worked on till the very end anyway.

On one of his last visits to the plant, Howard Green, divisional director of industrial relations for the Pennsylvania Corporation, bumped into Toucek in the yard. Green looked down quizzically at the tough, bantam truck driver. Toucek was a strange bird, a drinker, sullen, morose, moody; Green knew Toucek had troubles at home—he and his wife fought, and they had a retarded child. But the severance pay situation bothered Green because he knew Toucek thought of himself as shrewd and careful.

"Steve," Green said, "Tom Morgan tells me you haven't put in your application for your severance pay."

"Nope," Toucek said, "I been a Baker man for twenty years and I'm always going to be a Baker man."

The words startled Green. He hadn't known the depth of Toucek's feeling for the plant. He was to recall those words again and again. It was the kind of loyalty, Green said, you only found at Baker. And when you got it from a hard-bitten type like Toucek, you knew then how they all felt.

"Bull shit," says Toucek, talking in a hoarse whisper in his living room, in Farmington, Michigan, "those bastards knew just what they were doing when they screwed us, and I plan to get my fair share. Does 600 bucks sound like a fair share for working twenty years for them?"

Toucek lives in a nice brick house in Farmington, in the northwest part of Detroit. He sits on a flowered divan, and above him hangs a picture with flowers that match the divan. He is small, red-faced, with salt and pepper hair. There is a put-on toughness about him that becomes more real the more beer he drinks. He is a little man who drove a big truck and likes big trucks.

"I drove a short-haul semi for Baker. After the plant closed I could've got a job driving a long-haul semi, but the wife and I got an arrangement. She wants to work nights, so I got to work days. One of us has got to be at home with the kid."

The kid is a pretty eight-year-old child with reddish brown hair. She sits in the living room playing with her blocks. Her movements seem normal; it is only when she looks up and talks that you sense something wrong. Her eyes are not animated; her conversation is slow and halting. She likes to look at pictures. Toucek watches her with brooding eyes.

"I put her to bed each night. She won't go to bed for no one but me."

He pours himself another beer.

"I understand her—don't I, Anne Marie?"

The little girl looks up, smiles shyly, says nothing.

Toucek grunts. "It ain't so easy finding a job when you're forty-five. And it's impossible finding a job days. The wife and I had some rough days before the plant closed. We had some real rough days. Things got a little better during the closing. She sort of felt sorry for me. I'm independent. I don't take charity, handouts. What I got, I work for. What's mine, I take. I wouldn't take any unemployment comp. That's the same thing as welfare to me. It's for the niggers.

"After the plant closed it took me three weeks to get a job. I found one at a tool and die shop working days. They had a room in the back where they made gym tables. Long tables the kind you find in gyms they set up for Boy Scout suppers and ice cream socials. It was carpentry. I could do it, but I didn't like it. All the time I kept looking every chance I got to get back to truck driving. Then someone tells me about a job with a paper company. It was supposed to be truck driving but it turns out to be unloading trucks. Unloading huge rolls of paper into the shop. Hell, I couldn't take it. I ain't built for that. I worked there two months and I was pulling off this big roll with another guy when I fell off the tail lift and busted my leg. I was off for six weeks. They paid me, but the day I got back they fired me. They said business was slow and I was out. I din't mind.

"That was the summer of '66. I hung around for a while and the wife was good to me again, and then I got lucky and got another truck driving job, driving for United Paint around town, same as I did with Baker, only it ain't a semi but a stake truck. Still it's a truck and now we're fighting again, the old woman and me, but you know how those things are. What's the matter, honey?"

"What's this?" the girl says, pointing to a picture on her alphabet block.

"That's a cat," Toucek says softly, "a pussy cat."

"She asks me that a hundred times a day. I lookit her and I think, if it wasn't for her maybe we'd have broke up already. But we got to take care of her, and him too."

Seated in another corner of the living room, asleep, is a small, thin old man—Toucek's father. In his early seventies, he is almost completely senile. Toucek looks at him ruminatively and then pulls at his bottle. "He wasn't always like that. He used to be quite a guy. My ma died when I was twelve and I can remember him all right from then, a real boozer, a sheik, chasing after dames all the time. My ma died of a broken heart; he killed her, the old bastard."

Toucek's father opens an eye but Toucek is not embarrassed. He looks coldly at his father. "How's the sheik now, huh Pa?"

A vacuous grin crosses the old man's face and the eyes close. Suddenly there are the sounds of blocks falling, clattering onto the floor.

Anne Marie is crying. "The blocks all fall down, Papa."

"You knocked them down," Steve says gently. "Here, I'll help you pick'm up."

He helps her pick up the blocks, then gets himself two bottles of beer, holding one in his hand while the other swings by the neck between two fingers. In his other hand he holds some white papers.

"I take care of them both, her and him. I wouldn't be the kind of man he was for nothing. I'm a family man. I take care of my own; I look after things. Nobody gives me nothing; I don't take handouts. In fact, I *give*. I give to charities, to the Retarded Children's Fund. I don't take nothing. You see this house? Around it outside, I put in all the trees and shrubs myself, and the fence too. Every Christmas I put lights up outside, moving lights, and the people they come from blocks away to see Toucek's Christmas. I'm proud of this house. My old man gave my ma a shack to live in. Then the niggers moved into the neighborhood and made it worse. Now they want to come and live up here too. They want to move right up Grand River, but we won't let'm. I worked too hard on this house to throw it all away. I work too damn hard all my life, planning on things. You know what these are? They're savings bonds. I got two- maybe three-thousand dollars' worth." He pauses, and then grins slyly. "Maybe more. At the plant they used to laugh at me. Toucek he drinks too much. Toucek he's married to a lady riveter. Toucek he's got a retarded child and a senile old man and still he turns down 600 bucks.

"Yeah, well they're laughing out the other side of their fat mouths now. Some of them guys are doin' real lousy, I hear. They sold their future for a lousy 600 bucks. They give me that severance pay application and say here, sign it and you'll get 600 bucks, just for your name. They tell me I'm crazy not to sign, but I'm crazy like a fox, that's what. Sign away my rights? As long as I don't sign that piece of paper they got to pay me for my retirement pension. I'm forty-eight now. I'm gonna retire in 14 years, right? I'm gonna get a part pension from the place I work now cause the contract says anyone with 10 years seniority is eligible for some pension. But it won't be much. I put in 20 years at Baker, and that's where my pension's going to come from. I'm going to sue the bastards. They don't have my signature on nothing."

Toucek laughs harshly. "Rockwell, he's my friend. He says I'm a jackass for turning down free money. Well, I'll tell you something —there's no such thing as free money. You seen Rockwell lately? He's not doing too good, is he? How long did his 600 bucks last him?"

Toucek empties his bottle and opens up the other one.

"Jesus, it bothered them—the union and the company—that I didn't take the money and still stayed on to the end. Loyalty, they thought. Balls. What the hell do you want to be loyal to a factory for? I hear guys saying it won't close. Balls. Every man jack knew it was going to close and they knew who killed it. They did. They loved it and they killed it. Shooting dice, playing cards, crapping around, stealing. I stayed till the very end because I wanted to see it die. I wanted to go right down with it. And then step off and find another home. Well, I didn't. All I got now is this." He looks down at the hand pulling at his pants leg. "Now what's the matter?"

"What's this, Daddy?"

"For Christ sake, I just tole you it was a pussy cat."

She starts to cry.

"And take those goddamn blocks outa here too," Steve says. "I'm tired of looking at them. And you . . ." He reaches over and shakes his father. "You got a bed upstairs. Sleep in it, damn it. I'm tired of your snoring in here all time."

The old man opens his eyes looks at him and smiles. In disgust Steve lets him go. Anne Marie sits in the middle of the room and weeps hard, wracking sobs into her hands. Toucek surveys them both, his face red from the beer and his fit of temper.

"Ah—to hell with it," he says wearily.

He turns to me. "You better go. I got to put them both to bed."

On Pensions, a Fistfight,
and a Death at the Plant

May, 1964

For Stepan Toucek severance pay and retirement pension were intimately connected. If he gave up one, he could sue for the other. Although the union bargaining team led by Perry DeMoss negotiated on both subjects, they never linked severance pay to distribution of the retirement pension fund as Toucek had done.

"We saw them as separate items and bargained on them as separate items," Perry DeMoss says.

At the end of May, 1964, DeMoss summed up the union-company bargaining positions in two letters—one to Howard Green who had been present at the May 19 meeting, and one to Arthur Phelan who had not been present.

The letter to Green informed him that "since our meeting of May 19, I have contacted our regional director, Cal Koonz, and our legal counsel, Arthur Phelan.

"I am told that on the issue of pension moneys there is still room for negotiations. However, on the matter of severance pay, there are definite areas of disagreement."

In his letter to Arthur Phelan, DeMoss summed up the requests the union had put forward in the meeting of May 19—the reiterated request for benefits of $125 in severance payment for each year of service, and the requests for seniority transfer rights, and for more information on the pension plan now in existence.

DeMoss related to Phelan that the company's offer of $30 a year was "instantly and violently rejected" by the union bargaining team, and that there was only one area, he felt, where agreement could be reached—that was in the distribution of pension funds.

At the moment the only source of disagreement in this area lay in the language of the amendment to the plan. The plan had been originally drawn up and approved in 1955. Since no one had then foreseen the termination of the plant's operations, it had now been necessary to draw up an amendment describing in detail how retirement pension payments would continue to be distributed to employees already retired, since the Baker Color Company, a division of the Pennsylvania Corporation, would soon cease to exist. In addition, there were a number of employees who were expected to reach retirement age before the contract ended in December, 1965. They too would be covered by pensions. Finally, the company's actuaries had given strong indications that the plan was overfunded and that a good deal of extra money would have to be distributed among those employees not eligible for retirement. The question was how this cash was to be divided.

The union concurred with the company's decision to turn over the operation of the pension fund to a private insurance company which would distribute the funds in the following manner:

1. Pension funds would be used to provide pensions for life to the Baker employees who had already retired.
2. If there was still money left over, it would go to employees who were eligible for early retirement (age 60).
3. If there was still money left over [and there was], it would be divided among those employees whose continuous service began prior to November 13, 1963 (the date of the company's first letter indicating they were considering termination of Baker operations) and did not terminate until after that date on a basis proportionate to each employee's continuous service.

The language of this last clause provided some disagreement. In the company's wording of this clause older employees would receive more per year than younger employees. The union proposed that the amount per year should be equal for young and old alike.

"We did that, because we knew the majority of the membership would want it that way," DeMoss says frankly. "The older guys were in the minority."

The fact was that any amendment to the contract had to be voted on by the membership at large, and it was quite clear to DeMoss that the vote would be for equal shares per year for all. And that was how it ended, with every man not eligible for retirement benefits by the end of the contract period in December, 1965, receiving $40 a year for every year of service. This, in addition to severance pay of $30 a year, made a total package of $70 a year.

"It was a paltry sum for a man in his late fifties who now had no retirement income to look forward to," says Frank Robertson.

"These men—and I include the salary people too, though they received more severance and pension pay than the hourly people—were the truly tragic ones. The lucky ones were those long-termers who were eligible for retirement when the plant died. Among the salaried there were: myself; Tom Morgan; Lloyd Shearer, my production manager; Matt Gargan, supervisor of Shipping and Receiving; Jeff Barrett, who was the last man to leave the Fitzwarren warehouse. Some of the hourly got early retirement too. We all made out. But what about the others who just fell short? What was going to happen to them? I worried about those people. I advised them to get out; 'Don't wait for severance pay,' I told them, 'get a job as soon as you can, build up seniority in your new job.' I wrote letters for them, made phone calls. And some of them took jobs on their vacations—but they came back, they all came back and they'd say to me: 'Robbie, we're going out with you. We're going out with our heads up, just like you said.' "

Frank Robertson pauses to let the significance of this line sink in for the umpteenth time. He waits for a response, an assurance. Not receiving it, he goes on anyway:

"I could have wept with sorrow and with pride. The plant was holding together. It was going down magnificently. Men whom I had never expected loyalty from—men like Ned Rockwell who swore and cursed and made life particularly unpleasant most all the time—men like Ned proved loyal and courageous beyond anything I had a right to expect." He pauses and looking me straight in the eye says: "In that last year and a half Ned Rockwell and I saw eye to eye on everything."

There was, for example, the terrible fight in Building T that took place sometime near the end of May. Building T was the heart of the grinding department and it was about 2 P.M., Robertson remembers that he got a call from Lloyd Shearer, his production manager, that a bad fist fight had taken place over there. He hurried right over. Baker, like any other company, had its share of fights, and fighting, along with gambling and stealing, was held to be just cause for discharge.

Robertson hurried all the faster because Lloyd Shearer had been very ill lately and he knew this kind of thing upset Lloyd more than anything else. When he got to Building T Robertson saw several men standing over an older worker named Cottrell who lay on the cement floor with his face battered and bloody. Cottrell was in his early sixties. Standing nearby, still breathing hard, being talked to by Ned Rockwell and another member of the shop committee, was Stan Kasivich, a brawny, hard-working, hard-drinking, young Pole who had been with the company about ten years. As far as Robertson knew, Kasivich had never been in trouble before, though God knew they'd had their share of problems with Cottrell, a mean little man who openly aired his dislike of Negroes, Catholics, Jews —and who combined his bigotry with an infuriating air of superiority as he told everyone how to do their jobs.

From the looks of Cottrell lying there, moaning, it would be a long time before Cottrell told anyone anything again.

"You'd better get him to the clinic," Robertson said to the group of men surrounding Cottrell.

Two of the men picked him up and carried him out to a panel truck.

"I didn't really need anyone to tell me what had happened," Robertson says. "You could see it all right away. Kasivich had been drinking and Cottrell, thinking him drunker than he was, had started telling him how to do his job and probably telling him what he thought of Polacks in general.

Lloyd Shearer, looking thin and pale and upset, was standing there with Lee Jones and Jeff Barrett, who was foreman in the grinding department soon to be shifted to the warehouse, and John Franklin, the supervisor of the grinding department.

"What happened, Lloyd?" Robertson asked Shearer.

"What you're guessing, Robbie," Shearer said quietly. "Cottrell was baiting Kasivich."

"We've got just cause to fire them both," Lee Jones said eagerly. "Kasivich smells like a still, and according to Barrett, old man Cottrell started the fight."

Jones was happy; he liked firing people. Robertson ignored him and turned to John Franklin questioningly.

"I don't know, Frank," John said. "As far as I can make out, Cottrell was after Stan about a valve he didn't open. The mill's been grinding without pigment for over two hours. Isn't that right, Jeff?"

"That's right, John," Jeff Barrett said. "I caught it and was trying to empty out the tank when the trouble started."

Barrett was cautious, soft-spoken. He had been with Baker since

1932—thirty-two years. He had risen quietly through the ranks. From Frank Robertson's point of view, he was the kind of colored man (getting rarer every day) you could count on. In Robertson's eyes he had a sense of loyalty which someone like Perry DeMoss, born with a chip on his shoulder, never had. In 1958, Howard Green made Barrett a foreman, the only Negro to achieve this rank. He was a good foreman, a little timid, but the work got done. Robertson was aware that Barrett would often do the work himself rather than force a man to. He made good pay and, most important, Robertson could count on him. It was an unfortunate accident that a troublemaker like Cottrell with all his prejudices should wind up in Jeff Barrett's department.

"Who forgot to open the valve, Jeff?"

Barrett hesitated. "I guess it was Stan, Mr. Robertson. But he was helping me clean out the mess."

"He's run that machine for two years. What made him forget the valve?"

Barrett was silent.

"He was drunk," Lee Jones said curtly, "and he still is."

"You son of a bitch," Ned Rockwell said, "you'll have to prove that."

Lee Jones' head snapped around. Rockwell grinned. Frank Robertson shook his head. Rockwell had an extraordinary talent for getting people mad, changing the situation, putting management on the defensive by getting them to lose their tempers. And Lee Jones was a perfect foil for him.

"Calm down, Lee," Robertson said quietly. "I can handle this." He turned to Jeff Barrett. "All right, he forgot to open the valve. We've wasted a thousand gallons of paint. You're cleaning it out together with Kasivich. How did the fight start?"

"Cottrell was bugging him, Frank," someone in the other ring of men said.

"He knocked Cottrell down," someone else said.

"And he kicked him . . ."

"Twice . . ."

The story was fed into the machine and Robertson knew it would now grow and change and by the end of the day reach legendary proportions.

"We couldn't get Stan off of him."

"Cottrell started it; he said only a dumb Polack would—"

"So Stan just turned around and . . ."

Robertson looked at the spot, trying to visualize it. To his horror he saw, for the first time, blood on the cement floor. Where Cottrell had been lying.

"Get that cleaned up," he snapped. "The rest of you get back to work. Ned, let's you and I talk this over in my office."

"You want me there, Frank?" Lee Jones asked.

"No."

He turned to Lloyd Shearer. "Lloyd, we're all grown men here. Let's get this plant moving again."

That was all he said, but the groups broke up and everyone went back to work. Rockwell and Robertson walked back to the latter's office. They didn't talk to each other across the yard, but when they reached the office, Robertson shut the door and said:

"What are we going to do about this, Ned?"

The question surprised Rockwell. He was prepared to fight for both his men. The impossible old bastard Cottrell, the stupid drunken Kasivich. He was prepared to counterpunch, react, not to start the ball rolling. For a moment he didn't know what to say. Robertson waited for him, like a cat.

He shrugged. "You got just cause to fire them both, Mr. Robertson. I give you that. I hope you won't. Cottrell is a louse, but he's sixty-three and he's got twenty years here. You fire him and he loses all his benefits. Kasivich? He's . . ." Rockwell grinned. "He's just a dumb Polack. You let them be, give them both one more chance, I'll see it never happens again."

"Do you have any idea how much money we lost this morning?"

"I got an idea, Mr. Robertson, but look at it this way. A lot of the guys aren't themselves. Stan . . . he drinks OK, but he didn't used to drink on the job. OK, I found out he's got a bottle in his locker. I busted it and poured it out. I'll be responsible for him from now on. He's a good worker when he's sober. We both know that. He says to me he don't know why he hit the bottle, but maybe he's worried about not getting another job. He doesn't say that. He's too dumb to even think about it. He says to me that ain't it, he doesn't think the company is going to close the plant. He still thinks they're bluffing. But now he's drinking on the job. You figure it out. As for Cottrell, he's just an old man. He's so beat up now he won't be

talking the rest of the year. You give them both a break, Mr. Robertson, I swear to you you won't be sorry."

"All right, Ned, we'll let this one go. I know things are hard with
the men. Just make sure it doesn't happen again. You think Cottrell is going to be all right?"

"You couldn't hurt that hillbilly with a two-ton truck," Rockwell
said with a laugh.

He stood up. "I'm glad you came along, Frank. I don't think I'd
have kept my temper with that goddamn Lee Jones."

Frank Robertson grinned faintly. When you *really* lose your
temper, Ned, I want to be there."

Rockwell peered at him, and then he laughed, and Robertson
laughed too. Ned left the office. They understood what they understood. They were together in this one thing after all those years:
they were going to keep the plant going to the very end, no matter
what—drunkenness, fighting, stealing. All of that would take place
but through it all production would keep up right to the very end.
And each man had his own reasons.

Frank Robertson worked in his office the rest of that afternoon
but his thoughts constantly returned to the fight in Building T.
Lee Jones, understanding nothing, feeling for no one, trying to fire
everyone he could. (Get out of severance pay that way, and other
benefits too; save the company money that way, Frank.) Lloyd
Shearer, sick with a severe stomach disorder, a shadow of his former
self, standing there, a spectator unable to cope with the situation.
Jeff Barrett refusing to inform on any of the hourly, a foreman on
the surface but an hourly man inside. John Franklin disgusted with
the whole business, and Rockwell baiting Lee Jones, and deep down
having the kind of instincts you could appeal to. Instincts that
would keep the plant going.

Cottrell was sent home from the clinic and told to take a few days
off. Kasivich came back to work the next day, sober, and worked as
though nothing had happened.

And life went on. The fight was talked about for all of one week
and then another event took its place, a bigger event, a sadder event.
Will Calloway, the likeable, popular original finish salesman died,
and right inside the plant.

Will Calloway was one of the real old-timers. He'd started work
at Baker back in June of 1927, just fourteen months after Robertson

had. A tall, homely yet attractive man, Calloway moved up from being a clerk in the office staff to a salesman. He was never a great salesman, according to Robertson. "Will was too erratic emotionally. One moment he'd be up, the next moment he'd be down. He could go from jokes to anger in seconds. He was a worrier too, and the idea of the plant closing worried Will as much as it worried his boss, Harold Peterson, and Arnot, and the others. Will wasn't sure what was going to happen to him. He was only a couple of years away from retirement. Our plan," says Robertson, "was to phase him out slowly. There was no point in his driving back and forth to Cleveland all the time as original finish moved there; we were going to lessen his duties. Toward the end, just before he died, Will was doing pretty much what he'd done thirty-seven years ago when he started work. He was clerking. And nobody thought he minded."

Tom Morgan, the plant's last industrial relations manager, was a good friend of Will Calloway's. As Morgan liked to talk about his now-disappearing prowess as an athlete, so Calloway often talked humorously about his now-disappearing prowess as an actor. Calloway had been active in civic theatre groups in Detroit and the suburbs for as long as anyone could remember. He had even tried to recruit Morgan once for a walk-on part. Almost everyone liked Will —his jokes, his grins, his odd moods. He added a little something to the place, Morgan felt.

Because Morgan had been transferred from industrial relations to superintendent of the afternoon shift during the 1950's, he had to some extent lost touch with Will Calloway. Though often when he came to work at 3 P.M., he'd look in on Will and chin with him a little. Then he'd go into his own green cubbyhole of an office. The offices downstairs were across the hall from a sort of sick room the company had set up. It wasn't an elaborate affair, just two or three cots and some first aid equipment. If anyone had a serious accident, he'd be bundled up and taken over to the Compton Industrial Clinic down the block and across the street.

One afternoon, Morgan was sitting in his office when he heard a commotion and looked up to see a knot of men, sales people, coming down the stairs, sort of half-carrying, half-walking Will Calloway, who was trying to make a joke of it.

"What's going on?" Morgan asked.

"Old Will's got a little stomach upset," someone said, and Will laughed.

"A ham's a ham, Tom," he said.

They made him lie down. Morgan says, "The minute I took a good look at him I knew it was no stomach upset. He was white as a sheet, but he grinned at me, and winked, and then just lay there.

"We sent over to the clinic for a doctor and we stood around Will and talked about other things. Will watched us, and pretty soon he said he felt a lot better.

"The doctor came and put a stethoscope on him, and listened to him and said his heart sounded all right to him. By this time Will was feeling real good, making jokes and telling us he wasn't holding up production now because only the supervisors were here. And he sat up and asked for a cigarette, and we all had a smoke, the doctor too, and suddenly the cigarette fell out of Will's fingers, he closed his eyes, and fell down on the bed. The doctor jumped for him, did heart massage, breathed down his mouth. We rushed him to the clinic where they had oxygen tanks, but he was gone. He'd died right in front of our eyes. A joke on his lips at the last moment."

Will Calloway would be the first of three salesmen to die during the closing of the plant. Towards the end of that year Louis Arnot would die of a heart attack at home and the following spring Harold Peterson would take his own life.

The death of Calloway depressed everyone, for he was universally liked as a good Joe.

Looking back on it, Frank Robertson says, "I think now how I worried about the hourly people who were going to be without jobs. Maybe I should have worried more about people like Will Calloway, Louis Arnot, Harold Peterson, Lloyd Shearer, who was so sick all the time—management people whose jobs were supposed to be the same but had to be different because the production facilities were being moved. But, you know, we met so often with the union to argue about severance pay, seniority transfer rights, pension funds —we didn't have time to worry about salaried people, about management people who had no one to represent them. They got lost in the shuffle and it was my fault. Now . . . now I think about them all the time.

"I think about someone like Otto Mueller who was so loyal

through the years and got a rough deal at the very end. He was superintendent of the resin department and lost his retirement pension with just one year to go. What's happened to him? Or to someone like Henry Burns?—he wasn't salaried. He was hourly, but he was in exactly the same boat as Mueller. Both were just a year shy of retirement when the plant closed. What's happened to those poor guys? Loyal men, both of them, just born at the wrong time. I wonder what they're doing now."

Robertson Knows I'm
Driving a School Bus

Name: Otto Mueller
Age: 61
Birthplace: Detroit
Education: public schools
        B.A., Tri-State College, Angola, Indiana
Employment: 1927–32, Bell Telephone Company, engineer
        1932–65, Baker Color Company:
                laborer, foreman, supervisor, superintendent
                of the resin department
Married: Grace Courlander, 1933; two children, three grandchildren
Religion: Protestant
Residence: 87902 Happel Lane, Farmington, Michigan
Health: good

Frank Robertson wonders what has happened to the older workers who missed out on their pensions by a year or two—salaried men like Otto Mueller, the superintendent of the resin plant, and hourly workers like Henry Burns who drove a fork truck for Baker for twenty-five years.

Mueller is a large slow-talking, bald-headed man who lives in a neat little white house with aluminum siding in a new subdivision of Farmington. He is astonished that Frank Robertson wants to know what's happened to him.

"Why just last summer my wife and I drove down to Arizona and on the way we stopped in Arkansas to see the Robertsons. Frank knows I'm driving a school bus. I told him so."

Puzzled, Mueller removes his glasses, holds them up to the light, blows on the lenses, wipes them with his handkerchief, and holds them up again to the light. By the time he puts them back on his nose he has something figured out and he smiles widely, showing lots of teeth.

"I guess Frank is beginning to forget things. He's not well, you know. The plant closing didn't do anything good for him, and then he's had his wife's health on his mind all these years. As long as I've known the Robertsons—and it's a long time, over thirty years—Mrs. Robertson has been sick. Frank has got a lot to put up with." Mueller smiles again with all those teeth. He sits back in a clear plastic-covered easy chair. It is morning in his clean, well-furnished house. There is a big 295-square-inch television set, a hi-fi, a small white bookcase filled with Readers' Digest abridged books. All the easy chairs and the love seat near the hi-fi are covered with clear plastic. Off to the left is a small, spotless, modern kitchen with gleaming white tiles with colonial-type sayings printed on some of them. Mueller explains that these tiles can be used as trivets but usually they just use a pot holder since the tiles look so nice on the walls. Mueller is proud of the house which he cleans up every morning between 9 and noon.

"I do the cleaning and the cooking," he says with an apologetic smile, "water the plants and make the beds. And when the weather's good I've still got time for a little golf."

When the Muellers first moved here twenty years ago, the place was just fields. There wasn't another house around. Now there is a subdivision of twenty- to twenty-five-thousand-dollar homes.

"I bought about ten acres and gradually sold them off. I've only got one small lot left, and there's a For Sale sign out on it now. It's pretty late in the year to get it sold, but we're counting on the spring. My wife's going to retire from teaching at the end of spring and then we'll travel. We're going to see how we like trailer living. Did you see that trailer outside? It's an Airstream. If we like trailer living I plan to sell this house, and off we go. I guess, all in all, we were lucky. This house is all paid for, so's the trailer. Through the years the wife and I have been careful. She's taught elementary school for fifteen years now; we had luck with the stock I bought, and I guess I was luckier than I thought I was going to be when the plant closed."

When the plant closed Mueller got a job working for United Paint in one of their retail outlets, servicing painters who came in looking for advice. Then the construction business fell off last year.

It was harder than he anticipated getting a job at his age, so when he heard about this opening for a school bus driver, he took it.

Of course this job is just until his wife retires; then they'll both travel. At least Mueller hopes the job is temporary. Once before, he recalls, he took another temporary job—at the Baker Color Company, back in 1932. It was at the height of the depression, and a hard time to get work. He got the job through his step-father, Earl Higgins, who was the production manager. Mueller hired on as an ordinary laborer, a big step down from an engineer with a college degree, but he was grateful to get any job. All over Detroit people were being laid off. He himself had just been laid off at Michigan Bell where he worked as a cable engineer for four years and ten months. Suddenly in July the company announced they were laying off all employees with less than five full years of service.

Mueller smiles awkwardly. "I guess even then I was born at the wrong time."

He is referring to the fact that thirty-three and one-half years later when Baker closed its gates he was fifty-nine years and nine months old—just three months short of being eligible for a retirement pension. Lloyd Shearer, the production manager at the time of closing, whom Mueller worries about today, was luckier. Shearer was six months older than Mueller and got his pension. You had to be sixty to be eligible for early retirement. After thirty-three and one-half years of working at one plant to miss a pension by three months was, Mueller felt, like a bad joke. For a time during the closing period he thought he could talk the company into letting him work at least another three months. But the answer was no.

"I'd have gone to York if they asked me," he says, "but they didn't ask me. I'd have gone and worked three months or three years or however long they wanted me to work, but after thirty-three and a half years I wasn't good enough to be asked to go on for a few more months. Still, I was good enough to train the people that worked down there. They sent sixteen people up from their new resin plant at Newtonville for me to train, and I trained them and down they went again, but they never asked me down. After thirty-three and a half years I wasn't good enough to work another three months. But you know . . ." He stares at the creases in his sun tans, "even that I could take. That was the way the rules were. Everyone got terminated in December except Robertson and Tom Morgan

—they kept them on another few weeks. But everyone else ended with the plant. It wasn't that bad. I could accept the fact that I was born three months too late. The company had its rules and stuck by them. What really hurt me was the severance pay. I know I got a raw deal there."

Salaried employees at Baker who were not eligible for retirement pensions also received severance pay from the company, and a good deal more than the hourly employees received. Mueller received $8000 in severance pay in December, 1965. When he learned of the amount he was to receive he went to an accountant friend who pointed out to him that when the $8000 in severance pay was added to his $15,000 salary as Superintendent of the Resin Plant and both were added to his wife's salary of $8500 . . . then Mueller whose children were married and were no longer dependents, would be moving into another tax category and would be paying an enormous tax. Whereas, said the accountant, if Mueller could prevail upon the company to give him his $8000 severance pay three weeks later, in the calendar year 1966, then he would be saving close to $4000. For the following year the Mueller income would be reduced to Mrs. Mueller's salary plus stock dividends plus whatever part-time job Mueller got.

"It didn't seem like much to ask of them," Mueller says with his wide smile, the smile of an injured man. " 'All I ask is to let me work three weeks for you. Let me work into the new year a bit, and I can put the severance pay down as income for next year. I'll work for nothing. I don't want to get paid.' So I went to Robertson, and Frank thought it was a reasonable request, but the company didn't think it was. They said what if everyone else wanted to do this. It would be a company conspiring tax dodge and so forth. What it amounted to was that after thirty-three and one half years they wouldn't let me work three weeks for nothing so I could save myself four or five thousand dollars. I'm bitter about that. I'm very bitter about that. My pension loss, I can understand that. But that cruel tax loss, I can't understand that. Well, I guess that's the way big business is. They say they care, but they don't.

"They didn't have to close Baker either. There were things wrong, all right, but if they'd met the situation head-on, Baker could have been saved. I'm talking about the union. As long as I can remember the union ran the plant. They milked it for all it was worth, and the company let them. They were afraid of them. Tom Morgan, who was our negotiator for a long time, let them get everything they wanted. I've got nothing against Tom. He's a decent person. But he wasn't trained to be a tough bargainer. He didn't have the temperament for it. They ran roughshod all over him, all over us for that matter. It was the radicals in the union who closed Baker. DeMoss and Rockwell were the biggest radicals of them all. If they spotted anyone who was a good worker, they'd get hold of him and tell him he didn't have to work so hard. I know Perry DeMoss. Before he went over to the union, he worked in the resin plant for me. At one time he was looking after six kettles . . . three 500-gallon kettles and three 2,000-gallon kettles. He had to mix in three to four thousand pounds of solids for those kettles. When things would get busy, do you know what Perry would do? He'd sign out, saying he had some union business to do. And Rockwell the same thing. Why in the end, I don't think Rockwell ever did his work in the tankhouse at all. He sat around the cafeteria all day, wasting the company's money. It was people like Rockwell and DeMoss who forced the closing of Baker.

"I don't think the company really wanted to close down the plant. It doesn't make sense to be producing original finish for automobiles from a distance of 300 miles in Cleveland when you can be doing it two blocks away. The refinish business in York is something else again. The outlets for refinish are nationwide. But the original finish in Cleveland? There's one big outlet—in Detroit. It's foolishness. I know for a fact they've lost some of their original finish business. For instance, we made a good water primer for Ford. They moved it to Cleveland and the boys there let their tanks run out. They didn't meet the order and they lost that water primer business. At one time we had 94 percent of Chrysler's business. I know we don't have it now.

"If it hadn't been for union greed, Baker would have stayed open. We should have for once let them strike. We should have met them head-on just once. It would have straightened things out. But we were scared of them. As a result, they ran the place. The hourly never cared about Baker. The last two years, they first thought the company was bluffing. They'd announce to me the company was only trying to welsh on its contract, but when they saw it happening, when they saw equipment and raw materials being trucked out, then things began to fall apart. They began stealing. Paint went over the fence the way it never had before. I hear the colored have been painting houses all over Detroit with stolen Baker paint. They did prosecute a couple of colored they found with their basements filled with paint. Someone even stole a two-ton chainfall from Building T. Now how did they do that? The chainfall was used for hoisting materials on an overhead rail. How they got that out of the plant I'll never know.

"The plant fell apart after the explosion. Up till the explosion we were not doing badly. We were producing about 30,000 gallons a day. After the explosion, it was all over; it was a holding operation then, trying to keep old customers and transfer equipment at the same time. It was all ending, and I'm sorry. Because Baker was a good place to work. I've been in other paint plants and compared to them Baker was heaven."

The sun falls on Otto Mueller's bald head. A large man, he runs his hands nervously over the creases in his sun tans. A cuckoo clock in the kitchen chirps eleven. Mueller has nothing to do till three o'clock when he drives his school bus again. He has a 1966 Pontiac. He drives it to the school and leaves it there and returns about 4:30 P.M. with the bus. His wife is usually home by 3:30 P.M. She has a Corvair. His school bus transports high school students so he doesn't see his wife till he gets home. They usually have tea about a quarter-to-five and then she will cook supper. With his wife's job Mueller does not want a full time job. It would put him into a higher tax bracket. He makes $176 a month driving the school bus. And they have some income from stock dividends. Mueller has taken what was left of his severance pay after the "cruel tax loss" and invested it in stock. Pennsylvania Corporation stock. "It's gone up quite a bit," he says, cheerfully.

Trailer Going Nowhere

Name: Henry Burns
Age: 61
Birthplace: Detroit
Education: public schools
Employment: 1936–39, Ford Motor Company, assembly
             1939–65, Baker Color Company: jitney driver
Married: Ruth Gustine; three children: two married (three grandchildren); one unmarried daughter lives at home.
Religion: Protestant
Residence: 14397 Henry—northwest section of Detroit, Michigan
Health: mild diabetes and hypertension

Henry Burns prides himself on being a careful man, a law-abiding man, a man who takes care of himself and his family, who doesn't want anything for nothing, a man who plans ahead. He puts antifreeze in his car in September; the snow tires go on in October.

On one of the psychological questionnaires given to the men in the research study of Baker employees, the question was asked: "What would you do if an atomic bomb was dropped nearby?" Burns's answer: "I'd notify the proper authorities. Then I'd get my family and leave fast."

Burns is a square. There are right things to do and wrong things and 'Burnsy' as he was often called at Baker, always knows the difference. Yet for all this knowledge, he is a bitter man today. All his life he has done the right thing, planned ahead, worked hard, remained loyal to the company, and now he's in trouble.

"You didn't see it," he says, jumping off the sofa to peer out the pane in the front door—it's a warm October morning and he has left a tiny pile of leaves smouldering in the street which he is worried about the neighborhood children getting into—"I hauled it over to the garage to have some rewiring done on the brakes." He sits down. "It's two-tone, cream and green, got a green arrow on it, jalousied windows. Good little kitchen, wood cabinets, gas stove and electric refrigerator. Gas heat. Got a new water tank and electric brakes. We got it in 1961. Used it for vacations. Drove around Lake Superior, over to Kingston in Ontario, Thousand Islands. One summer I took my daughter and her children along and we drove down to the Smokies, right along the Skyline Drive. I've got a Pontiac Catalina, 8-cylinder; it never gave us any trouble. The kids love that trailer. Now . . . we use it for picnics. I put beer in the refrigerator. The grandchildren play in it on rainy days. Why not? It's not going anywhere. I had plans to trade it in for a larger one when I retired. It's only 16 feet. We were going to get a bigger one and take off to all the places we'd never been—California, the Rockies, Yellowstone, Florida. Now . . ." A noise outside makes him jump up. He peers through the pane in the door. "Damn those kids." He opens the door.

"You kids, stay away from that fire. You want to get burnt? Now beat it. Beat it."

He waits till they go, then he closes the door and sits down again. "Kids. You got to be a step ahead of them all the time. They don't know enough to look out for themselves." He breathes out. "I don't know what's the matter with me. I'm getting jumpy. I was never sick in my life. A little high blood pressure, maybe, and they been telling me I got some diabetes. They used that as an excuse not to hire me on at Fisher Body. One place my blood pressure is too high, another place my blood isn't right. Nobody says I'm too old. Nobody says it's the twenty-six years I already put in." He's silent. "Twenty-six years and they closed the plant when I had just a year to go before I'd be eligible for early retirement. I lost my pension rights. And when I lost the pension I lost our retirement. All the plans we made, the trailer. Now I'll have to work as long as I'm able and we'll see what happens after that. There's no use planning ahead anymore. And what the hell did planning get me anyway? Nothing. Absolutely nothing."

Burns is bitter about the union, the federal government, the company.

"The union could have done a lot better for us on the pension settlement. They let the insurance company get away with murder. The only one who made money on the pension settlement was the insurance company. I got 1800 dollars for my pension rights. That's all. For twenty-six years of work, that was my retirement pay, and the lousy goddamn government taxed me on that. They got laws in this country to protect rapists and burners. Who's going to protect an asshole like me? Everything's going wrong in this country. They were Communists marching in that Selma march, and the government protects them. That Russian—what's his name? Khrushchev—he said they were going to take over this country without firing a shot, and I believe him. This country's future looks goddamn dim to me."

Burns gets up and looks out the pane in the front door. There are no children near his almost extinguished fire. He paces the room.

"The company give us severance pay. They kept saying they didn't have to. But they had a reason for it. It was an incentive to stay. They gave severance pay for them, not us. It didn't make any difference. Most of us would have stayed anyway. Christ, just to start with, none of us believed they were going to close. That letter back in 1963, they mailed it to each one of us. I didn't believe it. Why, we were making money for them. Why would they want to close up a plant that is making money? Now I know a company never makes enough money, but I didn't know it then. Then we figured the whole thing was a scheme to soften us up for a concession in the contract. Rockwell thought so, so did DeMoss, everyone thought so. Then they start shipping stuff out. Then we saw. But it was a gradual deal; it could sneak up on you. They started making our paint elsewhere and it took a long, long time for us to notice.

"Then I figured, what the hell, I'll stick it out to the end. It was a good place to work. Why leave sooner than I have to? I'm healthy. Times are good. I'll take my severance pay and go out with my head up, like all the old-timers. We were loyal. We stayed on till the very end. I got laid off December 10, 1965. They took my jitney away from me a week before and shipped it down to Ohio. I just sat around. There were some guys drinking; I drank a little with them. There were some guys stealing. I didn't steal. I never stole. Most of the guys never stole. The company made a big thing out of the stealing, but you didn't have to do a hell of a lot to steal paint, for instance. They always let you take home cans of returned paint. They'd be cans with return labels on them. What the guys did now was switch labels from the returned paint onto new cans and take home new cans. But most of us just sat around in a daze. That last day, it was a funny goddamn feeling, I can tell you. I just came home that Friday afternoon.

"The next morning my wife—God bless her, she's the best woman in the world—she says to me, 'We're going to hitch up the trailer and take a trip.' And, by God, if that isn't what we did for the next three weeks. We drove that trailer up north. Visited friends in the Thumb area, then up to Traverse City where I did a little ice fishing, and then we went up in the U.P. and it was beautiful. I always liked the outdoors, fresh air, exercise, fishing, hunting. My wife was wonderful. I forgot all about Baker, about everything. I felt good. I was pretty confident about the future. We were going to put the 1800-dollar pension money and my 800-dollar severance into savings bonds. I had some friends advise me to buy stock, utility stock—that's supposed to be safe—but I don't know much about stock, and savings bonds look safe enough to me. I wasn't scared at all. That trip was wonderful. When I'd get back, right after Christmas I'd look for work. I wasn't going to collect unemployment compensation. That smells like welfare to me, charity. I don't like begging or beggars. I don't want anything for nothing. I always planned ahead and took care of my own. I was sure I could get a job. Times were good, I was in good health; I was only fifty-eight.

"Well, I'm going to tell you something, a man doesn't know how old he is till something like this happens. Every place I put an application in after we got back they said: 'Boy, you worked for them twenty-six years and they wouldn't take you along to their new plant?' I got lots of sympathy but no job. I looked all of January. I didn't take any unemployment compensation. I just looked every day. They found one reason or another for turning me down.

"The first place I went to was another paint plant, Riis-Moran. I figured they could use a man with paint plant experience but they were all fill' up, they said. Over at Fisher Body I saw they had an opening for a jitney driver. Well if anyone was qualified to drive a jitney I was the man. I drove jitneys at Baker for almost twenty-five years. I drove them when they were flat types, when they were electric fork trucks, and I drove the propane gas fork trucks. They read over my record and told me to come in and take a medical test. The M.D. gave me a test and said my blood sugar was too high.

They wanted to know whether I had a history of diabetes. I told them no, but they said they couldn't take a chance on me because of my blood sugar.

"Finally I got a job at Chevrolet Forge as an ash handler. Ash handlers don't handle ash. They got gigantic electric vacuums to do that. What an ash handler does is look after six gas furnaces, each one three stories tall. It was a big hot place, with a terrific amount of noise, the heat was tremendous, and there were lots of gauges I had to keep checking every couple of seconds. I was there a week learning how to handle it and then they threw me into it on the rotary shift. I had no seniority. I worked three shifts within one week. Days, afternoons, and nights. There were hundreds of guys around, but I didn't know anyone; I never got to know anyone. I never stayed on one shift long enough, and then there were those gauges to check, trying to stand the heat, the noise. I tell you it was awful. You wouldn't treat a horse the way men are treated in places like that. Lock them up in a prison like that. I came home one afternoon sweating all over and right at the corner up there, I blacked out. Pitched right down on the sidewalk. That night, I had a few drinks. My wife, God bless her, stood by me. I told her I was scared of that place. I was too old for that kind of work. She stood by me when I called in the next morning and told them I was quitting. I'd worked there a little less than a month. But I just couldn't take it anymore."

Mrs. Burns is a small, gray-haired woman with a cheerful face. According to her her husband was out of work for a month and beginning to lose confidence in himself.

"He was always so sure he could take care of things," she says softly. "It hurt me to see him not believe in himself anymore." She pauses; he has gone outside to examine the burning leaves. "I was getting worried about him. He always liked a drink or two, I know that he even had a drink or two at Baker, but it never interfered with him. But now he began drinking more and more. He wouldn't go near the trailer in our back yard. He said what was the use. He'd let me down, he kept saying that, over and over."

Mrs. Burns says simply that there were many hard moments but they tried to share them together and to keep them from the kids. The Burns have a son and two daughters. The son and the older daughter are married and have children. The younger daughter works at Burroughs as a keypunch operator and lives at home with them. She helps out. The son has a good job with an insurance company.

"I know the kids would help us if we ever got in trouble," Burns says, a few moments later, "but I'd die before I took any money from them. That would be the end of everything."

After he quit at Chevrolet Forge, Burns still refused to take unemployment compensation. And then in April, a week after his fifty-ninth birthday, he got a job as a sweeper at a firm that made plastic seat covers. He was paid $1.57 an hour. At Baker his pay at the end had been $2.97. One Saturday, shopping with his wife, he ran into a guy who used to work at Baker. The guy told Burns he ought to put in another application at Riis-Moran. They were hiring more guys. "Call them again," he said. "It won't cost you anything to call them."

Burns decided his friend was right, even though it had only been two months since he'd inquired at Riis-Moran and they had clucked over his twenty-six years put in at Baker and felt sorry and didn't have a job for him. Still he had nothing to lose, so he telephoned down there Monday morning and talked with the personnel man. They pulled out his old application and after a few minutes studying it, told him to come on down and see them. Burns went down the very next day. To his amazement they hired him on the spot. They even told him there was a good chance he'd be trained as a blender, one of the few skilled jobs left in a paint plant. He went home exuberant. Things had finally taken an upturn. He was back in a paint plant again. And he'd be making over $3.00 an hour, better than he'd done at Baker. He was happy. He and Mrs. Burns had a little celebration.

When he reported to work the next day there were more papers to sign. And among the things he had to sign he found a waiver of any claims to a pension from Riis-Moran.

"It was in their labor contract that a man had to have at least ten years' seniority to be eligible for a pension. And compulsory retirement was sixty-eight years old. I had just turned fifty-nine two weeks before. So I would just miss out on ten years if I worked to sixty-eight. I'd miss out by two weeks. After twenty-six years I missed out on a pension at Baker by one year, and now, if I live that long, I'll miss out by two weeks on a pension at Riis-Moran."

Burns, who prides himself on planning carefully, on thinking things through, does not see any connection between Riis-Moran turning him down two months ago when he was fifty-eight and signing him on now that he's fifty-nine.

"That's the way things happen," he says.

To add to his bad luck, the company changed its mind and decided to move a younger man into the blender trainee opening. Burns was assigned to a stockroom. After working for two months in the stockroom, he was given a jitney to drive. And he is now driving a jitney, the exact same kind he drove for twenty-six years at Baker. He's no longer exuberant or happy. He doesn't care anymore. "A job's a job," he says. "I just don't know what would happen to us if I got sick."

He refuses to think ahead now "because there's nothing to think ahead to." And he wonders what he did wrong. "Maybe I should have quit at Baker when I first heard they were going to close it down," he says, "But none of us believed it. When they began moving stuff out, we believed. But then there was the explosion. And you know what they did after the explosion? They started rebuilding part of the plant. Do you rebuild a plant you're going to shut down? We figured maybe they were changing their minds about closing. Hopes went up. It didn't hurt to hope, did it?"

He peers questioningly, as if suddenly an inner glimmer of the truth were dawning inside him, as if he were first realizing that perhaps it did hurt to hope, that a man who knows right from wrong, who puts antifreeze into his car in September and snow tires on in October, who doesn't want anything for nothing, who takes care of his own—this man can still not know what is going on, can still get screwed in the end.

"Maybe," he says, and stands up, "maybe I should have quit earlier at Baker. Maybe I should have said the hell with loyalty, the hell with eight hundred bucks of severance pay—what's eight hundred bucks? A month and a half pay, that's all." He stands up nervously, goes to the door and looks out through the pane. "Maybe I didn't do it right at all; I didn't look far enough ahead." He pauses. "Like those houses across the street. Do you see those four white houses across the street—the four down from the corner? Well, when we bought out here twenty years ago there were no houses there. Just a hill and a stand of oak trees. I bought this house figuring no one could build there because of the hill; we'd always have that hill and those oaks to look at. Then five years ago a guy come in and bought that hill and the oak trees. He brought in a bulldozer and two days later there wasn't any hill. He brought in a chain saw, and two days later there wasn't any oak trees. He sold the oak trees for firewood and with what he made on that he paid for the hill. Then he subdivided the land into four building lots and sold them for three thousand dollars apiece. Then he took off."

Burns turns, sits down on the sofa again, and clasps his hands. He is silent a moment. "I guess in this world some people can manage and others got to be taken care of. I always thought I could manage, but I don't think that anymore. For fifteen years I lived here and looked across the street and all I saw was a hill and some oak trees."

The Explosion

August 1, 1964

In June and July, despite transfer of materials and equipment, the Baker plant was still producing over 25,000 gallons of finish and refinish daily, and production efficiency was at a high of 18 gallons per man-hour. The warehouse located three miles away on Fitzwarren Street was as busy as it had ever been. According to Jefferson Barrett who had been transferred there in June as a supervisor on the day shift, the warehouse was shipping at least two hundred thousand pounds of refinish a week out to warehouses around the country during the spring and summer of 1964.

Both warehouse and plant were working six days a week, including the day shift on Saturday. On Wednesday, July 29, the word came down that the day shift was not to report this coming Saturday, August 1.

In view of subsequent events Neil Esslinger, a leader-checker at the warehouse, found this suspicious. "That made me think, looking back on it," he says, "that they did it on purpose. I think somebody got a good payoff on it. How come that Saturday of all Saturdays there was no one working at the plant?"

As a matter of fact, there were ten people working at the plant that Saturday, August 1: There was a watchman who had an office in the boiler room but who, fortunately for him, was drinking coffee in the cafeteria at the time of the explosion; there were two men trying to work out a problem with the computer in the main office building—an assembly line had not been functioning correctly and they were trying to figure out why not and how best to surmount the problem—and seven men were working in the testing lab on the third floor of Building 2.

Among the seven men in the lab was Willis Ingram, then 53, a small skinny Negro with amused eyes—an old-timer at Baker.

"We were mixing colors," Ingram recalls, "trying to catch up on a rush order. We'd been at it since 7 A.M. and were supposed to quit at 3:30 and we still hadn't come out with the right color. Finally Al Leto said: 'Let's take a break and come back to it.'"

They shut off the four experimental mixers. It was 1:55 P.M. Ingram remembers the time because he looked at his watch to see how close to 3:30 they were taking this coffee break. They were about to go downstairs to the cafeteria when suddenly the air felt funny. Sort of heavyish. Some loose papers and trash began skittering across the concrete floor at their feet, as though a fan were blowing from the next room. Later Ingram realized that the papers and trash were being sucked out of the building.

"What the hell—" someone started to say, and they heard a tremendous noise. Every window in their lab blew outwards.

Willis Ingram was not known for his swiftness afoot. Indeed, since he had returned from the state tuberculosis sanitorium at Northville last year, he had held a job which Perry DeMoss says was created for him. His health was improving but Ingram still moved slowly because of a chronic shortness of breath.

"I can tell you one thing," Ingram says today, "nobody got down those stairs faster than I did. I knew right away what was happening. The whole plant was blowing up."

Ingram and his coworkers ran down the three floors and when they emerged into the yard outside Building 2 it looked to Ingram as if a World War II air raid was taking place. The one great explosion was followed by a series of smaller but equally violent ones. Overhead black smoke was swirling up, and through the smoke Ingram saw an object go flying about thirty feet over his head. It was a huge drum of paint. It was followed by others. "They were being tossed in the air like depth charges lobbing off destroyers," he says. "15-gallon drums, 30-gallon drums, 100-gallon drums, all flying around over our heads. I knew one thing—we had to get out of there."

Ingram doesn't remember what the others did, but he knew he was not going out by the main gate because that seemed to him where some of the explosions were coming from. Instead he ran east to the Michigan Central Railroad fence, climbed it, though he hadn't done a thing like that since he was a school kid forty years ago, and began what was known for months afterward as "Ingram's great run."

He crossed the railroad tracks and ran east on West Morton, past the railroad blinker signs, the Fleetwing Gasoline Yards ("because if they ever went up that would be the end of Detroit"); he crossed a second pair of railroad tracks and sprinted by the Diesel training center, past a dry cleaning building out of whose windows some curious faces were peering. Ingram didn't wait for the light to turn green at Prairie and West Morton. ("You don't worry about getting runned over at a time like that.") He sprinted across the street, past the red brick Baptist church, a welding shop, the Hi-Hat Bar. A narrowing and broken sidewalk slowed him up a little as he ran past Zoro's Market, a drug store, and the Acme Floor Supply Company with a small sign advertising Pennsylvania Paints flapping slowly in the breeze. He crossed two more streets and ran past the Lutheran church and the fire station. Trucks were coming out of the fire station. He ran between them. When Ingram reached the corner of Livernois and West Morton, he stopped and breathed out. He'd run over a mile.

"Nobody put a clock on me," he says, "but it must have been damned good for a sick man."

Ingram believes it would have been even faster except for the last few hundred yards. People were coming the other way, running toward the disaster, and he had to run around them.

It had felt to Ingram and the others in the lab in Building 2 that the whole plant had blown up. This was understandable because part of their building—the north section where the grinding department was—*had* blown up. In addition the boiler house nearby blew up; Building 13, the resin plant, blew up; Building 8, the caustic and solvent wash building, collapsed; Building 14, the container and pigment storage shed, buckled under the heat, and all the main tunnels housing the solvent, the resin, and the service lines blew up. Later there would be considerable discussion whether the explosions started in the tunnels and spread to the buildings or started in a particular building and spread to the tunnels.

In his report to General Office, Frank Robertson described part of the scene:

> Building 5 was almost totally destroyed, suggesting that the explosions had begun there. The whole north section of the two-story building distintegrated while the south section remained without walls. The strength of the explosion was appalling.
>
> The intense heat in Building 8 caused its sheet metal construction to crumple. The equipment cleaning room which housed many combustible materials was completely destroyed by fire. This building was a complete loss.
>
> Building 14, which was also of sheet metal construction,

buckled. The pigment and container storage areas there underwent severe water damage.

The main tunnel exploded. The end wall cut-offs to the basements of Buildings 4 and 13 collapsed and thus the fire spread into the areas underneath these buildings. In Building 13 six resin storage tanks were ruptured. Five tons of foam powder were used to extinguish the flames in these areas and the operation wasn't completed till 7 P.M.

Outdoors there was havoc on a grand scale. Many of the outdoor drums storing finish and intermediate materials, exposed to extreme heat, ruptured and were jettisoned high into the air. Others were pierced immediately and spilled their contents into the tunnels which were now exposed to the surface. These flammable materials floated into the basements of Buildings 4 and 13 and fed the flames there.

Frank Robertson recalls the afternoon of the explosion very clearly.

"It was one of the first Saturdays I'd taken off in a long time, and the reason I'd taken it off was because it was my birthday. August 1st, 1964, I was 60 years old. Doris and I were going to go out to dinner later to celebrate, but right then we were working in the living room on her miniature collection. The phone rang. It's funny how you get about phone calls. Doris looked at me and said: 'Frank, it's going to be the plant.' And I said: 'Nonsense, we're not operating today.'

" 'Frank,' she went on, 'it's your birthday today. Don't go down there.'

"I said: 'Doris, it's not the plant.'

"But it was the plant. Paul Tilyard from the technical department. 'Frank,' he said, 'I just got a call—there's been an explosion at the plant. I'm going down there now.'

"Oh no, I thought. After years of safety measures, safety drills, when our production was holding up so well, when the transfer was going to smoothly—we had an explosion. That was what I thought. I heard myself telling Paul to make sure everyone on the fire list was called. He told me it seemed like a miracle but no one was reported injured yet. The fire and police were down there. The resin building was completely gone. I told him I'd be right down too.

" 'Doris,' I said, 'I've got to go. There's been an explosion at the plant.'

"She looked at me; she didn't say anything. I think she understood. She asked me if I wanted her to come with me. I said no.

"I drove down Grand River and pretty soon I could see smoke rising ahead of me. It filled the sky like a bombing raid. How did it happen? Sabotage? I'll admit it was one of the first things I thought of, but I didn't believe it. There wasn't a man at Baker who would consciously hurt our plant.

"It had to be an accident. The service lines. I kept coming back to the service lines in my mind. They'd been leaking for over two years. We'd patch them up and leaks would break out in other places. We should have overhauled them this spring but with the plant closing so near Frohman wouldn't give me any money for it. And now this.

"I turned down Oakman and the traffic soon stopped me. I could hear explosions; I could see drums of paint flying through the air. I could see flames coming out of three or four buildings. It was unbelievable, sickening.

"I left my car double-parked and forced my way to the plant gates. There was a mob of people around the gate when I got there. Fire engines, police, arson squad, and Baker people. Lots of Baker people—hourly and salaried. They'd heard the news on their radios. They were coming in from all over the city. Standing there, staring—production workers, clerical workers, truck drivers, maintenance boys, men and women—just standing there watching their plant go up in smoke. There wasn't a one of them that would have done this, would even have thought of doing it. This was their plant.

"A fireman barred my way. 'I'm Frank Robertson,' I said to him, 'this is my plant.'

"He took me over to the fire marshal."

Ned Rockwell was sitting in his living room watching a baseball game on television that Saturday afternoon when the phone rang. His sister, the one who lives in Oak Park, said, "Ned, thank God, you're there."

"What the hell are you talking about?" Rockwell said. "Where else would I be?"

"Baker blew up," she says. "Turn on the TV."

Rockwell continues. "I think she's kidding; I got the TV on already. Then I think she's too much of a dumb-dumb to make jokes like this, so I hang up and flip channels and while I'm trying to get something else the phone rings again. It's my other sister—the one that lives in Highland Park—and she says, 'Thank God you're there. Baker blew up.'

"Well, I can't get it on the TV so I get in the car and go down Grand River. The traffic was thick. It looked like everyone was driving down Grand River to see the fire. You could see the smoke from Grand River.

"Sure, the thought crossed my mind that maybe some jackass tossed a bomb or something. But I ruled it out right away. It was an accident. Later I got it straight from a guy in maintenance. A ball mill overheated; there were the usual sewer fumes. The place was closed up tighter than a drum Saturday, and no one around to watch it heat up. The only guy who could have been killed in it was the bolier room watchman, the caretaker, but he was having coffee in the cafeteria when it blew. The guy in maintenance told me the supervisor in that area had been told the ball mill was overheating but he didn't do anything about it.

"Some guys thought the company done it, and probably the company thought the guys had done it, but right from the first moment I saw the fires I knew it was an accident.

"I had to leave my car three blocks away and it was a real mess around the plant. The firemen and cops wouldn't let anyone close. And I didn't blame them. One hundred-gallon drums were being tossed over three-story buildings. The grinding building was gone, a box car was piled into the remains of the boiler room, and there wasn't a window left in any building. The lye tank was gone.

" 'Jesus Christ,' I thought, 'I hope nobody was killed.' I walked around trying to spot somebody I knew. Robertson was there talking with a fire marshal in a red car; Ray Kehoe, a supervisor on the second shift—a real tough cookie—was inside the gates directing things. He was telling the cops what to do, telling the firemen where to bring their hoses. I sneaked between two cops and went up to Kehoe. 'Look, Ray,' I say, 'it's me, Ned Rockwell. I got to get to my union records.'

"The records are in the tank house. He tries to talk me out of it, but I say I got to get them. I want my union records. He says if

that's the case he'll go with me. We walk to the tankhouse together, staying near the fence, the fires are everywhere and firemen
are running around us in circles. I turn to Kehoe and say: 'This is
it, Ray. It won't open again.' And Kehoe, that tough bastard, he
grins and says: 'We'll be back on Monday.' I didn't believe him,
but by God if some of us weren't back on Monday.

"We get to the tank house pretty soon and go in. I open my record
cabinet and the first thing Kehoe sees is some tools I stole, some
body filler, rubber gloves, dryer to work on my car. You know what
he does? Well, he was a big crook himself—stealing left and right,
and him a supervisor—but he turns his back and when I say I'm
ready to go he helps me bring out the records and all my stolen
goodies. Kehoe was supervisor of the thinner department on the
second shift. A real driver. If I owned a company I'd hire the
bastard. Anyway, he helped me carry the union records and my
stolen goodies to the station wagon and they stayed in the station
wagon for weeks.

"I stayed around for a couple of hours and watched them fight
the fires. There were lots of guys from Baker. They'd heard the news
on their car radios and came driving in to see."

Henry Burns was in his backyard watching his two grandchildren
climbing in the apple tree when his wife opened the back door and
told him someone had just telephoned to say the Baker plant had
blown up. Burns didn't believe it. He went inside and turned on
the radio. There was a newspaper strike in Detroit at the time and
the radio stations were giving extra coverage to news; sure enough,
two minutes or so later they repeated a bulletin about the explosion
at the Baker paint plant on West Morton.

"I'm going down there," Burns announced, over his wife's pro-
tests.

He took the two grandchildren with him. They got as far as
Grand River and Oakman before the traffic stopped them. Then
he walked, carrying one of the children on his shoulder. They stood
there and watched the fires licking out of the buildings. This is it,
Burns thought. The end of it. He says he felt absolutely nothing.

Otto Mueller was working in his garden when a neighbor drove
by, leaned out the window, and asked him if he'd heard about the
Baker plant exploding.

"I couldn't believe it," Mueller says. "There never was a more safety-conscious plant than we were.

"I got into my car and headed for Grand River. I hadn't gone a mile or so when I saw the smoke. I couldn't get close to it. By the time I got there they had the whole area roped off. I stood behind the ropes and watched. I didn't know what to think, though I knew the arson squad would be looking into it sure enough."

Tom Morgan was up north fishing with his son in his son's twelve-foot dinghy. He was on the first week of his vacation. They had just come back to the dock and he was tying up the boat when his wife came running out of the cottage. She'd just got a call from a neighbor who heard on the radio that the Baker paint plant in Detroit had blown up and twenty-seven men were killed.

"It sounded like a lot of baloney," Tom Morgan says. "For one thing I knew we'd caught up on our back orders and weren't supposed to operate the plant that Saturday. That meant there couldn't be twenty-seven men there. I didn't believe the whole thing until I got a long distance call from our daughter in Flint who said she just wanted to make sure I was up north. She'd heard the plant had a big explosion. Well, that meant it probably was true. It was as good a time as any to be on a vacation I thought, but I drove down Monday anyway. It was a mess all right."

The Lloyd Shearers live in a brick and frame house only about a dozen blocks from the plant. Shearer, Baker's production manager, had had a stomach operation the year before and was taking it easy on the couch. His wife, who'd been feeling poorly, was watching TV. No one had to telephone them about an explosion.

"We heard it all right," Shearer says. "Our windows rattled and the house shook. I went out the front door and looked outside. There was black smoke rising high in the sky. I knew it was in the direction of Baker but I didn't think it was Baker. We'd had our share of accidents before, but there wasn't a more careful, safety-conscious paint plant in the whole U.S.

"The wife said something had gone up nearby and I said: 'Yes,' but I was feeling so poorly I just lay down on the couch again. Pretty soon I got a call from Paul Tilyard and I told him, 'Paul, I won't be any good down there.' I just felt sick. The explosion was just another thing piled on. But after a while I got dressed and went down. Later I organized the supervisors into patrols to keep looters out."

The gang at the Fitzwarren warehouse that Saturday morning also heard the explosion. The warehouse is only about three miles from the main plant. According to Jeff Barrett, the supervisor on duty that morning, someone said: "Something blew up all right," but no one connected it with Baker. "We were busy," Barrett says. "We had lots of stuff to move, check, load and unload. We had drums and sacks of solvents and raw materials all over the place."

"Then the phone in the office rang. It was Bud McDermott's wife and she was half-hysterical. Bud worked at the warehouse and she worked at Sears and she'd seen a news interruption on one of their TV demonstrator sets that said the Baker plant had blown up and she wanted to speak to Bud. I told her not to worry. Bud was ten feet away. Nothing had blown up here and I got Bud onto the phone to talk to her. Then I told the guys what that noise was we just heard and we all walked outside. It was a beautiful sunny day. And there sure enough in the direction of the plant was black smoke rising high in the sky. We could hear the fire sirens coming from all directions.

"As soon as Bud hung up, the phone rang again. It was my nephew wanting to know if I was all right. I told him I was all right and for goodness sake to run over to my house and tell my wife I was at the warehouse and not at the plant and that I was all right.

"I went out of my way driving home after work that day. I drove by West Morton. There were still lots of people there and firemen and smoke. I wondered what it was going to mean. Would they just shut it right up? I never for a moment thought it was sabotage. Too many guys liked the place; too many guys were earning a living there. It was a sad business all right."

Neil Esslinger worked at Baker for eighteen years. He worked in the lye tank, at filling machines, in the shipping department, and, finally, in the warehouse crew under Jeff Barrett. He was known as a good worker. Today he works at Detroit Diesel, a huge GM plant which makes pistons and piston rings. It is a hot, noisy place and he hates it. He says he is not bitter about the Baker closing. They did what they had to do, Esslinger says. But he is certain, just the same, that it was a management plot to blow up the plant. He believes it was a plot that failed.

"It failed because the plant was so chopped up. Eighteen buildings. That's the reason the fire didn't do the damage they counted on its doing. But,"—Esslinger's eyes light up—"if they ever have a fire in their big, beautiful, new, one-level plant down in Ohio—boy, oh boy, won't that be something."

Henry Burns heard just the other day that a kettle over-flowed down at the new plant in York and spilled a few thousand gallons of thinner on the floor. "If I'd been down there," Burns says grimly, "I'd of dropped a lighted match into it."

But neither he nor Esslinger nor anyone else believe that a worker set the fire in the Baker plant back in August of 1964. "Christ," says Rockwell with passion and exasperation, "we loved that place too much to ever hurt it like that."

From a Report By Frank R. Robertson on the Probable Cause of the Explosion of August 1, 1964

As you are aware, extensive investigations have been made by the Detroit Fire Department, the Detroit Arson Squad, the Factory Insurance Association, and the Travelers Insurance Company as well as by Paul Tilyard, the plant Safety Engineer, and numerous other Baker management people. These investigations have pointed to three possible causes of the explosion: sabotage, an overheated ball mill that ultimately exploded, an overlong exposure of flammable materials. There was no proof of the first. All ball mills were found to be intact after the explosion, and no large discrepancies were discovered when inventory was taken of piped flammable liquid storage as checked against usage.

Relevant evidence was discovered beneath No. 19 ball mill. Before reading further into this report the accompanying photographs together with their captions should be studied.

(HERE WAS ATTACHED A SERIES OF PHOTOGRAPHS
SHOWING EXTENSIVE DAMAGE BELOW NO. 19
BALL MILL, INDICATING EXTENSIVE BURNING)

Without any other significant clues, the nature of the evidence below No. 19 ball mill indicates that this was the origin of the explosion. The spread of the fire would be accounted for by over 400 gallons of solvents exposed nearby in the building atmosphere.

Exactly what caused the spark that ignited the explosion may never be known. The following may be considered possibilities:

1. It is customary to leave some lights on in all buildings. A loose globe and bulb accompanied by the normal vibration of the building could have caused intermittent arcing and thus may have been a source of ignition. Under normal conditions, no solvent vapors would be expected to attain ceiling levels. Conditions beneath and around No. 19 ball mill indicate that conditions were far from normal.

2. There is the possibility of an ignition spark causing the explosion in Building 5 if one of the mill's ground systems and/or associated electrical circuits were faulty, providing at best intermittent electrical conduction. This could occur if one part of the system, because of grease, oil, resin, rust, were insulated from the rest of the system. The spark could have been produced if any part of the system was loosened due to building vibration and was grounding spasmodically. Because of faulty grounding an electric charge could build up to the point where it would leap across the gap of insulation, thus sparking.

3. There is also the possibility that as No. 19 ball mill was rotating it was throwing lacquer primer onto the back wall, the floor, and through the air—all of which raises the possibility that static electricity was generated. This hypothesis was shared by the inspectors from the Factory Insurance Association.

It is clear that many factors are involved that may have provided source of ignition. Such was the extent of destruction it was impossible to track down these clues.

What apparently can be positively affirmed is that the explosion began on the main floor of Building 5, center north area, and subsequently erupted into the tunnels.

The original alarm as recorded by ADT* was from Building 1. This was because the explosion compressed all the aero devices in Building 1. Building 5's aero signal was never sent in because it was instantly destroyed.

*

From the Recollections of Frank R. Robertson

August, 1964

Saturday. The oddest thing was the two phones. One dead and the other alive. It was about three o'clock when they finally let me in to go to my office. I stepped over the hoses and went into the main office building. It was a mess. All the windows were broken. Bits of plaster everywhere. Part of the walls and ceiling had fallen into my office. There were scraps of wood and plaster all over my desk and there were the two phones—the black local one and the gray one with its direct line to Pittsburgh. I picked up the black phone. It was dead. I picked up the line to Pittsburgh and it was alive. It was incredible. I pushed some scrap off my chair and sat down. There had to be a reason for that phone to be alive; I had to call Pittsburgh. I pulled out a notebook with all the office and home phone numbers for the general management staff in it. I knew none of them would be at the office now so I called their homes. I called Ike Kraeger first, I don't know why. There was no answer. I called Tom Frohman. His wife answered. He was out playing golf. The same for Wysse Allen. I called Alec Rutledge, the number one engineer in charge of plant facilities for the paint and brush division. He was out too. I hung up the phone and just sat there.

*The initials of the protection agency Baker employed.

Outside I could hear sirens still, and see firemen running across the yard with hoses. There were still fires in the tunnels, and Building 5, or, more accurately, what was left of it, was still smoking. It was hard to believe. Baker—the most safety-conscious paint plant in Detroit. How had it happened?

The phone rang. It was Alec Rutledge calling back. I told him what happened. He didn't say a thing. I told him to call Ike, Frohman, Allen, and to call me back later at home. Then I hung up and just sat there. What a birthday present this had been.

Sunday. A rainy day. Hard steady rain. Ike, Frohman, Alec Rutledge, and I walked through the plant. It was still smoking. One small fire truck was standing by. Supervisors were patrolling the grounds against possible looters. We made a tight-lipped foursome as we toured the devastated areas. Tom kept shaking his head and saying in that Texas drawl of his: "Frank, this is awful—awful—" Four buildings were completely gone including the boiler house without which the plant could not operate. The tunnels were destroyed. Ike kept mumbling: "No one got hurt; it's a miracle."

When we were done walking Tom said: "Let's go and talk somewhere."

There was no place to sit down in the plant, so we drove along Grand River Avenue looking for a restaurant. Most of them were closed. We finally found one called "The Snow Flake" open. We took a table in back, ordered lunch, and no one said anything for a while. Then Tom who was the senior man said: "Well, Frank, what do you think?"

I told him I wasn't capable of thinking. Truth was, I was thinking that this bunch had come down to make a decision and there wasn't one among them, even if he had the power, was capable of making it. Wysse Allen was the man, and he wasn't here. I wondered how much power he'd delegated. And I thought about the options open. There weren't many. They could declare the plant closed right now and ship what was left of the machinery down to York and Cleveland. But I'd been down to York just the week before and they were at least six months away from being ready to manufacture anything. That left two alternatives: move stuff out to all the other plants—Cleveland, Newark, Springdale, Torrance—spread it around in an attempt to hold onto the refinish business—or simply get out of the refinish business altogether. Cleveland could take the rest of the original finish business. They were taking almost 50 per cent right now.

There was a third possibility, to me more than a possibility. It was the solution, but I wasn't going to suggest it.

Frohman drawled, "Frank, what do you think we ought to do about it?"

Did he want me to play a game? All right. I asked, "What's the status of the other plants? Newark, Springdale?"

"No, sir," Ike said abruptly, "we can't do that. They're at capacity already."

That took care of option number one and left either going out of the refinish business altogether or rebuilding Baker. Did they want me to make that decision for them? Was there really a choice? I felt like laughing in their faces.

"Look," I said, "a decision's got to be made and got to be made now. There are people involved who are at home right now and don't know where to go tomorrow morning."

Frohman nodded. "Wysse Allen wants to know, Frank, if you think we can get this plant going in time to save the business. Because, as Wysse says, once we lose this refinish business, we will have a poor time retrieving it."

And with that new multi-million dollar plant going up in York they were damn well committed to an automotive refinish business. You don't often think of General Office being trapped by circumstances, but there they were too. They had no choice.

Alec Rutledge broke in with his brusque Scot's voice: "Frank will never open this plant again before the holidays, Tom. You will have lost the business before then."

Frohman looked at Ike. Ike said: "We don't know all the damage," Ike said, "but I'd say it won't be going before the first of the year, and only if Frank is lucky at that."

Frohman looked at me. "Frank?"

"Nope," I said. "You won't get me to put a date down."

"Now, Frank, not a date, but a round guess."

"Nope." Putting dates down was a game big businessmen played. I could talk about work conditions, and I did.

I told them I couldn't give them a date but that I thought we could have a fighting chance to save the business if certain conditions were met. If they gave me the green light, no studies, no red tape, no groups of maintenance engineers from Pittsburgh recommending first this and then that. They had to give me the go ahead to rebuild what I thought was necessary. And there was another thing. We had to be rid of the original finish business. Cleveland just had to take on all of it. They were doing nearly 50 percent right now. They would have to take on the rest.

Tom Frohman nodded and I knew then he'd thought this far at least.

I told him we had more of an inventory than he thought. Not much of it was destroyed, don't ask me why not. And the warehouse over on Fitzwarren was full to the brim. We had that going for us. And if I got the green light and no red tape in the rebuilding—and yes, there was one more thing.

"What?" he asked.

"Who's going to be in charge?" I asked.

Tom hesitated. "Well, you'll have Alec down here helping and I'll send Woody Martin and—"

"That's not my question," I repeated. "Who's going to run it; am I going to have the green light?"

Tom smiled. "Frank, events have surely turned you into a tiger." He shook his head. "I'll have to call you back from Pittsburgh on that."

So they hadn't come expecting to put me in charge. I didn't say anything more and neither did he. We ate then and I took them back out to the airport. That night about 9 P.M. I got a call from Pittsburgh from Frohman. I had the green light and the responsibility.

Doris had gone to bed. She was feeling poorly. I told her what had happened and that I wanted to take a little drive to do some thinking and that I'd be back in an hour.

I drove down to the plant. There were lots of people there. Portable generators had been set up and there were flood lights playing all over the yard. A second shift of supervisors was patrolling the area, and a special maintenance shift had come in to start cleaning up the debris. I greeted several people and walked around the yard. The rain had stopped, a ground mist was rising from different spots around the yard. And with the lights shining through the mist, bouncing off the rubble and the shadowy figures of workers and patrolling supervisors, it looked like a scene from London during the blitz. And I kept thinking: Are we sane to put heart and muscle into rebuilding this in order to close it up a year later?

There was no answer in my soul. Sanity never was a part of big business. I stood there in the ruins of Building 5 assailed by all kinds of doubts when I was suddenly aware there was another person standing near me. He was standing on a chunk of concrete, a small thin figure. I moved to one side to get a view of his face. It was Jerry Cowan, one of our maintenance crew. "Jerry," I said, "what're you doing up there?"

He didn't move. He didn't answer. He was looking up at the sky. I spoke again. "Jerry, this is Frank Robertson. I want to know what you're doing up there."

Jerry turned around and he said something I'll never forget. "Hello, Robbie," he said, though he'd never called me anything but Mr. Robertson before.

"Jerry, what're you doing up there?"

"I'm waiting for them to come again."

"Jerry, what in hell are you talking about?"

"Anzio," he said. "I thought it was all over."

He didn't say another thing but kept looking at the sky waiting for German planes or shells or whatever it was he'd lived through twenty or so years ago. I went off and got one of the supervisors and the two of us took him home.

The next day Jerry came back to work to help rebuild the plant. And he never said another word about it.

For two days after that, only maintenance people, supervisors, and a construction outfit came to work. Then on Wednesday we had some two hundred and fifty men working on the plant, rebuilding it. It was one of the most amazing, most heart-warming, saddest jobs I've ever seen done. We had to rip down the hull of the maintenance building; we did it ourselves, brick by brick, and I remember Matt Gargan saying, "We built it by hand thirty years ago, Frank, and we'll take the old lady down ourselves."

We had to do it by hand because the explosion hadn't made a clean job of it and the pile driver couldn't do it.

And then we rebuilt that old plant—all except one of the damaged buildings and we built a whole new boiler house. Everyone worked: truck drivers, mixers, cleaners, kettle operators, clerks, everyone had a hammer, a saw, nails, cement— there were no union rules, everyone pitched in to put the old lady in operation again. The Pittsburgh engineers just stood back and watched; they'd never seen anything like it. There were no coffee breaks, no pinochle breaks, men worked to rebuild a plant they loved. Windows, flooring, ceilings— people did things they didn't know they could do. Seven days after the explosion, seven days, we were shipping materials again. And by Labor Day—a little over a month later— we had finished rebuilding.

No company, no man had a right to expect the cooperation, the loyalty that those men gave in rebuilding the Baker plant. I felt guilty. Very guilty. I'll always remember that I knew what was happening and I couldn't do anything to stop it. When I told them the company wanted to rebuild most of the damaged areas, they believed the company had changed its mind about closing. They believed, every man jack of them, that it was their own future they were building. And, one way or another, I let them believe that.

Of Course We Thought They'd Changed Their Minds

"We'd been out of our minds to believe anything else," says Ned Rockwell. "Why should the company rebuild if they were going to move? I'm telling you, when we heard the decision that Monday that they were going to rebuild, it lifted spirits. It lifted my spirits. It lifted Perry DeMoss's spirits. It lifted Cal Koonz's spirits—if he had any to start with.

"Sure we pitched in. It was just like when you're in a family and you got an emergency, you all pull together, do what's needed to be done. Well, that's what we did. Everyone did, whether it was their job or not. Morale was high. I don't think anyone could have done anything better to bring plant morale up than to blow up the place and ask the men to rebuild it. Sure, looking back on it, it was idiotic and we were all a pack of dumb-dumbs. But not then. It didn't seem like it then.

"This don't mean I checked my brains. No, sir. We didn't come to work Monday and Tuesday. They told us only the maintenance department would be working. Well we had a grievance right there —we lost two days of work. And that bastard Lee Jones tried to recall the men back out of seniority. I wrote a grievance on that right away. We'd go back to work in order of seniority or Baker wouldn't rebuild. Well, they didn't argue much about that. We went back to work and we worked like hell and we put that plant back on its feet. Not Lee Jones or anyone. Us and Robertson and Tom Morgan and the old-timers. You can't buy that kind of stuff and they didn't buy it from us; we gave it to them, because, like jackasses, we thought this meant they were changing their minds. Christ, of course we thought they'd changed their minds, we'd been out of our minds to think anything else. We were tearing down buildings to rebuild them! Would anyone in their right mind do that so they could close up a plant a year later?"

It Was the Explosion That Killed the Plant

Name: Lloyd Shearer
Age: 62
Married: Shirley Davis—two children, both married
Employment: Baker Color Company, 1934–65; production manager, 1963–65
Residence: 14730 Ward, Detroit
Health: poor—hernia operation, stomach operation, ulcer; wife's health also very poor.

When Dr. Sidney Cobb of the University of Michigan's Institute for Social Research began his medical investigations of long-term Baker employees in June, 1965, his study group was limited to hourly employees—the "enlisted men."

"These are the men most affected by automation," Cobb explains, "the men most quickly displaced."

Cobb believed a study of salaried people would, therefore, have been less apt to show dramatic physical deterioration in health as a result of loss of jobs. "Having in general a better educational background, management people," Cobb said, "would be more mobile and thus better able to bounce back and find other work."

In the case of Baker, at least, this hypothesis would prove to be only partially true. Of seven Detroit-based salesmen (salaried personnel) in the Baker company, two had fatal heart attacks and one committed suicide during the closing. The plant manager, Frank R. Robertson, not in the study, is suffering from mucous colitis. Perhaps the sickest of the salaried people is the plant's last production manager, Mr. Lloyd Shearer.

In Arkansas, Robertson talked about Shearer—one of the real

old-timers—as a good friend of his, and a man who was trusted by all. Otto Mueller also talked about Shearer as a good friend and someone he was worried about.

Mueller says: "Sometimes I think I'm bad off, missing my pension by a year, and having to drive a school bus, but Lloyd Shearer, now, he's in a bad state. I dropped down one afternoon to see him and he's sitting there watching TV and he don't want to talk about anything. Sits there all day in his pajamas watching TV. His wife is sick too. Been sick a long time. I said to him, 'Lloyd, you ought to get out and do things,' and he says, 'What for?' He was making over tweny thousand a year at the end, and he got a pension to boot, but it's not doing him much good now, is it?" Mueller cannot supress a little hint of self-satisfaction; he smiles.

Another man who talked about Lloyd Shearer, the plant's last production manager, was Willis Ingram—the former tuberculosis patient whose mile run down West Morton to Livernois after the plant exploded has since become legendary.

"There weren't many good supervisors," Ingram says, "but Lloyd Shearer, now, he was all right. He was from the South but he give the Negro a fair shake. I'll tell you something: This guy was the only honest white man I ever knew."

And Perry DeMoss says, "Shearer was decent. He wouldn't doublecross you to Robertson. He was pretty sick during the closing. He had some kind of operation. You ought to go talk to him."

It turns out not to be so easy to talk to Mr. Lloyd Shearer. On the phone he doesn't see the sense of talking about Baker. "Talking won't open her up again," he says wistfully to me. But after some coaxing I get him to agree to a meeting. "I'm home every morning till noon," he says. "Then I got things to do."

Shearer lives on Ward Street, not far from the Baker plant. Indeed, Ward runs into West Morton Avenue about a dozen blocks west of the plant. West of Wyoming Avenue, West Morton is still largely white, though at the corner of Ward and West Morton there is a group of Negro women with shopping bags standing under umbrellas waiting for their bus. The morning I went out to see him the rain was coming down very hard.

Ward is a pleasant, tree-lined street of two-story houses, and the September rain comes down hard on privet hedges, flower beds, and a half-dozen little red and black FOR SALE signs planted in the middle of small neatly kept front lawns. Ward Street is a changing neighborhood.

The Shearer home is brick and frame and, like the others, two-storied. There is no overhang over the front steps and the rain comes down hard. The bell, pushed, arouses no spark of life inside the house. Pushed again, it evokes a slight jiggling of a venetian blind to the left and a woman's face peering out, the suggestion of a bathrobe or housecoat. The bell, pushed again, evokes definite action this time. A series of locks begin to come undone on the front door, the final lock being a brass chain that allows the door to open to a width of about five inches partially revealing a medium-sized, pale, lean man with sunken eyes and hollow cheeks and hands that flutter nervously at his bathrobe strings.

"I'm sorry, "Lloyd Shearer says. "I've changed my mind. I don't want to talk about Baker. My wife's sick. I been sick too. I'm sorry you had to make the trip here in this rain, but I don't want to talk about it. It makes my wife nervous to have visitors. We haven't had a visitor here in the past two years."

"Otto Mueller told me he's visited you, Mr. Shearer," I say.

"Mueller? Yes. But there's nothing to talk about. No point in it. Baker's all over. They treated me well. I got no complaints. Everything was fair and square and I don't want to talk about it. You can't come in. We don't have visitors. I'm sorry you got to stand out there in the rain." I have an umbrella in my car twenty feet away, but I know that if I leave to get it, he will not open his door, even this much, again.

"I heard a good deal about you from Mr. Robertson. From Willis Ingram, too. Mr. Ingram said that Lloyd Shearer was the only honest white man he ever knew."

Shearer's eyes light up momentarily. "Well, sir, I was brought up that way. I come from West Virginia. I was raised a certain way. I treated people as human beings and they treated me honestly back. I'm not treating you right, I know that. I'm sorry you came out here in this rain. I'm sorry it's raining on you right now but I've got nothing to say about the closing. I was sick during most of it. I had a hernia operation, ulcers too. I had stomach trouble from 1963 on. Three operations. I had another operation last year. I wasn't much good to anyone during the closing. It was a hard time for everyone. I worked at Baker for thirty-two years. They gave me this watch."

He extends his wrist through the open space. The rain falls on his gold watch.

"They gave everyone with over thirty years service a watch or a clock. I took the watch. We've got plenty of clocks in the house. It works good. I've got no kicks coming about anything. They treated me well through the years. It was a good place to work."

"What makes a place a good place to work, Mr. Shearer?"

"People. The right kind of people. That's the clue to a successful business operation. Oh, I don't mean to say Baker was full of angels or that everyone cooperated one hundred percent. We had our share of the other kind too. The union boys—they got away with murder, especially at the end. People like Ned Rockwell. You met him?"

"Yes. He's not doing too well right now."

"I don't care what happens to him. He was untrustworthy. Oh, you couldn't help liking the guy, he was a good family man, loved his kids, but he had a foul mouth and he was mean and untrustworthy. He didn't care about the plant but what he could squeeze out of it. Still, people like Rockwell were the exception. Most of them were pretty good guys. You treated them honestly and they'd treat you honestly back. That was the philosophy of Frank Robertson and it was a good one. I followed Frank right up the ladder: laborer, foreman, supervisor, superintendent. When he moved up from production manager to plant manager, I became production manager. That was in 1963. That was when I took sick too. I could barely get around those last two years. Look, you're getting good and wet out there. I got nothing to say about the plant."

"You got sick about the time they decided to close the plant?"

"No, sir," he says with a polite but firm smile, "I got sick back in 1963. They didn't decide to close the plant till after the explosion in August of 1964."

Suddenly I stop feeling the rain. "Didn't they decide to close Baker back in November of 1963?"

"No, sir," he says. "I don't know where you got your dates. We were making lots of money for them back in 1963. There was no point in closing us up. It was only when the plant exploded that they decided to close us up. It was the explosion that killed the plant. Nothing else."

"But, Mr. Shearer, there was a letter of November 13th, 1963, to every employee telling them the closing of Baker and the construction of a new plant in another place was under consideration."

"I never got such a letter. I never heard of such a letter. I was second-in-command of the plant then, I'd have known about it, wouldn't I have?"

"Mr. Shearer, there were meetings on the morning of November 13th. Mr. Robertson met with the supervisors, the clerical staff, the union committee."

The polite but firm smile seals the man off again. "No, sir. I don't recall it. I may have been ill that morning."

"There was another letter dated January 10th confirming the decision, saying the union had made no counteroffer and the company was going ahead with its plans."

"No, sir."

"And there were negotiations that went on through the beginning of 1964 between the union and the company, negotiations on severance pay and pension rights. There are verbatim records of these meetings."

"I don't know anything about it. Of course I was sick then so it may be what you're saying is so, but I don't think so. They were making money before the explosion. There was no reason to close the plant before then."

"Mr. Shearer, the company opened the new plant in York in December of 1965. The explosion occurred in August, 1964. They couldn't have bought land, drawn up plans, and constructed a six-million-dollar building in 16 months."

For a second his eyes waver, his hands flutter at his bathrobe sash. Then the firm little smile reasserts itself, intact. "Maybe what you say is so. But, sir, I worked at Baker thirty-two years. I worked my way up from bottom to next to top, and almost all of those years we made money. And we were making money when Frank and I were running the plant. Now you tell me, sir, what reason would anyone have to close a plant that's making money? Answer me that."

He waits. The rain is all over me—soaking through my coat; Shearer waits and when no answer is forthcoming, his smile widens.

"Exactly. There is no reason. It was the explosion that did it. There wasn't a building left intact from the explosion. That was when they made the decision. They had to. There was nothing left. Well, I don't miss it. I had enough. Thirty-two years, it was enough. They gave me this watch. I showed it to you already, didn't I? Other men chose the clock, but we have enough clocks. Listen, I want to apologize for treating you this way, keeping you out in the rain like that. You're all wet now, I see that. I'm sorry I couldn't ask you in though. My wife's sick. It makes her nervous to have visitors. Nobody's been here in two years except our kids. So you see I couldn't let you in. And I'm truly sorry you got so wet for so little."

"That's all right," I say. My socks, my underwear are soaked. I am so soaked I cannot think anymore.

Shearer extends his hand through the space permitted by the brass chain. To the left the venetian blinds jiggle shut. Then the locks on the front door slide shut.

Lloyd Shearer lives not far from the old Baker plant, but he also lives not far from the West Side Local. I found Perry DeMoss in his office drinking a paper cup of coffee; a puzzled grin comes across his lips when he sees me. "Hey, man, you look wet."

"I am wet."

"Let me get you some towels and a cup of coffee. I remember you take it black."

"Right."

DeMoss returns with coffee and paper towels.

"Where you been?"

"Talking in the rain with your friend Lloyd Shearer. He wouldn't let me in his house."

DeMoss is astounded. "No."

"He said he hadn't had a visitor in two years and I guess he didn't intend to start with me. He's sick."

"Lloyd was sick during the closing. I don't know what it was. A stomach operation of some kind. He could hardly get around. I'm sorry to hear this. He was a good guy. You could always get a fair shake from Shearer."

"He also thinks they decided to close up the plant after the explosion."

Perry looks surprised. "He knows that isn't so. He and I used to talk about the closing back in '63 and '64. They couldn't close a plant and build another one in a year's time anyway."

"That's what I told him."

"What did he say?"

"He said Baker was making money for the company; there wasn't any reason to close it."

Perry shakes his head, looks at the coffee in his paper cup. "He was a good guy too. One of the people you could trust at Baker. I wish there were more guys like him around now."

"You're pretty busy now, aren't you?"

The big Ford strike of 1967 had just been settled; the union was now working on GM and Chrysler.

Perry grins distastefully. "I'm busy all right, ducking flack. I didn't have anything to do with the Ford negotiations or any Big Three auto companies; it's my little guys giving me a hard time. One second I'm a hero to them, two days later they read what Ford settled for and I'm a bum. Christ, last week it happened right during the time span of one meeting. At the beginning of the meeting the chairman of the union committee gets up and says: 'Boys, Perry has just got us a raise of six cents an hour,' and they start cheering me and I'm a hero. The company had been offering three. The chairman was willing to settle for five. I held out for six and got it. Well, they cheer the hell out of me and I get up and make a speech. And the meeting goes on. About a half hour later someone comes in and says he heard Ford has just settled for ten cents an hour. Well, the place goes silent as a grave and then they start shouting at me, booing me, and the chairman says I've let them down. I'm a bum. Can you imagine that? A half hour ago I'm a hero, and now I'm a bum.

"I try to talk to them, explain the difference in the situations. I tell them with their little company the money just isn't there. I've seen the books. This isn't General Motors. But they won't listen to me. They don't give a damn. They want theirs. The guy across the street is a welder at GM and he's getting this and getting that. And they work as hard as he does if not harder and they want theirs. There's no satisfying them, and it's getting worse."

Perry is silent. Small, dark, usually cautious, something has triggered his emotions. Perhaps the picture of Lloyd Shearer locking his door, refusing to look at the past as it was. And his own remembrance of Shearer going out of his way to help the Negroes in the plant, sticking up for them when it wasn't popular to do so.

"And I'll tell you something else: I'm not satisfied with *my* salary, either. I'm not getting what I should be getting. I'm not getting any raises here, and you know why? That guy up there." He jerks his head toward the Reuther portrait on his wall "You know what he gets?"

"What?"

"Twenty-six thousand per year. Man, that job has just got to be worth fifty thou. He's up against guys drawing two hundred and fifty thou and he's beating them over the head. And he's only taking twenty-six, and the rest of us are getting paid accordingly. He's up on cloud nine. He's an idealist. He says he wouldn't be president of GM for anything and he believes it, and I believe it. But what about me? I got four kids and I know all about the cost of living too."

He looks up again at the picture with a quizzical expression. expression. "Someday he'll retire and things'll change. We'll make a little more dough." He shrugs. "So what've you been finding out in this book writing of yours? They tell you in Pittsburgh they moved because of the union?"

"Not exactly. It was pretty much as they said during the negotiations with you. The move was part of an overall corporate reorganization. They don't like unions, of course. They said frankly, if they had a choice they'd rather not have a union. Unions limit their freedom to make changes."

"You're damn right we do."

"If they had a union in York they'd cooperate completely with it, but they're going to fight like hell to avoid having a union in the first place. They aim to give their people a better deal than the union could give them. They think they've won. They had a Teamsters election a few months ago and the Teamsters lost their bid to organize the plant."

"Wait a second, man," Perry DeMoss says softly, leaning forward. "Are you trying to tell me that the new plant down in York is not a union plant?"

"The resin plant in Newtonville is unionized, but not the main plant in York."

Perry sits very still. "You know that for sure?"

"Yes. When I talked with Cal Koonz a while back he told me the York plant had been organized by the UAW, but it isn't so."

"He told you that 'cause I told him and someone else told me.

But you say it ain't so."

"That's right."

"Well, before you're out of this office I'm going to be on the phone to Cal and we're both going to be talking to Ohio. I can't afford to let a company get away from the union no matter where they go. If I let that happen I'll lose my job."

And he's on the phone even before I'm out the door and heading back into the rain.

It Was Good Business
To Be Decent

Baker In the Fall and Winter of 1964

Less than thirty days after the explosion of August, 1964, the Baker plant was back in full operation, minus the production of original finish, which had been transferred to Cleveland. The plant was now producing only refinish—packaged goods—in half-pints, pints, quarts, gallons. "We were doing a refinish business of a million dollars a month," Robertson says, and smiles ironically: "not bad for a plant classified as obsolete *before* an explosion."

From this point on, however, no new people would be hired. Robertson estimates that between the time of the first announcement of the closing, back in November, 1963, and the explosion in August, 1964, more than sixty new people had been hired to replace those (mostly transients) who had quit. After the explosion, those who quit were not replaced. In addition some jobs concerned only with the production of original finish were terminated. Altogether, Robertson estimates that only 6 percent of the hourly workers quit after the explosion and of those who quit less than 1 percent had high seniority. Robertson says he urged men to leave at this time, urged them to use their vacation time to try out new jobs, but the rebuilding of the boiler house had convinced many that the company had changed its mind about closing the plant. Still others believed it would close but they were going to "stick it out to the very end, going out like Frank Robertson said, with our heads up."

One group of workers Frank Robertson did not seek to relocate was the maintenance crews. They would be needed to keep the plant going to the very end and then to close her down properly. Robertson worked hard on keeping the morale of the maintenance boys high.

During this period Robertson wore two hats: that of factory manager concerned with production, and that of industrial relations manager concerned with morale, for he neither liked nor trusted his industrial relations manager, Lee Jones, popularly known among the men as "The Commander." Jones, tactless, brusque, egocentric, had antagonized almost every employee in the plant—hourly and salaried alike. Robertson had long felt that a stupid move on Jones's part could wreck the strange but very real harmony that existed in the dying plant. Towards the end of December, Jones made his stupid move.

It concerned a man named Hicks, Robertson recalls, a man who had reached the point where they were terminating him. Hicks had signed a severance pay application on which his length of time at Baker was listed. There was an error, an error the company made. Hicks had been out ill for four months and they should have counted him as him being on the payroll during this time. It affected Hicks's severance pay somehow, though not much; what it did make a difference on was the sickness and accident pay he'd receive and on any unemployment compensation he was entitled to receive after the plant closed. The error wasn't discovered until after the statement from the sickness and accident people arrived. Then it was realized that Hicks's record had been dated wrongly on the severance pay form.

"The point was," says Robertson, "that the man had signed his severance pay form, accepting the amount as binding. And Lee Jones figured he could stick by the original dates because the man had signed it, and thereby he could save the company a few hundred dollars in sickness and accident pay.

"It was Paul Tilyard, our safety engineer who had originally pointed out the error to Lee and Lee refused to change it. Paul came into my office one day—and mind you, Paul's a quiet one, not a squawker; he doesn't see trouble where there is none, but he knows a whole lot. He's an old-timer and what you'd call a kind of father-confessor to the whole plant. He came to see me and said: 'Frank, we're going to get a grievance on the Hicks termination and I want you to know, Frank, in my opinion they're right, not us.' "

"Well," I said, "I don't want any grievances, not at this stage of things. We're doing well, everything's going smoothly. We've all got things to do besides mess with grievances. If we're wrong let's correct it. Why don't you talk to Lee Jones about it?"

Paul looks at me kind of funny but doesn't say a thing and I get busy on other things. A few days go by and Lee Jones pops into my office. "Frank," he says, "we got a grievance on this Hicks business." And he started telling me the whole story.

"Look, Lee," I say, "are we right or wrong?"

"In my opinion, Frank, we're right."

"Now wait a minute. What makes you think we're right? Go get the records and we'll look at them together."

"Well, maybe technically they got a point."

"Look, Lee, let's give this man what he's got coming to him. Let's quit fooling with this. We're talking about two hundred bucks at the most."

"OK, Frank," he says and leaves.

I thought the whole thing was settled. You tell a man to do something and you assume he's going to do it. A few days later I'm crossing the yard and Ned Rockwell falls in step with me. His face is twisted up in fury and I know then he's been looking for me.

"What's the matter, Ned?" I ask.

"Are you going to back up that son of a bitch?" he asks.

"Which son of a bitch are you speaking of, Art?"

"Lee Jones. Holding out on that money to Fred Hicks."

"Oh, that's all settled."

"The hell it's all settled."

"It certainly is, Ned."

He stops and looks at me. "I got news for you, *Mister* Robertson. This is one thing we'll take to arbitration."

"You will like hell," I say, "because you don't have any case."

"Well, we'll see whether or not we got a case," he says angrily and stomps off. I know he'll be on the phone to Perry DeMoss in a minute.

I thought about it all for a moment and then instead of going back to my office I went down to the industrial relations office. Lee was at his desk.

"Lee," I said to him, "did you or did you not do what I asked you to do on the Hicks case?"

"Frank," he says to me, "I swear to you they don't have a case. We'll beat them in any grievance. Hicks signed that form. I got his signature right here."

I could hardly believe my ears. I exploded. I called him every name I could think of and I told him to change that figure on Hicks' form right away and get on the phone to Rockwell and tell him it was changed. We're not going to cheat that guy out of a couple of hundred bucks no matter what form he signed. Sure we could fight it out in arbitration and maybe win. I know that. We could go to court and maybe win but what on God's earth would we be winning? Nothing. We'd have hurt a man unnecessarily. A human being was involved here. It would have been cruel, sticky, and if it was legal, it would also have been unfair. We're too big to be trying to feather our nest at one man's expense.

And you know what else going to arbitration would mean? It would mean breaking the harmony, breaking up the pattern these men had, men working to the very end, going out with their heads up, men who loved this plant in a way Lee Jones could never understand.

Here I was skating on thin ice trying to keep a plant going and terminate it at the same time, trying to meet moral obligations to a man and do business too, and this rotten son of a bitch was going to throw a monkey wrench into the works.

I called General Office and spoke to Howard Green and told him Jones had to go. I wasn't going to put this plant to bed with Jones as my industrial relations manager. I wanted Tom Morgan back.

Howard didn't like Tom. He said Tom was too soft on the men and maybe he was right. But we were done negotiating, done bargaining; we were trying to stay in business and terminate, trying to transfer without losing a customer—we had to coddle the men now. It was good business to be decent.

Green understood. He called me back a few days later and said they found a spot in industrial relations for Jones in the Springdale plant.

I called Lee up and told him Howard Green wanted to see him in Pittsburgh. Lee went down there; they offered him the job and told him they wanted him to move right away. He came back to Detroit, came storming into my office and says he's not going to take that job. He's going to sit tight. They sent him here; he hadn't asked to come to this plant, and he was going to stay right here till the end. There was no future in Springdale, he said.

I asked him what kind of future did he see here.

He looked at me angrily and said he was going to finish with the plant. Just as though he had ties to Baker, and I thought: you're not good enough to put this plant to bed.

"No, Lee," I said calmly, "you're not going to finish out here. I'm going to tell you what I want done. I want you to go your own damn way. I told you how to handle the Hicks business and you did it your own way. You've lied to me about other things, again and again. As far as I'm concerned, Lee, you're finished here. You take that job down in Springdale. Monday morning your pay check will be ready."

He says to me: "Frank, you've sold out to General Office" . . . as if the idea of his being fired wasn't my idea in the first place. That's how his mind worked.

"I haven't sold out to anyone, darn you. I've fought for you in the past but you've embarrassed me. I can't trust you. I want to keep this plant going; these men are entitled to the kind of honesty you're not capable of giving."

Monday he picked up his pay check. And on Wednesday he walked into my office and asked me to approve an expense account he'd incurred when he was down at General Office two years back.

They fired him down at Springdale a little while later. And do you know what the son of a bitch is doing now? He's running an employment agency in Detroit. How do you like that?

Into Lee Jones' little green cubbyhole of an industrial relations office moved Tom Morgan. It was an office he'd occupied back in the late forties and early fifties and had enjoyed. An easygoing athletic man, Morgan liked industrial relations work. He liked people. Under the title of director of industrial relations he had helped set up golf and softball leagues, a gun club, chess and checker tournaments, bowling leagues, spring and summer picnics, even a hardball team that played in an industrial league. He had been successful, he felt, at keeping the place a happy unit. When Green became plant manager he bumped Morgan because he felt Tom was a poor negotiator, which was probably true. Green said he gave in too easily on grievances, wanted to be liked by the men. Well, that was one man's opinion. With emergency demands from Chrysler to meet, production schedules to maintain, the important thing was not to have walk-outs or wildcat strikes and Baker never had any of those. "Our job," says Morgan, "was to keep Chrysler going. We didn't have to make a job for Willis Ingram when he came back from the TB hospital but we did. And that kept the place moving and let us meet Chrysler's emergency demands. You couldn't have it both ways. Sure there were abuses and, you might say, the union ran the plant, but we stayed in business and we kept Chrysler going, and we made money. We did the things we had to do."

Frank Robertson agrees. Morgan, he feels, was the right man at the right time just as Rockwell was the right man at the right time just as he himself was the right man at the right time.

Toward the end of the year, a second salesman died—Louis Arnot. Arnot, a short stocky energetic and likeable man had almost thirty years in at Baker. A convivial man, a good dresser, a good family man who was always for showing you pictures of his wife and kids, Arnot's territory included all the Chrysler plants in the United States. He had enough energy for the job. It was true, too, that he'd had a history of nervous care, emotional problems, but it was nothing compared to his boss Harold Peterson, and Robertson more than once thought it undoubtedly went hand in hand with being a good salesman.

The announcement of the closing had taken Arnot, like the other salesmen, by surprise. And made him unsure. He was primarily concerned with original finish sales, and original finish production had been transferred to Cleveland, part of it before the explosion and the rest of it afterward. Louis was now working directly under Kahane in Cleveland, driving there two or three times a week, with samples from the companies, complaints, and coming back with new samples, responses, analyses. "Perhaps he felt a little bit like a shuttlecock," Robertson says, "I don't know." The old days when Louie or Harold or any of the salesmen could walk back to the lab and say, "Look, Jack, this is how that last batch of Chrysler Imperial paint came out, and this is the color they want. Now mix up some in the mills and let me have a look"—those days were gone. Now it was phone and drive, phone and drive. Especially during the shake-down days at Cleveland when they made a lot of mistakes and Louie was forever picking up after them with the auto factories. He wasn't a complainer like Harold. He just went out and did. He drove himself, and stayed as pleasant and convivial as always. Then one morning at the office, about 10:30, Robertson recalls:

I got a call from Mrs. Arnot's brother who told me Louie had just passed away. He'd got up that morning, felt all right and started shaving. He finished shaving and then told his wife he felt a little funny and was going to lie down for a minute. He died then and there, lying down.

I told the people in the office the sad news, called in Lloyd Shearer and some of the old-timers, and then went across the hall to break it to Harold Peterson. Harold was on the phone with a salesman in Pennsylvania. He looked up. "I know, Frank," he snapped, holding his hand over the mouthpiece. "Her brother called me too. But I got a problem here with some refinish for a '61 Plymouth . . ."

I left him there giving orders to his salesman on the phone. I went back into my office and told Lloyd Shearer I was going over to the Arnots' to see if I could be of any help. I went. There wasn't much I could do.

As I drove home that night I thought about Arnot who was only fifty-five. I thought about Will Calloway too, and about Harold Peterson snapping commands into the phone, so very near the edge himself. I thought about Lloyd Shearer who had been terribly sick the past year and was still not a well man now. All these people had secure jobs or had retirement pensions due them. If this kind of thing was happening to them, what on God's green earth would be happening to the others?

I didn't know, and I still don't.

One thing that was to continually amaze Robertson was the startling unpredictability of how people, hourly and salary alike, would react to the facts of job termination. There were some like Albert Lapin and Joe Nadeau, quiet workers in the resin department, who showed up dead drunk their last day and Nadeau made all kinds of crazy speeches till they took him home. There were many Robertson considered troublemakers, people, well people like Ned Rockwell who spent years blasting the company, complaining about this and that, who worked with a chip on their shoulders if they worked at all and who, when he'd call them in either to tell them the final amount of their severance pay or pension fund allocation, to tell them, in other words, that their working days at Baker were over, would respond not with a blast or a typical tirade but would sit there quietly, calm, cool, collected, and ask relevant questions, understanding the whole problem. And, on the other hand, there were those whom he had considered good and loyal workers, company men so to speak, who reacted in a completely unexpected manner.

One such man was Wilbur Fowler whom Robertson had hired during World War II when help was scarce. Fowler was a little quiet uncomplaining Southerner. Meek and mild, he kept to himself and worked long, hard, and tirelessly. He worked so hard and consistently that the union began to get down on him. Ruining it for other men, they said. Things got so bad that they began to threaten him bodily. His car, his wife, his kids. Robertson spoke to the union rep about that and countered with some threats of his own. Then later on he made Fowler a supervisor, taking him out of the union pale. Fowler continued to work hard, never complaining. As he had been a model worker, so he continued to be a model supervisor.

"Well," says Robertson, "there came the time to tell Fowler his job was being terminated and to give him the final amounts of his severance pay and pension allocation. He sat there and listened to me and then to my great astonishment he went completely to pieces. In all the years he'd been there I'd never heard a bad word out of Fowler. Now some of the foulest language I'd ever heard in my life poured out of him. Every four letter word imaginable. He was vicious. He cursed me up and down, cursed all of us. Told us he'd get us, threats, curses, on and on. Well, we finally got him out of there, but it was horrible. I didn't understand what had happened, but in time I'd see that kind of thing happen again and again and often from people you least expected it from. In God's truth there was just no way of telling how a man was going to react when you called him in and told him his working days at Baker were over."

Christmas Party at the West Side Local

Every Christmas, West Side Local ———— of the UAW gave a party for all of Baker's hourly employees and their families. It was a custom that everyone approved of. Wysse Allen, the former vice-president of the paint and brush division and the man who made the decision to close Baker, felt it was a good instance of the union's controlling men for management, doing a task that used to be management's. The union staff approved of the party too. Perry DeMoss used it as a forum to get to the men's wives and urge them to get their husbands to attend regular meetings.

And the men liked it too. Neil Esslinger, who was employed in Baker's warehouse, says the party was one of the few good things the union did. "They kept it free of politics," Esslinger says.

The parties were held on the Saturday before Christmas at the local hall. There were ice cream and cookies and a Santa Claus for the children. Usually one of the fatter guys played Santa in a suit rented by the union. He'd give each kid a toy and a balloon, and afterwards there was a noisy showing of Popeye cartoons. Then the kids would leave with their mothers and the men and wives with older children or with children who could get home themselves would stay for the regular meeting and soft drinks and cookies. Usually the speeches at the Christmas party were not about business, but at the 1964 party, Esslinger recalls, it was slightly different; there was a lot of talk about this being the last Baker party.

Ned Rockwell also recalls that particular party, but he remembers that there were as many guys still thinking the company was bluffing about the closing as took it seriously. The arguments for bluffing which included the old one about why would they re-build the boiler house if they were planning to shut her down, also took new fuel from a whole batch of new refinish orders that the plant had just taken on.

Rockwell made a little speech at that last party. "I wanted them to face facts. I told them the time to look for new jobs was now, when they had a chance to be selective, not when it was too late and you had to take what you got. I told them we were still negotiating with the company on a few items in the pension allocation and health insurance but it was a certainty Baker would close up some time this coming year and if I were them I'd look around now.

"And then someone asked me why I wasn't looking around myself and I told him 'If I look around who is going to take care of you bums?' It got a big laugh."

Perry DeMoss, who also talked about the closing at the meeting, repeated what Rockwell had said and added that the company had promised to send a personnel expert up from Pittsburgh who would help guys get new jobs.

"Christ," someone called out, "that's all we need is another expert from Pittsburgh."

That line broke up the meeting and they all went for the soft drinks. All except Orvie Blackburn who had brought his own bottle.

The thing about the Christmas party Neil Esslinger liked best was that you got to see for yourselves the wives and older kids of the guys you worked with. For instance, he'd heard the rumors about hillbilly Floyd Rink's family and about his sexy fifteen-year-old step-daughter, and there she was, and a well-built girl, all right, sticking right close to her ma.

Esslinger was also curious to see what Orvie Blackburn's wife looked like. Everyone knew that one of the reasons Orvie hit the bottle so hard was because his wife ran around on him. Mrs. Blackburn was a heavy, dark-haired woman, kind of well setup, and she was drinking Orvie's booze too. She was half-Irish, half-Indian and you could tell just from one look at her that old Orvie, the boozehound, would have a hard time keeping up with her.

Esslinger liked Orvie Blackburn. He worked with Orvie at the warehouse and when Orvie was sober there wasn't anyone worked harder. He was easy to get along with, though sometimes drinking would put Orvie in an ornery mood. Then he'd either drink himself into a stupor in some corner of the warehouse or else he'd work like hell, and he'd get mad when he felt like working and you didn't.

"One of the troubles with Baker," Esslinger feels, "they made it too easy for a guy like Orvie to drink. One of the bosses at the warehouse—Bill Gilreath—he liked a nip or two. And he wouldn't mind Orvie's going off into the corner with his bottle. But Gilreath always kept his head and after Orvie had a drink and went back to work, Gilreath would take advantage of him. When Orvie was in a working mood, drunk or sober, he'd work like a horse. One time Gilreath put old Orvie inside a semi to unload. The job called for two men and if the helper isn't around you're supposed to wait for him but Orvie, just like Gilreath knew, wanted to work and he unloaded the whole truck himself. Then Gilreath tells him, 'See, Orvie, you could do it alone. You don't need a helper.' And he tries to change the description of the job. You see how they operate? They'd make it possible for Orvie to drink and then try to take advantage of it. Well the union didn't let them get away with that.

"The union would help you now and then, even though most of the time they abused things as much as management. Mind you, I'm not against the union. I can remember back in the Depression, I was a little kid then and my dad, he was a farmer till we come to the city and he got a job at Cadillac across town. I can remember one snowy night he come home from work about 10 P.M.—he'd started work at 7 A.M., and here he was coming home about 10 and he had walked all the way across town in the snow because there were no buses or street cars—and he comes into our house and sets down and before my mom can say anything he says, 'Put some soup in my thermos and make me some sandwiches, because I got to be back on the job at midnight.' And my mom says 'You can't do that, you got to sleep a little.' And my dad he says, 'Yes I got to do that if I want to keep my job.' "

"When the union came in, they did away with that kind of thing. But after a while it went the other way, and that's where it is now. My old man was a firm union man and so am I, but still some of the things the union helps you get away with—my, oh my. Like Orvie's drinking. It would have been a good thing for Orvie if he'd been fired, and the company would have fired him but they were scared of the union. Or maybe if someone just really scared him at Baker about his drinking, because after Baker closed, old Orvie found out like the rest of us—there weren't any more Bakers. Other places, the place I work, for instance—Detroit Diesel; we make cylinder linings and pistons—well, that place don't give a damn about people. We got 5,000 guys under one roof and that was quite a change for me from sixteen guys in the Baker warehouse to this. At the warehouse we could step outside in the sunshine when we felt like it; right now we're 5000 guys locked up in a hot noisy prison. And take a little thing like vacations—only it ain't so little. At Diesel we get two-week vacations according to the contract just like we got at Baker. Only at Baker they gave us the vacation pay just before the vacation so you could actually go on vacation. At Diesel, do you know when they give you your two-weeks' vacation pay? In January. Where're you going in January? And when July and August come around and you're ready to go, you don't have that money, you spent it already and they know it and that's why they give it to you so you'll stay on the job. At Baker they made you take a vacation; it cost them a little more in bookkeeping but made it nice for the working man. At a big company like Diesel, they don't give a damn. They don't give a damn about the working man and about the conditions he works under. At Baker we had a safety-conscious boss—Paul Tilyard; if he saw one infraction he'd get on the foreman. No pallets standing; all aisles cleared. At Diesel, I've seen guys get hit with pallets standing up. All the aisles are blocked with boxes. We cleaned it up once when the president of the company was coming through. We washed down the machines and so on then, but most of the time it looks like Santa Claus' workshop at Christmas time. Every fire aisle jammed. And a place like that stays in business, and a place like Baker which cares abut its people closes up.

"But we stay in touch, us Baker guys. That's how I heard about Orvie. One of his cousins who used to work at Baker works with me at Diesel. Orvie had a whole bunch of hard-drinking relatives working at Baker. They were like a bunch of gypsies. Anyway this cousin told me that when Orvie quit at Baker he took a job with a land-scape gardener. (He always liked gardening and trees and stuff.) He quit a few months before he would have been terminated because he wanted to get into the gardening business while the weather was good. He got in but he didn't stay in. I guess they caught him nipping on the job so they fired him, this cousin says, and then Orvie got a couple of jobs in some tool and die shops over on the west side. He got fired from each one because of the drinking. There wasn't a one that would cover up for him the way we had at the Baker warehouse. Why, I can remember one morning

Orvie showed up, it was a Saturday morning, and he shows up at 8 A.M., an hour later then he should be there, and drunk as a skunk. I mean he couldn't walk. He drove his car down into the truck well off Fitzwarren which you're never supposed to do because that's where the trucks pull in to load and unload. Well we're all standing there goggle-eyed as old Orvie drives his car right into the truck well, and he opens the door and steps out and falls right on his face. Someone calls out, 'Get that man back in his car; he's in no shape to walk.'

"Wasn't that funny? We all laughed at that. Well, someone got Orvie off in a corner where he could lay down and sleep it off. And someone else put his car away. He was still on a bender from Friday night and he come to the only place that'd take him in— Baker.

"I guess it got rough on Orvie afterward. His cousin told me that after he got canned from the last tool and die job he got another job as a landscape gardener because that was his first love and he lasted a while on that and then he got fired there too because of the drinking.

"Orvie had two kids, both married now, and good kids. When they were smaller he'd take them to church every Sunday. He could never get his wife to go to church. She'd laugh and tell him she'd do what she goddamn well pleased. And I guess she did. Old Orvie took the kids to church and then come home and hit the bottle. Sometimes with the wife but mostly because she'd be out boozing with some boyfriend.

"I guess it got worse at home after Baker closed. The kids were out of the house, both married, and this cousin tells me sometimes Orvie'd come home half-drunk and the wife'd have some guy there and Orvie'd just lay down on the couch and sleep it off. It was Labor Day 1967, the cousin told me; he was there with another cousin and Orvie's married daughter and the wife, and they were all sitting around the living room drinking and talking and Orvie gets up and he makes this crazy little speech saying: 'I love my wife. I love my family. I love my kids.'

"They all laugh, but that's what he says. Then he goes into the bedroom and closes the door. They go on talking. There's a shot. They run in. Orvie has blown his brains out in the bedroom with a shotgun.

"Old Orvie. They didn't do him no favors by letting him drink on the job. He did his share of the work though. He always would. I guess where he went after Baker they couldn't be expected to know that."

February 10, 1965

Employees of the Baker Color Company,
a Division of the Pennsylvania Corporation
———— Unit of West Side Local ———— UAW
Greetings:

All of us know that to be tossed out of a permanent job when one is in his middle years is a bad thing. We know this is true from a money standpoint, and we suspect it may be equally true from a health standpoint. Accordingly we have asked Dr. Sidney Cobb at the Institute for Social Research at the University of Michigan to make an extensive study of this matter.

Dr. Cobb has proposed to study in conjunction with us a group of men who seem likely to lose their jobs either due to automation or to the closing of a plant. He intends to follow closely this group of men from the time they lose their old established jobs through their period of adjustment, and conclude it after they are definitely established in their new jobs.

We are asking you to join with Dr. Cobb in his research study by participating as volunteer members. There are several good reasons why you should become a member of this study and cooperate with Dr. Cobb and his staff of nurses. First, this is a chance to do something positive for your union and for the cause of organized labor in general. Second, we believe that, at very little time cost to you, you will be making a major contribution to medical research. Third, from a personal outlook, you will have professional people keeping track of your health over the next few years.

Each of you will hear directly from Dr. Cobb about the details of his research study. It is my understanding that participation in the study will require no travel or other expense. Information will be obtained from you by nurses who will come to your home. Your contribution of time should amount to about one hour a month or twelve hours a year. This may vary depending on the situation, but your time spent should not exceed this by very much.

It is my sincere hope that you will see your way clear to helping Dr. Cobb for his work should prove of extreme importance to our union. Your shop chairman and union rep join me in this hope as is indicated by their signatures below. If you have any questions, I am sure your shop chairman will be glad to answer them.

Fraternally yours,
Cal Koonz, Director, Region 1-A UAW
Ned Rockwell, Shop Chairman
Perry DeMoss, Union Rep, West Side Local, UAW

The Head That Stands
Out Above the Crowd

Sidney Cobb, a tall, lean New Englander who in his own phraseology, had "enough medical practice during the Battle of the Bulge to last me a lifetime," returned from World War II determined to go into research, and specifically, research in psychosomatic medicine in which he had a long interest.

While working as Director of the Neshoba Associated Boards of Health in Ayer, Massachusetts, Cobb commuted to the Harvard University School of Public Health where he studied the epidemiology of rheumatoid arthritis. The more he studied arthritis, Cobb says, the more he was convinced of the relevance of sociological and psychological factors.

In July 1952, Cobb was invited to continue his research into the epidemiology of arthritis as a member of the staff of the School of Public Health of the University of Pittsburgh.

After a five-year study of arthritis using a sample of the Pittsburgh population, Cobb looked for a "closed population"—people who lived and worked in the same place, a stable sample that could be observed month after month.

He found his closed population in the nuclear age community of Oak Ridge, Tennessee. He spent three years studying that community and concluded that while most physicians in their consulting rooms found rheumatoid arthritis to be a crippling disease, in the field, arthritis was quite common and generally a mild disease that would under certain psychological and sociological circumstances turn into a crippling form. What were those psychological and sociological circumstances? One of Cobb's conclusions was that losing a job could exacerbate existing arthritis and might even produce new arthritis.

In 1957, a year before the Pennsylvania Corporation launched the corporation-wide study of strengths and weaknesses that would ultimately point its finger at the Baker plant in Detroit, Cobb found himself casting a larger net into the sea of psychosomatic illnesses. His studies at Oak Ridge and elsewhere were turning up interesting data not only on arthritis, but on ulcers, heart disease, mental ill-ness, tuberculosis, and even cancer. Cobb now began to look around for another closed population to study, preferably an industrial organization.

"A company produces a product," Cobb says. "In the process it affects the world around it. It may pollute rivers, air, change the landscape—it may change people's lives, affect their personalities and their health. I was interested in what industry does to the health of human beings—specifically in how psychological trauma such as the loss of a job affects all facets of a man's health."

In 1961 Cobb moved his operation to the Institute for Social Re-search at the University of Michigan where for some years there had been in progress studies on the effect of shift work on hourly workers, organizational stress and middle management, the relation-ship between occupational status, self-esteem, and productivity, the meaning of a "good job" as opposed to a "bad job," and what hap-pens to a man when he retires.

Even more telling than this last, Cobb felt, would be what hap-pens to a man's health when his job was taken away from him in the prime of his life. "If we understand that," Cobb says, "then a lot of things like 'good jobs' versus 'bad jobs,' retirement, occupational stress, might fall into place." To find the meaningful problem and attack it, "to hit," in the words of an old teacher of Cobb's at Har-vard, "the head that stands out above the crowd."

The head that stood out above the crowd, Cobb felt, would be a company shutting down its factory permanently, whether it was because of automation or relocation for marketing reasons. Cobb began looking around for a likely candidate. In December of 1963 he received word that the ——— corporation was considering clos-ing their adding-machine plant in Detroit. Cobb and a colleague from the Institute for Social Research visited the management of ——— who listened carefully to their proposal for studying the men before and after termination. "They told us they'd give us an answer in a week's time," Cobb says. "A week later we went back to Detroit, and were driven with several of the top executives to the Detroit Athletic Club in a Cadillac, wined and dined and told 'no.' It was obvious that this issue was a threat to management, and there was a distinct fear of the union."

It occurred to Cobb then that it might be more sensible to begin with a union. The UAW, he knew, had long been interested in the idea of a guaranteed annual wage. They might be interested in any study that showed the importance of stable employment. From talking with their rank and file, the union staff knew what happened to men during layoffs, what happened to them when a plant closed because of automation and relocation, but a scientific study might buttress their own insights.

Cobb got in touch with the officers of Region 1-A of the UAW. The UAW was immediately interested in the study and not only did they help Cobb find a plant about to close—the Baker Color Company—but they gave Cobb $2,500 in seed money to get his project started.

This was back in February of 1964, during the midst of union-company negotiations on severance pay and the pension plan. In September of that year Cobb received additional funds from the U.S. Public Health Service.

"Our first move back in 1964 was to reduce a set of ideas or hypotheses to operational forms. For instance, if we wanted to find out how much a man changes his self-concept (a) as he first learns about an impending job termination, (b) as it becomes a reality, and (c) as it appears no new job will be forthcoming, we had to design the right kind of apparatus to find out these things. It meant designing questionnaires, profile charts, card games, a whole battery of psychological tests, and then deciding on what kind of accompanying physiological testing could be reasonably done in a man's home. Blood samples, blood pressure, urine analysis, body weight, and physical health questionnaires."

Cobb and his team, which consisted of six nurses, two bio-chemists, and a psychologist, worked up a battery of physiological and psychological tests. They decided to limit their study to workers who were 35 years or older, had at least three years of seniority, were married, and were their family's principal bread-winners.

"We were trying to hit the head that stood out above the crowd," Cobb says.

Of the 120 people who fitted this category at Baker, about half were unwilling to participate in the study—some because they didn't see how it would help them, some because they didn't want any help. Ned Rockwell, who was instrumental in getting men to sign up for the study, told Cobb why one man—Darrell Gunn—wouldn't join the study.

"And it's too bad because he would have been perfect," Rockwell said much later. "Gunn just about cracked up when Baker closed. He was a guy who knew more than his education—a real intelligent guy. He told me he couldn't be bothered with this study. Said it was for dummies like me, and the men who needed help. I remember he got a charge out of arguing with the lawyer at Baker. Used 75 cent words with him that nobody else there understood. He's a card-carrying journeyman. That gave him a good chance to get a job. He worked at Chevy or Ford—I can't remember which—but he quit because he said he was afraid of the big machines. Then he went from job to job. Now he's working at Nonshatter Glass. Old Gunn, smart as he was, never believed Baker was going to close till he was laid off. Now he won't be happy no matter where he is. Boy, he would have been perfect for your study."

Cobb ended up with 58 hourly workers in all. Because he had to approach the plant through the union, there were no management employees in the study. Something Cobb now regrets. At the same time Cobb and his team began studying the 58 hourly employees of Baker, several control groups were set up in other companies not terminating.

"The initial visits by the nurses," Cobb says, "took place seven months before the Baker plant closed. They were "get acquainted" visits, and they were also aimed at getting historical data. We needed a profile of illness and illness behavior, of past illness patterns and past employment history. We know, for instance, that at model changeover times in Detroit the local hospitals begin to fill up. Are people really sicker when they are temporarily laid off jobs, or are they just complaining more? Do aches and pains bother people more when they're not working, or are they finding a sick role preferable to an unemployed role?

"We inquired therefore about past health: Arthritis, ulcers, aches, headaches, colds. We took blood pressure, body weight, blood samples. We left a two-week health diary with each man, asking him to keep notes on how he felt each day. Some of the men didn't keep it up too well, so that when the nurse returned to pick up the diary, she would have to ask him to elaborate on his notations. Most of the nurse's questions on this two week later visit, however, were aimed at profiling emotional patterns—anxieties, or happinesses, resentments, depressions, and so forth. We began to call this second visit in each round, the visit on which we picked up the health diaries, the self-identity visit as opposed to the first or health visit.

"The Baker employees in the study each received two visits before the plant closed. Then the nurses made another round of visits as soon as the plant closed. There was another round four months afterward, another eight months afterward, twelve months, and we are still finishing up our twenty-four-month and final visits and in the process of putting our findings together.

"We hope we'll be able to find out what happens to a man's health when his job is taken away from him and he's still in the prime of his life with people dependent on him. We're also curious to know why some men are able to cope with job loss and others not, and can this be predicted? What happens to the health of an obviously rigid type like Ned Rockwell or Henry Burns? What are their chances of adjusting to a new life? What happens to a man like Jerry McNerney, the prison guard, with his high fear of failure? What are his chances for adjustment? Paddleford, another man with a high fear of failure, lost his hair twice and yet he has, on paper at least, managed to cope. Why? What about the health of those hourly workers who didn't hang on to the end waiting for severance pay but got out and found new jobs? And all the marginal people? Marginal in intelligence and skill—men like Floyd Rink, Dave Masiak, Albert Lapin—what happens to them physically, emotionally, occupationally?"

By May 1965, seven months before the plant closed, Cobb's nurses were visiting Baker men in their homes after work. They found a good many who admitted to being apprehensive about the plant closing; some who cheerfully insisted the plant wouldn't close, that the company was only bluffing, and others who just seemed apathetic.

One who seemed apathetic was Willis Ingram, former tuberculosis patient and hero of the legendary mile run down West Morton Avenue when the plant was exploding.

"The company's got to do what they got to do," he told Nurse Ann McHugh. "I'll look around when the time comes to look around."

Two years later, by the spring of 1967, Ingram still had not found work and Nurse McHugh and Dr. Cobb were very worried about him. In addition, Ingram found his house on Samson Street had been condemned by the city to make room for the new Chrysler Freeway. Within one week Ingram had lost his job of 29 years standing and the house he'd lived in for more than half of those years.

This combination of circumstances and the fact that for two years Ingram was doing nothing, apparently fast becoming unemployable, led Cobb to believe there was a good chance of Ingram's tuberculosis reactivating itself.

That this did not happen; that, indeed, Willis Ingram would turn out to be one of the few genuine Baker success stories, coping successfully with job loss beyond anyone's wildest expectations, would amaze Cobb as much as anything in his study. The discovery that Ingram was a success however, and not a failure was due to a set of circumstances that, Cobb admits wryly, no one could have predicted.

A Little Bit Here,
a Little Bit There,
I Make Out

Name: Willis Ingram
Age: 56
Married: Ruby May Hargrove
Children: Linda 28, married; Arthur, 21 student at Wayne State University; Roy Morris, 20, soldier in Viet Nam
Religion: Baptist
Education: 6th grade, Georgia
Occupations: farmer
              1933–34, CCC
              1935, Midland Steel Company, laborer
              1936–65, Baker Color Company:
                  lye tank, warehouse, stock checker, janitor lab technician, canning machine operator
Residence: 14309 Garfield, Detroit, Michigan
Health: underwent surgery in 1950 at Herman Kiefer Hospital. Thoracoplasty, or removal of ribs for treatment of tuberculosis; 1960, tuberculosis reactivated itself, hospitalized Mayfield Sanatorium, 11 months; now returns to Herman Kiefer every 6 months for checkups; complains of shortness of breath, also bursitis in shoulder.

Willis Ingram was born in Valdosta, Georgia, 56 years ago. His father died the year he was born. Ingram's first job was picking berries when he was thirteen for 28 cents an hour. His last job at Baker was working a canning machine for $2.97 an hour. It was a two-man operation. One man would work the spigot that squirted paint into the cans—either pint, quart, or half-gallon cans, while the other man would put the lid on and tighten it. It was not an unpleasant job, according to Ingram. If you had an interesting partner, you could have some interesting conversations. When the line slowed up and no empty cans were being delivered, he and his partner would sit down and play a little bid whist. "The great thing about Baker," says Ingram, "you didn't have to look busy when there was no work. Other plants when there's no work and the boss comes by you got to pretend. At Baker you didn't have to pretend. It's a big difference."

Before he worked in canning, Ingram's job was in the lab where he was working when the plant blew up. Before the lab job he worked as a janitor for two years. "It was a special job," Ingram says with a twinkle in his eyes, "they called it the Willis Ingram job. The union made them give it to me." He laughs softly, remembering.

Ingram made a good recovery although he still goes to Herman Kiefer hospital every six months for X rays and a checkup. He improved so much that by 1963 he was back on regular duties, working in the lab as a technician. That was his job when the first letter from the company was posted, the letter advising Baker workers that the home office was considering closing down the plant.

"I remember that letter OK," Ingram says today. "Other guys may have thought the company was bluffing, but I didn't. I thought right away they would close it. They were making money, but, like one of the Pennsylvania people said once in a speech to us, they could be making more money somewhere else. I can understand that. Who doesn't like to make more money?" He grins. "Hell, I got no special feelings about Baker. I stuck to the end to pick up my severance pay, that's all. It was no question of loyalty. It was a question of money. Baker was a good place to work, and that's all. And even at that, it was the union made it that way. Not management. They didn't give a damn about us. That Robertson, he was the most two-faced man I've ever met, and I worked under him 29 years. He's just like—what's his name? you know, the governor—Romney. They both speak with forked tongue, especially about colored folks. Robertson, he'd say one thing to your face and another thing behind your back. And when the union would get after him and pull something good for us, Robertson would give in but afterward he'd try to grab off the union chairman by giving him a supervisory job. They did that with one guy after another. Matt Gargan, he was union chairman once and when he became a supervisor he was the worst enemy any of us had. He was two-faced too. I'll give Ned Rockwell credit for sticking to his guns and Perry DeMoss was too smart for them in the first place. It took a long time for them to realize how smart Perry was."

It also took a long time for them to know how smart Willis Ingram was. I heard about Ingram from Sidney Cobb when we first discussed the possibility of a book on the men of Baker. He told me then he had one man in his study who had a long history of tuberculosis and who was coping so poorly with impending job loss that he, Cobb, was predicting that his tuberculosis would reactivate itself.

Sometime later I talked with the nurse who was handling Ingram —Mrs. Ann McHugh who has a master's degree in public health. Mrs. McHugh told me that when she first interviewed Ingram in May 1965, seven months before the plant closed, he was apathetic about everything except his health. He seemed to have no notion of where to look for a new job. In addition to this, his house was in the process of being condemned by the city to make room for the new freeway. It wasn't much of a house, Mrs. McHugh reported, wood and tar paper, clean and neat inside, but not much of a structure. Ingram, she said, seemed equally apathetic about future housing. "The most important thing in life to me," he told Mrs. McHugh, "is taking the next breath."

Ingram was terminated from Baker on December 3, 1965. He got what he considered was a fair price from the city for his house. And with it, he bought a two-family house on Garfield, in the heart of the ghetto. He rented out the bottom half to his daughter and son-in-law. He rented out a room in his own apartment to his brother who worked at Ford, and his younger son, who was a part-time student at Wayne State University and worked in a tool and die shop also, paid him a small amount of money each month.

Mostly Ingram complained about his health to Mrs. McHugh and said it was his poor health that stood in the way of finding a job. No one wanted to hire a former tuberculosis patient. He wasn't certified to lift anything over 35 pounds and he found he had to sit down and rest quite often. His unemployment compensation had run out. In addition, he told her about an invention of his—he couldn't tell her more than that because it was a secret—but someone had stolen the plans, and he was very upset.

In subsequent visits in 1966, Mrs. McHugh noticed no improvement in Ingram and she became quite concerned about him. In addition to his complaints about shortness of breath, Ingram spoke of some bursitis in his arms.

In the spring of 1967, Mrs. McHugh said she noticed another development in Ingram's behavior. He seemed to evade her questions and the tests he was to take; he didn't take his usual interest in discussing his health symptoms. He still hadn't a job and when she asked him how he was supporting himself, he'd shrug, point down to the apartment below and say: "A little bit here, a little bit there. I make out."

"He seemed," Mrs. McHugh said, "anxious to get me out of the house. I would usually arrive about 11 A.M. Mr. Ingram would still be in his pajamas. He wore a bathrobe and the moment I got there he would start looking at the clock. He told me he didn't have time to fill out the forms, and that he felt all right. He let me take his blood pressure, which was good, but he did not want to discuss his health. No, he hadn't got a job. Who would hire him? The only time he showed any interest in anything was when he asked me if I knew anything about the men suing the company. He had heard that some of the men who were having a hard time getting jobs were suing the company for health compensation, and that some lawyer was helping the men collect for health damages. He had heard that anyone who had worked at Baker for twenty years and was now having a hard time getting or keeping work could sue and collect. Had I heard? I said I'd heard rumors but didn't know anything about it. He seemed disappointed. Then the phone rang in the dining room and he went to answer it. Mrs. Ingram, who is cheerful and neat, came and talked to me while he was on the phone. When he was done he came back in and said I had to go because he was going out. I asked him where he was going but he wouldn't say. He said he didn't see how he'd have any chance for a job with his health being the way it was, and he didn't want to talk about it anymore. I left."

As far as Mrs. McHugh was concerned, Willis Ingram was a sick man. In choosing a sick role over an unemployed role he was on his way to being truly sick. Dr. Cobb, after a visit to Ingram, during which he gave him a physical checkup, was inclined to think that it was only a matter of time before the tuberculosis reactivated itself. In Cobb's mind, Ingram was linked with Jack Ramsey, Dave Masiak, Ned Rockwell, Albert Lapin, and several other Baker employees who, unable to cope with job loss, had assumed sick roles and were very close to illness if not already ill. Ingram's case might have been left that way if the city of Detroit hadn't exploded into violence the following June. That changed everything.

In June of 1967, a police raid on a "blind pig" on 12th Street in the heart of the Detroit ghetto triggered what some have called riots and others, rebellion. The destruction left many ghetto buildings and homes in ruins. Anyone who watched TV news films of the looting of stores and markets and their subsequent burning will recall seeing whites looting as well as Negroes, a fact which led many at the time to state this was not a racial clash but a war of the have-nots against the haves. Yet anyone who in the next few months visited white homes in the northwest part of the city, beyond the ghetto, or took the expressways into the center city to visit Negro families could tell instantly that Detroit was a different city from what it had been before. White families talked about their loaded guns by the doors, about their plans for protecting themselves. The white man was not welcome in black neighborhoods; it was hard for a white to get a cup of coffee in a black restaurant without feeling the tension. Detroit had polarized racially, and the atmosphere was such that Dr. Cobb's nurses, all of whom were white, were having a difficult time making appointments, no less getting information, from the black respondants in the Baker study.

And so in July Cobb hired a Negro interviewer—Mrs. Ginny Frazee, a handsome, intelligent woman in her mid-forties, a former social worker—to take over some of the Negro respondants in the ghetto. Mrs. Frazee, a graduate of Spelman College in Atlanta, had been born in Detroit, and raised only a block or so away from where Willis Ingram lived on Garfield. "It wasn't yet the ghetto then," she recalls. "There were only two other Negro families on the block beside us."

Mrs. Frazee's father was a physician whose patients were white and black. He was a much respected man. The Frazee house, a solid-looking two-story brick house, is now the parsonage of the Baptist church next door. The elementary school where Ginny, her sister, and her brother went is still there and used. Now the neighborhood is all black, but there are still some people there who remember her and her parents. Some of the same stores are there, though the ownership has changed hands many times. Some of the same stores that were fire-bombed during the June riots Mrs. Frazee can remember as stores where black youngsters got a hard time, even in her day. "Whenever I drive around and look at the ruins," she says, "I keep noticing that the ruins are selective. And, God pity me, I don't mind one bit."

Although she was not trained as a public health nurse, Mrs. Frazee—who now lives in a handsome modern home 45 miles west of Detroit, in Ann Arbor where her husband is a communications engineer—found herself interested by the Baker study and the fact that I was writing a book based on it. "Not that I believe all of the study," she says to me, her lips curving in an ironic smile, "I hate words like 'blue collar worker' and 'environmental threat.' In the ghetto, environment is always a threat, and ghetto people know how to bounce back. They're used to being pushed around. The Institute for Social Research is studying the wrong people; they ought to be studying the white middle class and what happens to *them* when they lose their jobs.

"Mr. Ingram spent most of his time putting on an act for Ann McHugh," Mrs. Frazee says. "Take that stolen invention of his. He made that up too. It's an old southern Negro trick. You give the nice white lady what you think she wants to have. Mr. Ingram gave her a sick role because he knew that was what she wanted, what the study wanted. And all the time, Ingram was coping better with his job loss than any of the others. He's making a lot more money than I am and Ann McHugh too. I wouldn't be surprised if his income matched Dr. Cobb's."

Mrs. Frazee remembers quite clearly her first visit to Willis Ingram. It is clear in her mind because for her it was a visit back into the past.

"I drove around the old neighborhood for a while, past the house we lived in, the Baptist church my sister and I used to sneak into—we're Methodists—past the school we went to. I hadn't been back in years. It felt funny. I was a stranger in the neighborhood. I said hello to some children playing near the Ingram house and they just stared at me. I didn't belong there.

"From Ann's description I expected to find Ingram living in a dump. But it was a far cry from a dump, believe me. He lived in a nice, neat, two-story brick house. The Ingrams lived on the second story, and the steps were all laid with linoleum. And at the top of the stairs there was a glass door with a little curtain and a shiny brass knocker.

"When I got inside their apartment the first thing I saw that it was a spotlessly clean place. Immaculate. Mrs. Ingram had a lot of the furniture covered with that clear plastic—the sofa, and a love seat in the corner of the dining room. And then there was Mrs. Ingram herself, pretty and stylishly stout, if you know what I mean, wearing an embroidered apron. She looked content. She just didn't look like the wife of a dying man, no more than the living room she led me into looked like the living room of a dying man. There was a glass coffee table and on it little plaster dogs, turkeys, a Mexican pheasant. There was an expensive hi-fi set off to one side and a bowl of wax fruit on the hi-fi. There were two or three big comfortable leather chairs. Over the mantel piece were three hand-painted pictures of birds.

"The dining room was even bigger than the living room. A big table set for breakfast for three—at 11 o'clock. Also, and it was funny, there was a bunch of yellow legal pads lying there next to a small blue telephone. I took a good look at the phone. My husband works for Michigan Bell, and I recognized that phone as a Princess Pat trimline model, the new kind with the built-in dial. And the phone matched the blue wall paper. And there was also a large portable TV set in the dining room, and for a moment my head swam: Was this the home of the job failure Ann McHugh had been telling me about?

"And then, all of a sudden, the dying man himself appeared: small, thin, a small round gray head, and he stood there in an undershirt, bathrobe and trousers, scratching his head. He hadn't expected me. He had expected a white nurse. He looked at me, disheveled and in a bathrobe and used to playing a comic role, but his eyes gave him away. They were alive and smart and if you couldn't tell from all the expensive things in the house, you could tell from Willis Ingram's eyes that this man was in charge of himself and his life, and his home. He was the boss here.

"Where's uh . . . what's her name?' he asked me, in that high comic voice of his.

" 'Mrs. McHugh and I had to switch some of our case load, Mr.

Ingram,' I said. 'I hope you won't mind my interviewing you.'

"He nodded, as though all along he'd expected something like this to happen. Then he said, 'Look here, uh . . .'

" 'Frazee. Mrs. Frazee.'

" 'Yeah, well look here, Mrs. Frazee, I told that other lady I wasn't interested in this thing anymore. My health is fine now.'

" 'For the sake of the study, Mr. Ingram,' I said, 'we can't have people dropping out. And there are only a few more visits to make after this one. I do hope you'll finish this important research study with us.'

"He sort of snorted, and then looked at his watch. And then up at me. 'What did you say your name was?'

" 'Ginny Frazee.'

"Well, Mrs. Frazee. I am a busy man. Right now I've got to eat breakfast. If you want to talk to me while I eat breakfast, why, that's all right with me, but then you got to go.'

"Mrs. Ingram invited me into the dining room to have a cup of coffee with them. I joined them at the table. Their son who goes to Wayne State came in and sat down too. He was quiet and shy and respectful of his parents. Mrs. Ingram served the three of them a big breakfast—bacon and eggs, hot biscuits, and coffee. And Mr. Ingram ate with great appetite, joking about the long time research studies took and how it must be a pretty good business. I had one of Mrs. Ingram's biscuits; it was delicious and I told her so. She laughed softly saying she'd been making biscuits longer than she cared to remember. After breakfast was finished, the son left for school and Mr. Ingram and I went into the living room. He let me take his blood pressure, but as soon as that was done he tried again to get rid of me.

" 'Now, Mr. Ingram,' I said, 'I drove 50 miles to see you this morning. And I'm not leaving until we go through these questionnaires.

" 'Now, Mrs. Frazee,' he said sternly, 'I just don't have time for your questions.'

"I said, 'It only takes a few minutes and I—'

"At that moment the phone rang. Ingram looked at me annoyed. 'You see, I got business.'

"He went back into the dining room and closed the door. I heard him talking into the phone softly and then I heard him say: '273 in the box for a quarter. Got it.'

"I stood there a moment and then started laughing to myself. The last piece of the puzzle had just fallen into place. Everything was clear now. The hi-fi, the color TV, the furniture, the Mexican pheasant, the banker's hours he kept. And I stood there, giggling, thinking about poor Ann McHugh telling me how this man was failing, apathetic about getting a job. I was still laughing, when the dining room doors opened and Ingram came out. He stopped short and looked at me warily.

" 'What's so funny, Mrs. Frazee?' he asked.

" 'Now Mr. Ingram,' I started to say.

"But the phone rang again. He gave me a look and went back into the dining room, closing the doors behind him. I listened again for a moment and then started laughing again. I sat down on the couch and took the questionnaires out of my case and put them on the coffee table. When Ingram came back in, he looked startled at the old familiar questionnaires spread out on the coffee table.

" 'Now see here, Mrs. Frazee,' he said, his voice rising, 'I don't have time for this. You got to go.'

" 'Now you just sit down, Mr. Ingram,' I said, grinning, 'I am not going to leave until I ask you about your health. And don't you worry about that old phone of yours. You go and answer it as much as you want to. I was born in this neighborhood. I grew up over on Duggan Street. I went to Dubois School right down the block here and then to Northeastern High School. I went to the Bethel AME over on Blashford. I was about born here, Mr. Ingram; I grew up here till I was eighteen; you just go right on with the phone calls and I'll ask you questions in between.'

"For a moment Ingram's face was blank as he was deciding how to take this. Then he grinned and scratched his head: 'You know, huh?'

" 'I know.'

"And we both laughed."

"I asked him the questions I was supposed to ask, reading them word for word, and he answered them easily, lying a little sometimes to give me what he thought we'd like to have for our study, and then laughing when I accused him of not being honest. The phone rang continually, interrupting us, and he'd go into the dining room and write down the bets on the yellow pads. He didn't bother to

close the doors anymore. 'Number one, two, three for ten cents in
both races,' I heard him say one time. 'Nine, nine, eight in the box
for ten,' he said another time. 'Honey, I know you're due for a big
hit today.' As I listened I knew why this was a bad time for Ann
McHugh or for anyone else who wanted to see Ingram. He probably had to deliver his numbers by one or two o'clock. If they were
using numbers from the stock market on which to pick winners,
they'd have to be all set by 4 P.M. Most of the time they used the
afternoon horse races to pick the numbers. They'd have to be set
by 2 o'clock then. Probably he'd drive the numbers over to the
house himself with the money. I wondered if he did his own collecting. Later, when we got to be friends, Mr. Ingram told me he had
a man and his girl friend collecting for him. 'I'm not well enough
to go around collecting,' he told me solemnly, 'I'm a gambler, and
I'll gamble on anything except my health.'

"During our visits together Mr. Ingram told me he'd gambled at
Baker. He'd had a book at Baker, but he hadn't done much with it.
Just let friends and relatives play on it. He hadn't been in business
yet. The man who has a book in the numbers game is like a stock
broker with a private seat on the exchange. He is privy to betting
on numbers. To play the numbers game, you either have to have a
book yourself—not many do—or you have to work through someone who has a book. Like a stockbroker, Mr. Ingram takes a commission on every transaction. He keeps thirty cents on the dollar,
though the dollar bet is often broken into ten dimes. If a client hits,
Ingram gets 15 percent of the winnings. The numbers game is the
Negro stock market, and Mr. Ingram is a full-fledged stockbroker.

"He told me he had always thought about going into it full time,
but until Baker closed he never had the opportunity. After it closed,
he used his severance pay and pension rights money to set himself
up in business. He needed capital. This was because after collecting
the numbers he had to pay ahead to the 'house.' And then afterwards collect from his clients. He used his Baker severance pay to
pay ahead.

"Mr. Ingram never came out and said exactly how well he was
doing, but he told me at one time he was carrying a woman who
owed him over five hundred dollars. Putting one thing and another
together from what he said, I figured out he was making about four
hundred dollars a week, getting up at 10:30 in the morning, sending

a son to Wayne State University, living in an immaculate, attract-ive two-family brick house and going every six months to Herman Kiefer hospital for TB checkups.

"He complains every now and then about shortness of breath, but he is very much the master of his house. He has, in the jargon of the social scientists, 'coped pretty well with environmental threat.' "

In the spring of 1968, Ginny Frazee invited me to go along with her on one of her periodic visits to Ingram. She telephoned ahead and, she reported, while Ingram was not terribly enthusiastic about his nurse-interviewer being accompanied by a man writing a book about the Baker plant, he did agree to see me and talk about old days at Baker.

Our appointment is for 10:30 A.M. We are on time, but Ingram isn't. Mrs. Ingram informs us, with a tiny smile, that Mr. Ingram has gone out. Ginny Frazee stifles a grimace of annoyance and we thank Mrs. Ingram. For a half hour or so we drive around the neighborhood on the chance that Ingram is hiding next door and might return once we've left. We go back to Ingram's house and we are in luck, for just as we finish parking the car another car pulls up and double parks in front of the Ingram house.

"There he is," Ginny says. I see a small thin gray-headed man wearing a windbreaker, get out of the car. "Hello there, Mr. In-gram," Ginny calls out.

Ingram looks up and sees us. A slow smile breaks over his features. "Looks like you're in luck."

"Yes," Ginny says, "aren't we?"

We follow him into the house and Mrs. Ingram, who must have seen this from the window, is ready with a pot of coffee. We sit down in the living room with the hi-fi, the pictures, statuettes—it is all just as Ginny Frazee had described it.

"Well, Mr. Ingram," Ginny says, after we are seated, "you won't believe it but this fellow is writing a book about the Baker closing."

"That so?" Ingram says, and turns to me. "Why do you want to do that?"

"He thinks it's an interesting story, that's why. A plant it was good to work at closing, and a lot of people getting hurt by it."

"That so? A lot of people hurt? Well," he says, nodding gravely, "I hear there are some that miss it, but—I'm not bitter. You talk to Jeff Barrett yet? Do you know him?"

"No."

"Let me set you up with him."

He goes into the dining room and picks up the blue Princess Pat trimline phone (the phone with the built-in dial) that goes with the blue wallpaper and he dials.

"Jeff," he says a moment later, "this is Ingram. Willis Ingram. How're you? Listen here, I got a fella here. A writer. I want you to talk to him, tell him all about Baker. He's writing a book. Yes, a book. You ought to talk to him." He puts his hand over the mouthpiece and says to me: "You want to see him this afternoon?"

"Tell him I'll call him tomorrow."

"Jeff, he'll call you tomorrow. How's your wife? That's good. You say hello to her for me. Take care now."

After a few more words, Ingram hangs up. He comes back into the living room, a little air of cockiness swinging from the edges of his thin shoulders. "That was Jeff Barrett I called for you," he explains. "He was *salaried*. He's not doing too well now though." He shakes his head sadly.

Ginny Frazee leans forward. This, plus the waiting for him, is too much. Her eyes have a gleam in them. "But *you* are doing well, Mr. Ingram. *You* look just fine. Tell me, how do you do it? Do you have a job now?"

Ingram, startled, gives her a wary glance. "Oh, I get a little disability pension. And you know I got the rent from downstairs." He grins a little defensively.

But Ginny won't let him go. "Still, Mr. Ingram," she says, "you've got so *many* nice things here. The color TV, that hi-fi, you must be doing *very* well, Mr. Ingram."

"Now, now, Mrs. Frazee, you know how it is," Ingram is grinning widely, now, "A little bit here. A little bit there. I make out."

"Oh, I bet you do," Ginny says.

And they laugh together.

The file of Willis Ingram, which had been placed with the files of workers unable to cope with job loss, has now been placed among the files of those who at the moment are coping successfully.

And Sidney Cobb smiles ruefully. "I worried about this thing. Originally the study was designed without Negroes. There weren't enough long-term seniority Negro workers at Baker for us to get a scientific sampling, and at the present time in our society there are too many differences between Negroes and whites to lump them together. Negroes tend to have higher blood pressure than whites; self-identity problems are different in Negroes and whites. Ideally, we should have done an equal study on whites and Negroes, but there weren't enough funds for that. As it turned out the number of Negroes in our study—15 percent of the men—was too small to allow us to test our hypotheses accurately. And finally, it was quite clear to us early in the game that Negro respondants ought to be interviewed by Negro nurses or social workers. We'd seen how a Negro respondant clammed up when his Negro interviewer brought a white interviewer along with her.

"I told the union that for the scientific accuracy of the study, I would prefer not to have any Negroes in it. The union rose up in arms. All men are the same, they told me. They accused me of discrimination. They themselves were working hard to eliminate discrimination and prejudice, and so on. I think I finally convinced them that it wasn't a matter of prejudice but of getting a good scientific sampling. I pointed out to them that I was not taking women in the study. The bulk of women who worked at Baker were married and didn't have the same need for a job as the men had. They may even drop out of the labor force when the plant closed. And the number of women who were actually heads of households was too small.

"The union got the point then, but they had a public relations problem on their hand and they told me I had to take Negroes in the study and that was that.

"And so we did. And it's going to be a pain in the neck in the analysis. But some things we learned are of interest. To start with, there was a proportionally higher participation of Negroes in our study than whites. I think part of this was due to Perry DeMoss's telling them to get into it, and they trusted Perry completely. And part of it was due to a need for medical care. The other thing we learned was that the Negroes in our study were less able to cope with job loss than the whites. Ginny Frazee's idea that the ghetto-dweller, being used to hard times, is thus better suited to cope with them, just isn't borne out by the facts, by our physiological tests, nor by the low number of Negroes getting new jobs. Our study shows that automation hits the Negro harder than it hits the white; there are fewer winners among the Negroes than the whites, and Willis Ingram, who fooled us so beautifully, is, I'm sorry to say, the exception rather than the rule. He was a very clever and intelligent man who was probably waiting all his life, without knowing it, for the break he got when Baker closed."

Fridays Were Sad Days

The Baker Plant, May–June, 1965

Frank Robertson says he was vaguely aware of a health study going on after work hours. He'd heard one or two reports from Tom Morgan, but not much more than that. He wouldn't have paid much attention to the study anyway, for that spring, about the time Cobb and his research team were starting their study, Robertson's own personal managerial juggling act was becoming more complicated than ever. In February, General Office had informed him that the York plant would be ready to open in July, and so he had adjusted the production schedules accordingly. In May, he began laying off some of the seniority men. "We'd let them know on Monday that Friday would be their last day," Robertson explains. "Some of them had a hard time believing it; others just nodded. Fridays became sad days around the plant. There would be a lot of handshaking with the man leaving, perhaps a drink or two at the bar across the street. Men worked right up till noon on their day to go home. Then I'd go over to their department and shake their hand and thank them for being so loyal. Some of them I'd get jobs for, others I'd written or telephoned recommendations, still others just weren't sure what they were going to do. There were tears from time to time. It was easiest on those men who could cry, I always thought."

Then, suddenly, in June, General Office dropped a bombshell. Ike Kraeger called Robertson and told him that the York plant was having unexpected problems and it was going to be delayed about five months. They wouldn't be able to open till December. Robertson just had to keep Baker going and producing another four or five months.

The news floored Robertson. To transfer operations, to keep producing so as not to lose a single customer (and, in one case, to take on a new and big customer), to keep men happy, help them find new jobs while making sure key people stayed on the old job, to terminate some and not others—and now not to know when it was going to end. It was an impossible mental and physical juggling act.

The situation at the Fitzwarren warehouse finally broke the logjam. More and more stock was being put into the rented warehouse on Fitzwarren until it was overflowing. Stealing was on an alarming increase at the warehouse. In February, Robertson signed a contract with Pinkertons to keep the warehouse under surveillance. But even as this was happening more and more stock was being placed in there. The situation had become intolerable.

Robertson made a phone call to General Office to tell them he was coming down there. The next morning he flew to Pittsburgh and met with Frohman and Wysse Allen in Allen's office.

"You've got to let me start this thing," he told them angrily. "It's going to be a marathon if I can get the help to keep it. I have one hundred and forty truckloads of stock of all colors and types that has got to get down to York. I can't keep it any longer. I will not be responsible for it. This has been horsed around and played with till I'm sick."

Frohman and Allen looked at him. What had happened was that no one had been prepared for the miracle Robertson had wrought. The high production, the high efficiency, and now proof of this—a warehouse filled to overflowing. They had been caught out in their miscalculation.

Frohman said: "Frank, the truth is you're making us all here at General Office look kind of funny."

"It's not me. It's my people," Robertson said bitterly. "They been making you look funny. And would you like to know why?"

"Shoot."

"You won't like it."

"Shoot anyway."

"You wrote us off. You let us alone. You let me take advantage of the psychological reactions of people. And it could have gone otherwise."

Wysse Allen spoke quietly. "You walked alone, Frank. You walked alone."

"I was used," Robertson snapped at him too.

They were silent. Then Tom Frohman said: "Frank, why don't you go down to York and get them moving on this stock matter? I think that's got to be the answer."

And so Robertson flew from Pittsburgh down to York, Ohio, where he could see that no progress had been made since he'd been down there a month or so before. He talked to the factory manager, a man named Donald Lockhart, and for a half hour Robertson listened to *his* complaints. Finally he said: "Now look, Donald, I was down here a month ago and things are still setting in the same places. So I'm going to have to break our friendship. I've tried everything I know how to help down here. I've pleaded, I've begged, I've threatened. Nothing's been done. Not much, anyway. When I go back to Detroit I'm calling in trucks. And I'm concentrating my people. And we're going to start shipping it to you, at the rate of seven trucks a day."

"We can't take care of it," Lockhart said.

"Get on that phone and tell someone you can because I'm going to start shipping the minute I get back to Detroit."

"You can't do that."

"The hell I can't. Wysse Allen told me to close that plant and, Mister, I'm going to close it."

"We won't know what to do with it."

"Months ago I asked you to get some rented space down here."

"We don't have authorization for it."

"Damn it, whose responsibility is it?"

"I guess it's mine."

"Then get the authorization and start renting space because those trucks will be rolling the day I get back."

Lockhart got on the phone to Pittsburgh, got authorization. Robertson returned to Detroit. The next day trucks started rolling out of the Fitzwarren warehouse.

The stealing went on, however.

"Stealing had to go on," Ned Rockwell says, "that warehouse was jammed with goodies going out much too slowly. The men on all the shifts there, the men who went there from the main plant, all knew their time was going to be up soon so they began helping themselves. Some of these guys were out-and-out crooks. Other guys were just getting even.

"Nobody wanted that kind of trouble. Because it meant grievances. Even if the guys were crooks, you had to stand up for them somehow. So we had grievances on the stealing, especially after Robertson put Pinkertons on over there. We tried to settle the grievances in Steps 1 and 2, at the worker–boss–area-committeeman level. But I can remember one incident that was too big right from the start. It was too big because the dumb-dumb stole too much and it was too big because the company had invested a lot of time and expense in tracking him down.

"So on this dumb bastard we had to go to Step 3 of the grievance procedure—a meeting between the union committee and Perry, for the union, and Robertson and the management. The guy was a plain crook but he was a union man too and I fought hard to keep him out of jail."

A Grievance on Stealing

Grievance No. 9—discharge of Robert Spitler and Walter Remus
April 16, 1965
Union–Management meeting thereon

Statement of grievance by union
We are protesting the company's suspension of R. Spitler and W. Remus whom the company alleges took company property without receiving permission. The union asks that both employees be reinstated immediately with receipt of all monies due them.

Step 3. *Company response:* On Thursday, April 8, 1965, Mr. Spitler and Mr. Remus were suspended pending the completion of an investigation of certain of their activities as employees of this company. The investigation has now been terminated and its conclusions have led us to discharge Mr. Spitler and Mr. Remus for infraction of General Plant Rules, Intolerable Offense Rule No. 1. Mr. Spitler violated this rule on February 23 and 24, March 25, and April 5, 1965. Mr. Remus is held to have been in violation of this rule on April 5, 1965.

NOTE—Step 3. In order to avoid placing a criminal conviction on Mr. Remus' personnel records, his lawyer on 4/14/65 requested that the company drop its prosecution charges against Remus if he agreed to resign from the company. Upon receiving this request, the company agreed to it. Remus resigned as of 4/15/65.

Discussion
Company statement: The union was told that on February 8,

1965 surveillance was placed on activities in and around the Fitzwarren warehouse. This surveillance showed the below results re: the above grievance. The surveillance personnel are available as witnesses on behalf of the company.

Feb. 23, 1965—10:20 P.M.   Spitler was observed backing his car into truck Well No. 1. Surveillance observed Spitler placing 3 cartons of paint stock in his car trunk. After locking trunk, Spitler drove out of the well.

Feb. 24, 1965— 3 P.M.   Spitler was observed at his home removing said cartons from the trunk of his car and placing them in his garage.

8:18 P.M.   Spitler backed his car into Well No. 7.

9:27 P.M.   Spitler's car was still in the well.

11:03 P.M.   Spitler drove his car out of Well No. 7. His headlights were off until he reached the street. The car left the vicinity of the warehouse. (Spitler's card was later observed to be punched out for 12 P.M.) The car was observed to be riding extremely low from the weight in the trunk. Spitler drove much slower than he usually did. He drove to Marco's Cocktail Lounge on Lassiter St. and parked in the lot behind the cocktail lounge. During the next half hour four cartons labelled "Baker Automotive Finishes" were observed on the rear seat of Spitler's car.

March 25, 1965—10:02 P.M.   Spitler drove his car completely inside Well No. 2.

10:12 P.M.   Spitler drove his car out of well, left it parked on the apron, closed exterior door to well and re-entered warehouse.

10:16 P.M.   Spitler left the warehouse, opened exterior door, and drove out in his car. He drove around the area in a circular pattern, and then drove to the Michigan Bar on Grand River. His time card was later observed to be punched out at twelve midnight.

10:32 P.M.   Spitler left the Michigan Bar and drove out of the neighborhood.

10:48 P.M.   Spitler again parked his car in the rear parking lot of Marco's Cocktail Lounge on Lassiter. Again several Baker Automotive Finish cartons were observed in the rear of Spitler's car. The back seat of the car had been taken out, making more room available there.

By prior arrangement surveillance people were to contact company officials whenever an employee drove his car into one of the Fitzwarren wells. Contact was made in this case and the surveillance people were instructed to detain Spitler. This did not happen because Spitler had loaded his car and left the area while the telephone contact was being made. A second member of the surveillance team followed him. By the time Tilyard and Morgan, the company officials, arrived at the warehouse, Spitler was gone.

April 5, 1965—11:50 P.M.—Spitler backed his car completely into well No. 3 and closed the exterior door.

Because arrangements on March 25th had failed, the surveillance team was instructed to move in the next time a car was driven into a loading well. Accordingly, the surveillance people went into the warehouse, identified themselves and proceeded to Well No. 3 where Remus was in the act of putting several cartons of BAL 7000 (quarts) into the back of Spitler's car. The trunk of Spitler's car was open and the surveillance men observed three cases in there. In addition Remus had a carton in his hands and was about to put that in too. Remus was getting his cases from a pallet which had been taken to the truck well for more efficient loading. Upon arriving at Remus's side, the surveillance men asked him why he was putting paint in this car. Remus replied, and the language is exact, "Bob Spitler asked me to put this paint in his car for him. This is his car." The question was asked again by the second surveillance man and Remus's reply was the same.

After this the surveillance men and Remus walked to the warehouse office, Tilyard and Morgan were notified by phone, and Spitler was sent for. When Spitler arrived and the surveillance men identified themselves he asked if they were arresting him. He was told he was not being arrested and could leave if he wanted to but they were asking him to stay in the office. Spitler left the office, went to his car in Well No. 3, and started removing the cartons of BAL 7000 from his car. When a surveillance man who had followed him observed this and asked why he was taking the cartons out of his car Spitler replied: "I'm going home." He then asked the surveillance man if he was under arrest or could he go home and again he was told he could leave if he wished. Whereupon he started to curse the surveillance man and a second surveillance man who came into the immediate area. He soon quieted, however, and went with the surveillance people back to the warehouse office. An area union steward was there and he and Spitler discussed the matter in a corner of the office.

Mr. Tom Morgan arrived at the warehouse about this time. Spitler moved his car which he had emptied, from Well No. 3 and parked it on Fitzwarren. He came back into the warehouse and Morgan and the surveillance men talked with him. Spitler denied any knowledge of his doing anything wrong. Tilyard arrived, and while he talked to Spitler Morgan called the police, gave them the background of the situation, and asked them to come. The police then attempted to find out from Spitler what he was doing but Spitler just repeated that he wasn't doing anything wrong. Remus also denied doing anything wrong. The police requested Spitler and Remus to return with them to the 15th precinct for further questioning, and Spitler cursed and swore. The police then informed him they would take him in one way or another. Remus was quiet and raised no fuss. After a few more moments of arguing Spitler and Remus accompanied the police to the 15th precinct. The two surveillance men, Tilyard and Morgan, drove to the 15th precinct where they informed the police that it was the company's firm intention to press charges. The matter was left in the hands of the police. The surveillance team plus Tilyard and Morgan returned to the Fitzwarren warehouse where all the cases that had been in Spitler's car were set aside for evidence.

April 6, 1965—9:00 A.M.—Assistant Prosecutor, Arthur Monahan, advised Tilyard and Morgan that Remus's charge ought to be reduced from larceny in a building to simple larceny. He also informed them that Spitler could not legally be charged with anything, despite surveillance team reports of previous activities on Spitler's part.

Tilyard and Morgan filed a complaint against Remus, and proceeded to Recorder's Court where Remus's attorney obtained an adjournment from Judge Keller. A hearing was set for April 14, 1965. The company filed no objection.

April 14, 1965—Before Remus's case was called before Judge Keller, Remus's attorney met with Morgan and the police detective assigned to the case and asked Morgan what the company's reaction might be to a suggestion on his part that the company drop charges against Remus and accept his resignation. It was felt that a conviction would be a severe mark on an otherwise clean record and would make it extremely difficult for Remus to get a new job and support his family. Morgan advised Remus's attorney to write up such a proposal and have it signed by Remus as well as himself. This done, the company dropped charges against Remus.

April 15, 1965—At a union-management meeting this morning, the union was informed of the action so far in the case against Remus and that the discharge of Spitler had gone through and would not be changed. The union's argument was that since there was no criminal evidence against him— as witnessed by the assistant prosecutor's statement that Spitler could not legally be charged—then his discharge was not for just cause. Furthermore, it requested the company to pinpoint the exact incident he was being discharged for.

The company argued that its surveillance reports on Spitler's activities over the past weeks as described above was more than justification for his discharge.

The union wanted to know why the company hadn't had Spitler arrested before April 5, 1965, since they had been following him around previously and had eye-witness accounts. The union claimed that by permitting him to continue his activities unmolested the company was in effect sanctioning Spitler's removal of material from the warehouse.

The company replied that no moves were made against Spitler earlier because the company wanted to know exactly who was engaged in these activities and the amount of material being removed and on one occasion Spitler moved too quickly to be detained. The company cannot subscribe to the argument that its careful procedure in determining who was doing what could in any sense be interpreted as giving Spitler a license to take material out of the warehouse and into his car.

Rockwell says, "We met with them again about a week later and Perry DeMoss came along. They didn't back down then, but I talked with old Robertson a lot about this case. Spitler was a crook, but with things the way they were, that warehouse sitting there full of goodies, he'd have to be something special *not* to steal —and he had put in quite a few good working years at Baker. I finally persuaded Robertson to let Spitler resign the way Remus had rather than discharge him. The main reason is that under the pension agreement a man having been discharged—not terminated, mind you, but discharged—loses all rights to his pension benefits. This way he keeps his pension benefits but loses his severance pay, of course."

Rockwell was successful with all the other "discharge for cause" cases that year, too. He was able to persuade Robertson to allow the offenders to resign and thus save their pension benefits. Their discharges were not always for stealing. There was a case that went from May to August of that year—the case of Melvin Hodges, who had taken another job while he was supposed to be on sick leave. The company found out about this, discharged him for cause and required him to repay his sick and accident benefits which he had received from June 4 to July 5. When Hodges had put in for sickness and accident pay he denied having another job. At Rockwell's prodding, the company agreed to accept Hodges' resignation as of May 19, 1965.

Rockwell says: "Most of these guys didn't know what they were doing. They were just all churned up inside. You know, I used to hate Robertson in the old days, his sneaky ways, but you could talk to him now. And I could tell he was as grieved about the closing as I was. He really understood about the men. He and I spent a lot of time together talking about why these poor dumb-dumbs did the things they did, and we both grieved for them. If old Robertson is as sick as I am today, it's because we both loved that lousy place too much."

From the Recollections of Frank R. Robertson

July–August, 1965

Thursday. "A bird in the hand is worth two in the bush, Charley," I told Charley Hazzard this morning. Charley had been offered a job at United Paint and was wondering what he should do. Should he give up his severance pay to take it? With his fourteen years his severance pay would come to about $400. Not much compared to a good job now. But Charley, a steam fitter, wasn't sure. He wants that severance pay That's *his* bird in the hand.

Making phone calls for two boys from the resin department. Both good workers being terminated tomorrow. They came in and asked me for letters. I'll give them letters but a phone call sometimes works better.

Finished the second call when Harold Peterson came in. A shipment of astro-blue paint for a Plymouth Valiant had been sent back from Atlanta. It hadn't matched. He'd gone over to the lab with it to ask them to do a test, but no one was there.

"Well, Harold," I said, "they're probably out on a coffee break. Try them again in ten minutes."

During those ten minutes Harold sat in my office cracking his knuckles and telling me that this was what it was going to be like when the plant moved. No lab at all. One enormous coffee break. "That's foolish thinking, Harold," I said. "All you do is call York and your salesmen send the paint back to York. If anything it will be a lot easier to telephone York than to keep running over to Building 2."

Harold nodded, but I could tell he wasn't hearing a thing. He started talking about his boy.

I listened, but my mind was elsewhere. A note on my desk saying Johnny Johnson wanted to see me. I had an idea what it was about. Some of my maintenance boys I'd heard were beginning to get job offers. This was one group of people we could not afford to lose until we shut the whole plant down. I wanted to keep this bunch together no matter how little work there was for them at times. These were my own boys. The elite of the plant. They'd never have trouble getting new jobs. I'd raised them myself. They could repair every machine in the plant as well as run it. I was determined not to let them bust up until it was all over. Each week I had to send General Office lists of men to be terminated and it was Ike Kraeger who noticed that not one maintenance person was being laid off. He telephoned me about it and wanted to know if it was my intention to keep the maintenance boys together till the end.

"That's right," I told him.

Ike, a goddamn jug head if there ever was one, wanted to know what in hell I was doing that for. Did I need *all* of them?

"Yup," I said trying to restrain my temper.

"What for?"

I said to Kraeger. "Did you ever put a plant to bed? Did you ever handle people? The answer to that is no. If you're not perfectly happy—and I've told you this twice before—you get yourself a new boy and get him here tonight."

"Now, now, Robbie," he started.

"Then lay off me, damn it," I said, and slammed the phone down on him and all of General Office.

Harold Peterson said he was going to give the lab a call. I picked up the phone and called the lab. The men were back. "Harold," I said, "why don't you send someone over with the paint and you go home and take a nap? I know how hard you've been driving yourself lately, and the sales charts show it."

Harold shook his head. His old energy was flowing back in him. It was incredible what a few supporting words could do for him. "I don't need a nap, Robbie. I'll straighten this thing out; I've got to fly down to Nashville tomorrow. I'm firing our man down there, and I've got a red-hot salesman from Technico going to take his place. This closing has thrown things out of whack; we've had more complaints from distributors than ever before but I'm going to rattle the dead wood hard."

We hadn't had any more complaints than before. It was just that Harold was magnifying them more during the closing. It was him the closing was hard on, not the Nashville salesman. I suppose I should be more patient with him. He is a magnificent sales manager when all is said and done. He drives himself hard, and if I could only take away his worries about the closing, a closing that shouldn't really affect his job anyway. . . . Perhaps I should try not to let my mind wander while he rattles on. But you can pay so much attention to one man and then another needs your time.

Mrs. Parkinson stuck her head in the door and told me Clarence Fritts was here to see me. Did I want to talk to him?" I was startled. Fritts retired last year. What the deuce could he want?

Mrs. P. said he wanted to ask me something.

Fritts started at Baker the year after me. He lacked the energy or drive to move up to a supervisory position. But he had always been a conscientious worker, loyal, and trustworthy. He came in, looking the same. We shook hands.

"Robbie," he says to me, "my nephew who works over at the warehouse on the afternoon shift says you been giving recommendations for men wanting new jobs."

"That's right, Clarence," I say, puzzled.

"Well . . ." and Clarence Fritts grins, a little embarrassed, "I thought I'd come in and get one."

"You must be kidding. You're over a year retired, Clarence."

He chuckles. "I know, Robbie, but you never know when you'll need something like that and besides when Howard told me what you were doing for the boys, I got to thinking I don't have any signature of yours on paper."

I start laughing. "Clarence, I'll send you a job recommendation in tomorrow's mail." We talk for a few minutes and then he leaves and I'm left wondering about it all. Has a panic set in among retired workers? Are they worried about the company continuing their pension? It occurs to me I should have asked Clarence this, but I didn't. He made it seem as though he just wanted my signature on paper, and perhaps he did. I don't know. Isn't the union filling its retired workers in on things? There's just too much for one man to cope with.

Friday. Handshakes with 12 employees, but the big event of the day took place at 4 P.M. at the main gate when, believe it or not, Austin Wagle who works in the grinding department

and has twenty-two years seniority tried to walk out of the
plant carrying a ladder. The guard called me and John Franklin the super of the grinding department, and John and the
guard brought Wagle and the ladder over to my office. It
was a 5-foot aluminum step ladder. I couldn't believe it.

John and the guard brought Wagle in. I told Mrs. Parkinson
to get Ned Rockwell on the outercall. There'd probably be
no union ruckuss about this but I wanted to make sure. For
one thing, at least twenty men had seen Wagle walk out with
the ladder. As the guard said: "I started to let him go. He
was carrying the damn thing like it was his own. Then I says
to myself that's a company tool." Another reason the union
might not kick up a fuss, I thought, was that Wagle was not
one of their favorites, he'd worked too hard through the
years.

While we waited for Ned Rockwell, I tried to gauge Wagle.
He'd moved up slowly to where he was making $3.00 an hour
as the operator of a ball mill. Now he sat there, looking down
at his knees, frightened. John Franklin who liked him was
upset. He kept saying: "Austin, you must have been out of
your mind to carry out something like that. You can be fired
for cause. You'll lose all your severance. You got 600 dollars
coming to you; that ladder isn't worth 600 dollars is it? And
all your pension money . . . for a 5-foot ladder?"

Wagle just sat there and looked miserable. I guessed he was
fighting back tears. A man in his 50s.

Rockwell came along finally and with his usual choice of four
letter words wanted to know what was going on. When I
told him, he looked at Wagle incredulously. "Jesus, man,"
Ned said, "you'd have to be wearing a mighty big shirt to
sneak that ladder out." The guard laughed but Wagle didn't.
And neither did Franklin. And neither did I.

"Austin?" I asked Wagle gently, "just what did you think
you were doing with that ladder?"

"I don't know, Mr. Robertson. I honestly don't know."

"Did you know you were carrying it out the main gate?"

"I don't know," he repeated. "I don't know."

"As John Franklin told you, there isn't a ladder in the world worth all the severance pay and pension money you can lose." He nodded, looking down at his knees. "We can fire you for just cause, you know that?"

"Yes, sir."

"But I'm going to give you a break. We're going to pretend it was an honest mistake on your part. You thought you were taking the ladder over to Building 1 and got mixed up and walked out the gate."

That did it. He burst into tears. The guard turned away and I looked over to John Franklin and told him to get Wagle out of here. Rockwell shook his head. "This sure beats all, don't it?"

"It sure does," I said.

But it didn't. A few weeks later a two-ton chainfall disappeared from the yard, and how someone got that out under his shirttail I'll never know.

In the wake of the Wagle incident, I've done a lot of thinking about stealing. More and more of it is going on. Mueller tells me he saw two colored boys hoisting paint over the fence. An inventory from the warehouse shows that a lot of stuff is missing there. We've already caught two men stealing paint there and fired them both. Yet, I didn't fire Wagle. Why not? Because he'd been a good worker. Because it was a kind of temporary insanity, a striking back at General Office. People are just not themselves these days.

Friday. Stan Powaluk came in to say goodbye to me. I wrote him a job recommendation and asked him what his plans were. He said he had none but was thinking of maybe going into a handyman business. Helping old ladies, general house maintenance and window cleaning. I asked him if he needed tools. He said sure, so I wrote a note to Johnny Johnson over at maintenance to give Stan some secondhand tools, hammers, a saw if we had an old one, any old wrenches, squeejees, sponges. After I did this I realized this was one way I could cut down the stealing. Give the stuff away. There are hundreds of items York wouldn't be needing and it would cost the company hundreds of dollars to auction them off when the time came to sell the machinery—why not give the old stuff away now?

Tuesday. Yesterday I gave three old Stilson wrenches to an old-timer from shipping and receiving and Tom Morgan reported to me today that he stole a fourth before he checked out for good. Maybe it's not the things they want but some kind of revenge. Maybe it's simply that some people would rather steal things than ask for them. I'm still telling them to ask me for things.

Thursday. We've got a Pinkerton guard on full time at the warehouse. Starting today.

Monday. I've been averaging two hours a day writing, telephoning, and sometimes going on visits to help people get jobs. Tom Morgan's been working too. He's not so keen on making trips to other plants, but I've told him it's part of his job.

Tuesday. Had lunch with Oscar Potts today, over on Grand River. He wanted to find out how the closing was going, and I could remember back almost two years when I'd bought him lunch at the Dearborn Inn and asked him how his closing at Ace-Marvin had gone. Oscar was curious to know why my plant hadn't fallen apart and I told him I didn't know for sure, except that these men were being loyal beyond any idea. You're loyal to your country, your flag, but not to a cold-blooded company that doesn't care about you. Oscar wryly remarked it probably had something to do with the way I was handling things, and I had to admit to Oscar that I was learning things. Like stopping trouble, clearing production bottlenecks during the closing. In the old days, I used to go sailing right in there and get to the heart of the matter. Now I hang around the troublesome area, sort of making it known

I'm around, and when the time is ripe, the men kind of invite me in. Sometimes I've had to spend a whole day in and around an area, but I never barge in. Things have a way of opening up better. Oscar listened to me, chewed on his toothpick, and said: "And when they lay you off, Frank, what in hell are you gonna do?" I laughed and said I wasn't thinking that far ahead, Oscar.

Wednesday. No sooner do I tell Oscar Potts what a managerial genius I am and how smoothly things are going, then I have my most serious problem since a year ago when the Fred Hicks thing broke and I got General Office to fire Lee Jones.

10 A.M. I get a call from Ned Rockwell who says the committee wants to have a meeting with me. Five of them come on over: Ned, Dick Tyner, Wayne Bender, Jimmy Bailey, and Rudolph Bimmler. Ned gets right to the point. "Frank," he says, "some of the guys have been offered good jobs but they got to take them now, and not next month when maybe they're on your schedule to be terminated. Since it don't make any difference to you really, we want you to terminate the guys on this list right now."

He hands me a list with six names on it, including one of my maintenance boys. I smell the trap. Five of these boys are scheduled for termination within a couple of weeks but the man from maintenance isn't. Ned's trying to hide the man in the middle of the list. Johnny Johnston told me his boys were getting offers and getting restless too. A lot of paint companies would be after their knowledge and skills. Some of them, the smarter ones, had quit, given up their severance pay and taken jobs, but others had assured me they'd be sticking it out to the end. They were going to collect their severance pay. Undoubtedly some of the others on this list had jobs lined up too and now they wanted to have their cake and eat it too—that is, to have their new jobs now and their severance pay too. Well, I was not going to do that. If people wanted to quit, that was their business, but they couldn't quit and collect severance pay too. I knew this had to come up sooner or later and I was surprised it hadn't come up sooner. What it all amounted to was that I was running this plant with a captive crew and only now were some of them realizing the terms of their captivity.

I told Ned I couldn't do it. "This is illegal," I said. It violates the terms of the contract. If I did this for these men, I'd have to do it for anyone and everyone. Our closing would go to hell, and you know it."

Then Ned did what I figured he'd do. He became the Ned of the pre-closing days. He turned on that old temper of his and called me a whole bunch of names, most often "heartless son of a bitch." And he snarls: "Robertson, today's the first time I felt like cussing you since you became plant manager. Before you became plant manager I hated your guts."

"Yes, you did."

"Well, since you been plant manager you been pretty decent —up till now. Now you're your old self again."

"Ned, keep still a minute, will you, and let's go through this again. I'd like to lay these men off. I'd *love* to see Tony get located right now. But if I do this what am I going to do about Dave, about Buck, Angelo, about everyone else in maintenance? Or anyone else I need to put this plant to bed?

"To hell with them."

"Ned, you're being ridiculous."

"By God, I'll tell you how ridiculous we're going to be. We're all going to stop working, aren't we?"

"Yeah, yeah—" says the rest of the committee.

I say: "OK, if that's what you want."

"And what in hell are you going to do then?" Ned jeers at me.

I look at him and I think: I can do as good a job losing my temper and cussing as you can, Ned Rockwell. So I say angrily: "I'll tell you what I'm going to do, goddamn it. I'll transfer the remaining business out of here so goddamn quick your head'll spin."

"Where'll you transfer it to?"

"That's none of your damn business."

"Well, we're gonna strike. That's what we're gonna do."

And Ned gets up and so do the other members of the committee and they stomp out angrily.

Tom Morgan shakes his head. "Frank, they're going to strike. What're we going to do?"

"They're not going to strike," I say calmly. "Ned won't let them strike."

Just the same I thought it might be a good idea to see Ned again. There was a tanker being unloaded over by the tankhouse, but since it was a little after closing time I figured the best place to catch Ned was in the parking lot. So I went over to my car pretending I was going home, and looked around through the corner of my eye to see where Ned was. Lots of other people going home but no Ned. I spot Matt Gargan getting into his car and I ask him where Rockwell is. Matt is his supervisor. Matt says: "Why that scriggly son of a bitch. I heard what he told you today." And he looks back at the tanker being unloaded inside the gates.

"Don't tell me Ned's working overtime unloading that truck?" I ask.

"He sure as hell is," Matt says.

I go back inside the plant and saunter by the tankhouse and sure enough there's Ned unloading the tanker. He doesn't look up; I don't look at him. I walk by as if I've got business elsewhere. Then a few minutes later I come sauntering back and when I'm ten feet by him, Ned explodes: "What in hell's the matter with you, Robertson? You got the high hat or something you won't even speak to a guy?"

I stood there and looked at him without expression. He says:

"Hell, about this afternoon, I just wanted to see if you could get mad."

"Well then, Ned," I said, "I can blow my stack just like you can."

"I don't know why in hell you don't do it more often. Why, if I was in your job . . ." And he tells me he wouldn't have my job for all the tea in China, and everything's all right again.

We both know there's not going to be any more talk about strikes or walkouts or Frank Robertson laying off people illegally so they can collect their severance pay and get a new job too.

Thursday. How lost you get in details. How much you thrive on problems. And when the biggest problem of all is staring you in the face, you don't even see it. Maybe because you know all along there isn't anything you can do about it.

Twice last week Harold Peterson asked me to have lunch with him and both times I couldn't make it. Thank God, I somehow had the sense to eat with him yesterday and today. Yesterday we talked over some of the methods of handling distribution from York and I had Harold pretty well convinced that basically things wouldn't change without the lab and the plant production in the same city with him. Today, he was in my office again and said he wanted to buy me lunch and I said all right, and we went over to the Terrace Lounge on Greenfield, a pleasant place. I bought Harold a scotch and soda and I had a bourbon old-fashioned. I was pleased to note that Harold was not acting jumpy or nervous. Perhaps that should have warned me. He complimented me on how well I was doing that impossible job of mine.

"That's to your credit, Harold, not mine," I said sincerely.

But Harold told me that this plant wouldn't be closing if they'd made me plant manager five or ten years ago. And he knew how hard it must have been for me to have incompetent men, one after the other, put in over my head. People who had no real feeling for Baker, for the men, for the product. He was very flattering. I had never really heard him talk this way. He usually just talked about himself and his problems. But he seemed to have reached a kind of serenity and I enjoyed listening to him. Then he quietly apologized for his behavior the past year or so. "I know I've been a pest to you, Frank, all these months."

"That's not so, Harold."

"Yes," he said, and smiled. "I know how much I've hung myself around your neck. But no more. Everything's going to be all right. I was bothered that the factory was leaving us, but I can see the sense of it now."

And on he went, assuring me that everything was going to be all right. And as he talked his nervousness really seemed gone. I actually believed him. He told me Jim Sweeney, his assistant was doing a fine job, and that things were never better in distributor sales. This afternoon he was going to do a little more work and go home early.

I told him I thought that was a fine idea, and then the food came and when we finished eating we went back to work. Harold left, as he said he would, about 3 P.M.

At 5 P.M. Jim Sweeney, Harold's assistant, came into my office and shut the door. He had just got a call from Mrs. Peterson. Harold had gone home early and his wife had to go out to Hudson's in Northland and wanted him to come with her. Harold said no, he had some work to do. And then he kissed her which he rarely did, told her to drive carefully. She had her own little car. He waved her out of the driveway and she went off to Hudson's. When she came back, he was dead. In the garage. He was 59 years old. Making over twenty-one thousand dollars a year. He wasn't going to have to relocate; nothing much would have changed for him except he'd have to telephone the plant in York rather than walk over to the plant across the yard. He had a history of psychiatric care, which no one but Tom Morgan and I knew about.

I called Tom and he came right up and I told him what happened, and I told him and Jim Sweeney that not a word about this was to get out. It was going to be a heart attack. Then Tom and I drove to the Peterson home. It was hard to believe that Harold and I had just had lunch a few hours ago. He had seemed so calm, so above the storm. I should have been warned. But I'm glad I at least had lunch with him. It would have been awful if I'd turned him down.

Right now I've got to consider Harold Peterson a casualty of this awful closing.

Friday. The news that Harold had a heart attack is all over the plant. Everyone is very quiet about it.

At noon I shook hands with ten men being terminated today. One of them wept. I told him it was only a matter of time before we all joined him and I wished him luck.

Doris and I ate out tonight. She wanted to know who had been terminated, and asked me more about Harold Peterson. I told her again it was a heart attack but I think she suspects. I changed the subject and she began talking enthusiastically about Arkansas. Her brother had caught a huge bass down there and he sent us a picture. She knew the kind of boat we'd buy once we got down there, one of those boat floats. We talked about the Ozarks and how we would probably give them a try. I owed it to her. Arkansas had still another thing going for it. It was far away. I had the feeling that as soon as *I* was terminated, I'd be wanting to go far, far away.

"You're thinking about Harold Peterson again," Doris said suddenly, accusingly.

"No, I'm not," I said.

He Came Out Looking
For Cartons

Name: Jefferson Barrett
Age: 62
Married: Lillian Dixon, 1940; died 1950; two daughters, both married;
    two grandchildren. Remarried—Alice Buckmaster, 1952.
Religion: Protestant
Education: high school, West Virginia
Occupation: 1932–65, Baker Color Company:
                         lye tank, shipping and receiving, lab techni-
                         cian, resin dept., grinding dept., supervisor,
                         shipping and receiving, supervisor at Fitz-
                         warren warehouse
Residence: 33210 Crest St., Detroit, Michigan
Health: good; wife very ill, stroke victim, diabetes.

Jeff Barrett who was a supervisor at the Fitzwarren warehouse at the end of the closing remembers Harold Peterson well.

"I'd have to," says Barrett, "it was his warehouse. Baker had seventeen warehouses around the country and Peterson was in charge of all of them. Ours on Fitzwarren was the main one. We shipped paint to the others. That last year we were shipping out almost 200,000 pounds a week of refinish. We'd ship them out in 17-, 30-, and 53-gallon drums. We were shipping thinner and other paints in cartons—pint, quart, gallon cartons and five-gallon pails.

"Peterson came out a lot that last year. He'd check on every last detail. Make sure the label of the distributor was spelled right, no detail was too small for him. He was a hard-driving, stern man. He had no small talk for anyone. He was always all business.

"Another reason Peterson came out a lot that last year was because of the increase in stealing going on there. Guys were stealing paint, buckets, ladders, scales, machine parts, tools. There were no guards till February when the company put Pinkertons on. They caught one fella driving his car right into the well and loading cartons of paint into it."

Barrett remembers Peterson's last trip out to the warehouse. "Of course," he says softly, "we didn't know then it was his last trip. Some paint had disappeared a couple of nights before and we thought here comes old Harold to give us hell again. He drove right into the truck well which no one is supposed to do. I thought, 'Oh, boy, he must really be mad now.' But he wasn't. He got out of his car and came over to me and he says: 'Jeff, I need some empty cartons. You got any extras?'

"I guess I stared at him. He says, 'We bought a new house and we're moving in a couple of weeks. I need some cartons.'

" 'Well sure,' I say. 'We got plenty of cartons.' I got out a batch of cartons—flats, broken down you know, and put them into his car. He just stood there and watched me. And when I was done he thanked me and drove off. He didn't go checking on anything at all. Two days later he was dead. I heard it was a heart attack. And just when he had bought a new house. He was a hard driver, Mr. Peterson. Hard on the men, hard on himself—too hard, I guess. And I heard he didn't have much luck from his son."

Barrett is silent. He dominates the living room, a tall handsome black man with gray hair, a man of dignity and grace and strength. He drives a two-year-old Buick that Frank Robertson helped him get at cost; he owns this old but solid and well-kept brick house, and he considers himself lucky. Lucky despite his own share of bad breaks. In a backroom, Mrs. Barrett sits in a wheelchair watching a portable television set. Two years ago she had a stroke and lost the use of the left side of her body. Since then a reactivation of her diabetes has made the loss of her right leg a certainty. Next week the Barretts are going to the hospital for final tests. Jeff is not optimistic. "We've had a skin graft, but the surgeon thinks she's going to have to lose the leg."

Mrs. Barrett, incredibly thin and gaunt, manages a smile. "Yes, Jefferson is wonderful," she says softly, "he takes care of me and does everything. I'm sorry I can't be more of a hostess to you."

Barrett bathes and feeds his wife, cleans the house, cooks, irons, shops, does the laundry.

"I don't mind it," he says, "though sometimes I've just got to get out of the house. Even just once a week. Sunday nights some neighbors come over and sit with my wife. I get out to our social club to play a little contract bridge or just talk with the boys. It's hard. But it's harder on her. There's nothing we can do about it. We've had some bad luck—" His face brightens as he adds, "But we've had some good luck too."

Among his good luck Barrett counts first his two daughters—both of whom hold college degrees from Johnson Smith College in North Carolina and both of whom have married well and are working. One is a school teacher in Columbus, Ohio, "not far from the new plant in York," he says ruefully. The other is a cancer technician in Detroit. Both girls are from Barrett's first marriage. His first wife died in 1950. Barrett took her back to their hometown—Taswell, West Virginia—to bury her. There, on a subsequent visit, he met the lady who would be his second wife and would bring up his girls.

Barrett is very proud of his girls and of his second wife. "She's a brave woman," he says. "You will never hear her complain."

Barrett says that another piece of good luck was his working at Baker for thirty-three years.

"It was a good place to work," he says, leaning forward in his chair, his eyes lighting up, "it was like a big family. We had good times, picnics, ball games. The men all got along. Just before the end, in December of 1965, the hourly had their last Christmas party. Ned Rockwell, the shop chairman, came to me and said, 'Jeff, we're having a farewell party at the hall. I'm not inviting you—you're salaried, but a lot of guys'd like to see you and say good-bye.'"

Barrett chuckles. "It was a long time since I'd been to the Christmas party. I was made a supervisor back in 1952, but I always got along with the men. I liked Ned. He worked under me at shipping and receiving for a while." Barrett grins. "When Ned became shop chairman he stopped working so hard. Perry DeMoss too. When Perry became chairman he stopped working so hard too. The truth is, those last years the union ran the plant. I'm not against the union; I was a union man myself for more than twenty years, and we needed the union badly in the beginning.

"I went to work at Baker back in 1932. I started as an equipment cleaner in the lye tank. All people of my race started there and usually stayed there. A man named Ed Clifton was my first foreman. The lye tank was hot, full of hot pipes, steam, and I remember there was a 150-watt bulb burning over our heads that only made it worse. The light through the window was all we needed, and somehow that bulb got to infuriate us. We didn't need it. It was the straw that broke the camel's back. Well, one day my partner, Sam Marshall, turned it off. A minute later the light went back on. Sam turned it off again, and sure enough the light goes back on again and our foreman, Ed Clifton, is standing there and he says to us: 'I turned those lights on. You might stumble and hurt yourselves.'

"We didn't need that light. He was just making things hard for us.

"In the thirties we had an inner plant union that didn't do much good. During the Depression when things were bad, orders came down to only work a half day till 1 P.M. This same foreman I was telling you about, Ed Clifton, put the notice on the board and he tacks on this too: 'The colored will work till noon.'

"I got angry. I told Ed to come on down to the lye tank and tell us that. I'm not a politician but when he come down I found myself speaking for all the colored there. I told him it wasn't fair the white get to work till one o'clock but the colored have to quit at noon. We feel you are prejudiced against us because we are black.

"It was as though no one ever said that to him. I told him he's got to see it from our point of view. I was boiling mad. I knew I just couldn't stand there that way without doing something I'd regret, so I grabbed the trash and began dumping it. I started working. And everyone else started working and Ed stood there. A little later that notice was taken down and everyone worked till one o'clock.

"But in those days management could do that to you. They could discriminate against you because there was no union for them to be afraid of. Now there's a union, and they're afraid. Now maybe they're too afraid. Now it's gone the other way. And I know because I became a supervisor.

"Paul Tilyard came over to me and told me, 'Jeff, it's about time you became a supervisor.' When I thanked him, he said: 'Don't thank me, my friend, you've earned it.' So overnight I was boss over guys I'd been working with for twenty years. It could have been bad,

but it wasn't. They knew they could trust me. The other supervisors would be running off to Frank Robertson, but I never did. I
didn't trust Robertson and I didn't like him. He helped me get my
Buick two years ago at cost, but I still never liked him. He played
favorites with people, and I knew he didn't like the colored. No
matter what he said. He talked one way to you and then another
way about you. He made foremen into toads. Mueller, Matt Gargan, John Franklin, Johnny Johnston, Jim Sweeney—they reported
to him all the time. He was an underhanded man, Frank Robertson
was. Lloyd Shearer was the only one who stayed independent and
honest. He was the only salaried man you could trust, and he was a
Southerner at that.

"Maybe Robertson felt he had to operate that way. I don't know.
But it wasn't good. I know he had his problems. When I moved
over to salary, I could see problems from the management's point
of view. There were times I just couldn't get guys to work. They'd
say it wasn't their job. Sometimes the job I'd be asking them to do
would be easier than the one they were doing. And it was only five
feet away, but they wouldn't do it. It was out of their classification.
And they'd pull all kinds of tricks to goldbrick and they'd sneer at
you. They knew the company wouldn't back you up, while the
union would always back them up. The pendulum had swung the
other way. Perry DeMoss and I were on opposite sides of the fence
then. I liked him and I respected him as a man, but we weren't
friends anymore.

"I believe in the union still, even with its abuses. And I guess I'd
probably be better off right now if I'd been hourly and had union
protection. I was just sixty and I got early retirement when the plant
closed. I didn't want it but what could I do? I'd been making good
pay—over $9000 a year. Our plans were that I'd retire at 65, rent
this house out and go back to Taswell to live, and travel a lot. I
thought maybe I could give bridge lessons, teach contract bridge.
But my wife's stroke December 13, 1964, and the plant closing
changed all that.

"It was Sunday morning. She hadn't been feeling too well for
sometime. The diabetes, rheumatism, arthritis—but she'd got up
about nine o'clock and was in the kitchen. She'd just made the
coffee and poured herself a cup when suddenly the cup began to
shake in her hand. She sat down on a chair, and her mouth was

shut tight. I sent for an ambulance. It was a massive stroke. She lost the use of all her muscles on the left side.

"In those days I was working at the warehouse. When she got back from the hospital I got a girl to come in and take care of her. The warehouse wasn't like the plant; you could duck out and make a call. So I kept in touch with her. There were 27 people working at the warehouse and two-thirds of them were under me. I was hoping that even after the plant closed they'd keep the warehouse, just to stock the distributors in Detroit. But they decided not to. They decided to ship up from York. I started hoping they'd ask me to go down to York. I would have gone. York isn't far from Columbus where my older daughter is. It would have been pleasant, living near the grandchildren, but they told me they weren't taking anyone. Which wasn't true. They took lots of the salary. But I can see it from their point of view. I was 59; they could get a younger man more cheaply. Robertson told me then I was going to have early retirement, and that's what I got.

"Right now I get 102 dollars from social security, and 330 dollars in my pension. I tried to get a job after the plant closed. I'm strong and healthy, but most everyone told me I was too old, or they wanted me to work for 25 percent less. I took unemployment compensation for 26 weeks and we kept on the girl who took care of my wife for that long, but then we let her go and I took over. We would have lost money paying her and me working at one of those old man jobs.

"We've gone through our bonds, and now I don't know. I pay 350 dollars a year on taxes on this house; six-fifty a month for health insurance to the Mutual Life, and that's 100-dollar deductible. The company set it up for me. They pay 75 percent of the balance after 100 dollars. We just got a bill for 155 dollars from the surgeon for the skin graft on my wife's leg. And she's going to have to go back into the hospital next week for tests and for them to decide what's going to happen next."

Barrett is bitter about the company on one score: He feels they owe him vacation pay for 1966. He worked all of 1965; he's entitled to three weeks' vacation, and he is bitter about that. "To the day I die," he says, "I'll know that they owe me three weeks' vacation pay. They gave it to Robertson and to Tom Morgan, but not to any of the others."

Barrett has heard about the industrial compensation suits that have been taking place recently. He's heard that a lawyer has said anyone who worked for twenty years or more at Baker and has no job now can get money on a health claim. Lungs, headaches, backaches, asthma—working in a paint plant over a long period of time never did anyone any good. He's heard that Willis Ingram got over $4500 on his settlement. Barrett worked for 33 years at Baker, and 20 of those years as an hourly employee, but he's afraid to see a lawyer about suing the company. The company could monkey with his pension, and he has no union to protect him.

Still, despite his wife's illness and the fact that he has no real job though he feels young and strong enough to be working, Jefferson Barrett thinks of himself as a fortunate man. Like Willis Ingram he is master of his house. It's true that as master he must play the servant—he must cook, sweep, iron, clean, feed, bathe, market—but he is doing it and doing it well. It is a true feat. And he is proud of his wife and her courage. And proud of his daughters and the stability of their lives and marriages. And perhaps most of all he is proud that the Baker men he meets occasionally on the street still think of him as one of them. "Because I always think of myself as a Baker man too," he says.

Baker in the Summer and Fall of 1965

It was eighteen months now since the company had first announced its intention to close down Baker. Nevertheless life at the plant seemed to flow on much as it had before. Trucks rolled out to warehouses; salesmen came and went, conferences and meetings were held as usual, and as late as the summer and fall of 1965 some of the hourly were still debating whether or not the company intended to close the plant. Some workers had left, others had been hired, most had stayed on at their jobs, even bidding on new ones within the plant, as though all the jobs would be there forever.

With the delay in the opening of the plant in York, Ohio, terminations at Baker had indeed slowed down, and by summer it was clear that those who were quitting for new jobs had done so. The rest—the great majority—were going to hang on till the end to collect severance pay, though the answer they still gave Frank Robertson was "We're going out like you said, Frank, with our heads up."

According to Robertson, of those who stayed, most worked hard. It takes more man hours to produce refinish which must be broken down into gallons, quarts, pints, and half-pints, than it does to produce the huge drums of original finish. Nevertheless, though overall paint production was down at Baker because the original finish had been moved to Cleveland, the plant's efficiency ratio—gallons of paint per man-hour—was as high as it had ever been.

This is not to say there weren't complaints and snags. Robertson says that one of his hardest jobs at the tail-end of the closing was explaining to his foremen why Ned Rockwell was permitted to spend so much time in the cafeteria. One day, however, a foreman from shipping and receiving came over to Robertson to tell him that Rockwell was not doing union business in the cafeteria or answering complaints, he was playing pinochle, and he'd been doing that all day long.

Robertson walked by the cafeteria and sure enough Ned was in there playing pinochle. Robertson didn't say anything then but a day or so later when Rockwell was in his office on some business, he mentioned the card-playing.

"I told him I said sure he could spend as much time in the cafeteria as he needed on union business, but that didn't mean playing cards.

" 'How do you know we weren't discussing company problems while we were playing cards?" Ned asked.

" 'Well, were you?'

" 'You're damn right we were.'

" 'All right, Ned,' I said, 'but it's hard for me to understand how you can be discussing serious problems while you're down there playing cards. However, you told me that you were discussing business while you were down there playing cards and I'm not going to call you a liar—but maybe you are.'

"Ned just sat there and looked at me and grinned and we went through it a second time, and he says: 'I guess you just don't believe we were discussing business, do you?'

" 'Ned, we discuss a lot of business over a lunch table, over a drink, and I suppose you could discuss business while you were playing cards. Anyway, it's a little late for me to make an issue over that, isn't it?'

"Ned didn't say anything. He just sat there and grinned. And after a while we got onto other matters, probably a grievance the shop committee was preparing."

Grievances, according to Robertson, were part of the game. And the company gave in on most all of them. "We had to," he says, "we'd gone this far and now the end was in sight." He smiles. "Perhaps Ned Rockwell really was thinking about his grievance business during those long pinochle games. They tried to milk the company right to the very end."

During those final months, Robertson told the supervisors to leave Rockwell alone. Sitting in the cafeteria playing pinochle he was, more than ever, in Robertson's opinion, a living sign that the men weren't taking any guff from the company.

"Besides," Robertson adds, "there just wasn't that much work for Ned to do anyway. Before the explosion we used to get in nine and ten tankers a day that the tankhouse crew had to unload. Now we got maybe one a day. There wasn't that much for Ned to do around the tankhouse. And he had to be around the plant for just that one. Sure he could have been raking the yard—" Robertson laughs at the idea of the union chairman sweeping up, and shakes his head. "But he couldn't do that, and besides, we had Big Dave Masiak for that job. That was Big Dave's department."

Robertson is silent. In talking about Rockwell, he grins, laughs, remembers with vexation and amusement their spats, but there was nothing amusing about Big Dave Masiak. Masiak was a punching bag for both union and management. Robertson remembers Masiak clearly because Masiak was an old-timer and because Masiak's record was one that Dr. Sidney Cobb particularly wanted to see when he visited with Robertson after the plant closed. And Robertson also remembers Masiak because he had urged Big Dave to look around for a new job, not to wait until the end.

"But I couldn't budge him," Robertson recollects, "and I think I know why. I'm pretty sure Dr. Cobb thinks this too: We made Baker too good a place for him and for others like him. Some years back Masiak hurt his back loading a truck. Though he was checked out as OK by the medical people, he still complained a lot and the other men didn't like working with him. Nor was he doing his job. So we made a special place for him. Sweeping the yard. We gave him his own department. And he swept. He did a job no one else did. He paid his way. Masiak was very important the last few months . . ."

Robertson's voice trails off, as though even he doesn't believe what he's saying. He shrugs. "I've always believed that every man is a human being. And every industry has a reasonable debt to society in the area of people like Dave Masiak. If we hurt them because we took care of them and then had to let them go, that's not our fault. It's the fault of the rotten world we live in. Don't you think?"

The Invisible Cripple

Name: Dave Masiak
Age: 55
Birthplace: Detroit
Education: eighth grade
Employment: handyman—odd jobs till 1935
       1935, Ford Motor Company, open hearth, Rouge plant
       1951, Sposito's Banana Warehouse
       1951, Baker Color Company:
              shipping and receiving, given janitor's duties in
              1964
Married: 1952, Helen Dembowski; 3 step-children
Religion: Catholic
Residence: Dearborn, Michigan
Health: poor—diabetes, hypertension, arthritis, obesity.

They let Dave Masiak go on Friday, October 29, 1965. He had fourteen years' seniority at Baker, twelve of which he had worked at shipping and receiving, and the last two years, the years of the closing, he worked as a janitor.

Opinions vary on Masiak as a worker. Robertson says that he did an honest day's work, even as a sweep-up. Tom Morgan says he was a goldbricker, both as a truck unloader and as a sweep-up. He says there were times Masiak would come to work an hour late and it was a nice day and someone would greet Masiak saying "Ain't it a great day to go fishing?" and Masiak would turn right around and go fishing. One afternoon Masiak showed up at three o'clock, just when the day shift was going home, carrying a string of fish he'd caught out at Edison Lake.

Dr. Cobb rates Masiak as marginal in intelligence. Because of Masiak's low intelligence level, he, Cobb feels, could not cope with the plant closing either before or after. Masiak's health problems which dominate his world today are mostly due, Cobb feels, to this inability to cope with the plant closing.

Masiak himself dates his health problems to that day early in 1964 when he got hurt at the plant. He remembers the circumstances clearly. He was unloading a truck and slipped between it and the loading dock and somehow got pinned by a drum. He strained his back and it has never felt right since.

He can date the incident because it was about the time the company sent every man that second letter saying they were definitely going to close, only most of the guys were still arguing whether it was a bluff or not. Masiak today insists he knew they meant it. "That's the way it is," he says with an amiable toothless smile. "When you have to go you have to go. I can't blame them. I don't think about it anymore."

What Masiak now thinks and talks about mostly is his health. He was one of the few Baker men to keep up his two-week health diary faithfully. He can remember exactly where and when he ached. Now he sits in his living room and tries to make a fist for the nurse.

"You see," he says, "I can't do it. It hurts so bad."

It hurts so bad from the arthritis, he says. He can hardly walk. His knee joints hurt, his back hurts, he has the arthritis in the spine a lot. His feet hurt too but the feet hurt from the diabetes. Every night he soaks his ankles for a half hour in cold water and they still hurt after that. The worst is the high blood pressure, because it's the high blood pressure that's preventing him from getting a job. He could control the high blood pressure and his excess weight and the diabetes and the arthritis with medicines, but the medicines cost money and he doesn't have money because he doesn't have a job and he can't get a job because of all the things that hurt him but especially the high blood pressure. He hasn't worked a day since Baker closed more than two years ago. There was that job opening in one of Dearborn's elementary schools—a janitor's job, sweeping up, the kind of thing he did at Baker toward the end. He went down to the Board of Education office and filled out an application. But they told him he had to take a physical at the Board of Health. And he won't go down to take the physical. "I couldn't pass it," he says. "My blood pressure is too high. I got to wait till I feel better."

This was over a year ago when he filled out the application. He won't withdraw it. This way he's still looking for a job. He's job hunting. Now though, he's not sure he could handle a janitor's duties. He read in the paper about plant guard openings. There's less work involved. He thinks he may take a crack at that when he feels better. He's not unemployed, he insists, he's sick.

Fat, toothless, a whining wreck of a man, he rates lowest in self-esteem of any of the Baker men on the psychological tests given by Dr. Cobb's nurses.

Yet it was not always like this with Masiak. In fact, it was once the opposite. Esslinger, who likes to work hard and respects those who do and has nothing but contempt for those who don't, recalls working with Masiak in shipping and receiving and he can remember when everyone called him "Big Dave" with respect and how strong Masiak was. "He was one of the strongest men at Baker," says Esslinger, and others have testified that Masiak was one of the few men who could handle the big drums by himself.

Masiak's early records at the company show many disciplinary actions. Gambling in the plant, stealing, fighting. Before he got married Masiak ran with a tough crowd in Detroit. Some of his buddies ended up in prison. They drank hard, lived hard, and found their money where they could. Masiak doesn't talk much about those days now but once in a while he talks wistfully about going back to Hamtramck and visiting some of the bars where when he used to come in the bartender would automatically set up a double whisky and say, "How're you doing, Big Dave?" He was tough then and afraid of no one.

Marriage softened him a little, he says. He got married in 1952, just a year after he went to work at Baker. His brothers and sisters had all the time been after him to settle down, but he liked his freedom. He liked going where he felt like at night, doing what he felt like. He liked taking off for fishing whenever he wanted to. He was crazy about fishing. When he was fishing he never wanted to be doing anything else, even drinking. But there comes a time when a guy should settle down. Part of it was finding Baker. He knew after the first few weeks that this was a good place to work— no one bugging you, all the guys liked it there. So when his brother Mike insisted he come over for Sunday dinner and finally meet that widow they had been talking about for a year, he went over.

She was a small quiet woman, the kind you didn't notice at first. She looked like nothing would bother her. The kind he liked. Mike said: "Dave, this is our neighbor, Helen Dembrowski. This is our Dave."

Just like that it was. They ate and they talked about how every-one was going to take a cottage on Lake Michigan next summer and how the kids were getting bigger and how nice Helen's kids were and how they took care of themselves and earned their own spend-ing money and how Helen's Rudy had left Helen with enough money to take care of herself and a house too. Pretty soon he had a few beers and he began to talk too. He doesn't remember what he said but it must have been OK because no one told him to shut up. The little widow was his own age, and she didn't have so bad a figure. She must know what she's doing, he thought. She had gray quiet eyes like she knew what was going to happen, which was more than he did. Anyway, he offered to take her home and when they got to her house she introduced him to her son Ron, a tall kid with pimples who shook hands and disappeared. She told him Ron had a job as an usher at some movie house, and how all the kids had got their own jobs. He made a drink for her and for him. He heard the other kids come in and go upstairs and heard her saying, "It's all right, Dave." He thought, *They know*. And he said, "I guess it is all right."

And it was. He had got himself a home and a family, just like that—a good marriage and a good job. Well, he still had the good marriage. They had hard times now but Helen had taken a job work-ing in a milk depot mornings, and the kid, Ron, still a bachelor, helped out some. But the job was gone. And the health was gone too.

If he'd only been more careful the day he hurt his back at the plant, because that was the beginning of it then, the beginning of the constant aching pain in the spine, the knee joints, the finger joints. He couldn't lift things anymore. They kept him on. Baker was good about that. They gave him a job as a sweep-up. It meant taking a pay cut from $2.70 an hour to $2.40, but it was an easy job and he could handle it. It was a funny job for him to have because that's what his old man did for the city of Detroit for twenty years after he came over from the old country. But he made more at Baker than his father made from the city. And it was easier work. It let him move around the plant, talk to guys in different depart-ments, play the numbers a little like he used to in the old days. He didn't think much about the plant closing. Especially after they rebuilt it. Life seemed to go on like it always did. Looking back now he thinks the union could have got the men a better settlement. He thinks he may be sore at the union, but not at the company. "That's business," he says, "if you got to go you got to go."

He didn't look around for other work before the closing. None of the guys he knew did. They all stayed on till they were terminated and picked up their severance pay. His back hurt so then he wasn't sure what kind of work he should be looking for. A friend of his ran a window-washing business and he told him he could have a job. But the first time he went up to wash windows he got all dizzy. He didn't take that job. And then there was the decision about the bait shop. All his life he'd wanted to run a little bait shop—sell night crawlers, worms, lures, flies, rods, hooks, sinkers, nets, waders —give guys advice. He knew a lot about fishing. He'd fished most of the lakes and rivers in both the Lower and the Upper Peninsula of Michigan. He could sit behind the counter and tell people what was best for them to buy, where to go. He and Helen often talked about investing his pension money and severance pay in a bait shop. Rent a store somewhere in Dearborn. But at the end he got scared. Suppose it didn't work out? He'd lose every cent of the pension money and severance pay. So they didn't open a bait shop. They banked the money and spent it piecemeal for food, medicine, utilities—and now there was none of it left.

For a long time he counted on that janitor's job at the Board of Education. He told everyone he was going to take that job, but the arthritis and especially the blood pressure were too much.

He looks at the portable blood pressure unit the nurse is wrapping up. "I bet it was high, wasn't it?" he says with an ingratiating, toothless smile.

"Not too bad," she says. It was 276 over 110—high enough.

He nods. He knows. No one can fool him about his health. He knows better than any doctor or nurse how sick he is.

"Is Mrs. Masiak still working?" the nurse asks, wanting to change the subject.

Masiak smiles in his trying-to-please-you fashion. Three of his front teeth are missing. There's no money to replace them. Someone's also told him it is impossible to get a job when you got missing teeth. No one wants to hire a man with missing teeth.

"She's still out at the dairy half-days."

"Do you get any other help?"

"The kid helps out. He pays us ten dollars a week for his room.

The wife brings in thirty." He grins weakly at the idea of three people living on forty dollars a week. "I'm sure glad the house is paid for."

His hands flutter nervously over his shirt buttons. "Say, did you happen to hear anything about some of the Baker guys suing the company?"

"A little," the nurse says.

"I got this letter from a lawyer."

He gets up to look for the letter. For a fat man who hurts he moves quickly. Indeed, as you sit there and watch him and listen to him complain about how he hurts in every joint of his body, you realize that he cannot sit still. Even when he sits, his feet shuffle, his fingers flutter or tap the ends of his chair, and he is ready to spring up and move about the room, constantly talking as he does, usually about his health and how it hurts him to move. Now, though, as he looks for the letter, he talks about the lawsuits he's heard about. "The lawyer says I should come see him. I left it here I thought. He says it's in my self-interest. Maybe my wife took it with her. I don't see why she'd do that. I hear some of the guys are getting a lot of money. I heard Don Taylor got more than five thousand. He wasn't sick at all. I got sick at Baker. I hurt my back at Baker that day. That's where my health started going bad. Right in the spine. The arthritis started there. I guess I'll wait till she comes home; she's probably put it somewhere. Do you think I ought to look into it? I hear the company is settling all those compensation suits."

He sits down again, in a different chair, under a crucifix hanging on the wall. His fingers begin tapping the ends of the arm rests. "I guess it can't hurt none to see a lawyer. What do I got to lose?"

"Did you ever do anything about that job at the Board of Education?" the nurse asks.

He gives her the helpless smile; it is similar to the amiable, hurt smile of Otto Mueller, the former superintendant at the resin plant who is now driving a school bus. The smile of men to whom life has dealt bad deals, about which they will not complain too loudly.

"I'm going to look into that as soon as I feel better," he tells the nurse.

"Mr. Masiak, they're probably wondering what's happened to you. You ought to go down there."

"I should. You know I read in the paper about a job as a plant guard. That's not as hard as sweeping. I think maybe I'll put an application in for it."

"What about that bait shop?"

He smiles. "Yes, I'd like to do that OK."

"What do you do with yourself all day, Mr. Masiak?"

"I read the paper. Watch TV. I sleep. I like to sleep a lot."

"Don't you do any more carving?" The nurse turns to me. "Mr. Masiak is a wonderful carver. He carved the big totem pole out back."

Masiak's face brightens. "I saw a man do it on TV, then I tried a few. The big one out back, a lot of people liked it. I'd like to carve some more but my fingers won't take it. I can't move them so good anymore. I got the arthritis right here."

"In the joints."

"Yes."

"How about your knuckles?"

"They hurt bad. And in my spine and my legs. It hurts getting up after sitting down. It hurts getting up after lying down. It's hard to get up in the morning. I can't garden anymore. I used to like looking after the wife's garden, but I can't do that anymore."

"What about your doctor? Have you been seeing him?"

"I saw that welfare doctor you told me about. For a while he gave me some free medicine, but—" His voice trails off.

The nurse knows. The welfare physician has simply grown tired of seeing Masiak. For a couple of months the welfare physician did pay attention to him. This came about because one day Masiak told the physician that he was going to commit suicide, he felt so lousy. The doctor paid attention, gave him tranquilizers. The pills made Masiak feel better. He kept coming back for them. But the trouble with suicide threats is that they only work once, maybe twice. The welfare physician stopped believing Masiak and cut off his free medicine. Now the welfare physician doesn't want to see him anymore. In his eyes, Masiak is a malingerer.

Sidney Cobb disagrees. "A welfare physician is trained to treat specific organic illnesses. He's not interested in depressed states. He's not trained in psychosomatic medicine. Masiak with multiple diseases has multiple complaints. A welfare physician by nature is prone to classify anyone with multiple complaints as a chronic complainer—i.e., a malingerer. And," Cobb adds, "you can imagine what this does to Masiak's already low self-esteem."

In Cobb's opinion, Big Dave Masiak is practically totally disabled. He is genuinely unemployable. His blood pressure is much too high; his headaches are bad, so is his arthritis, his diabetes, and obesity, and he is getting worse each day. He sits in his living room, rocking in his chair, unable to sit still even though it hurts him to move. He talks all the time about where it hurts, says he is still job hunting but is afraid to try seriously for a job. He reads the newspapers backwards to front, starting with the Help Wanted and working his way to the page one headlines. He knows all the local, national, and world news. He knows where all the jobs are, but he doesn't want to leave his living room, and he doesn't leave except on Sundays when he goes to church with his wife and his stepson, Ron. Masiak has six brothers and three sisters, but he doesn't want to see any of them, because he doesn't want any of them to see him. He is ashamed of himself. He feels guilty that his wife is working. He feels guilty because they don't have a car. They're the only family that has to walk to church, he says sadly.

If a man is totally disabled—blind, legless, armless—he can, at the age of 50, receive $300 a month in social security. Masiak, in Dr. Cobb's opinion, is totally disabled, but his disablement doesn't show on the surface. He is an invisible cripple.

At Baker there was a place for him, he functioned there. Now there is no place for him. His health and concern about his health has become Masiak's job, his way of life, his functioning. When he is not talking about his health, he is usually asleep.

"I like to sleep," he says. "When I sleep nothing hurts."

The Masiaks live in a small two-bedroom frame house with Johns-Manville stone facing on the lower part. There is a green aluminum overhang over the front door, and a green welcome mat underneath. The driveway to the small, well-cared-for but carless garage is lined with white stones that years ago Masiak found up north, brought back, and painted.

In the middle of the backyard stands a five-foot painted totem pole. Copied from the work of the Indians of the Pacific Northwest, it has fierce gods, beaked and awesome, stacked one on top of the other, defiantly challenging a hostile world. Immortality, courage, and belief—and all carved by "Big Dave" Masiak in the days before the arithritis got to his fingers and he stopped believing in himself.

The Rumor Mills

October and November were months of tension, trauma, and rumors both inside and outside the Baker plant. Outside the plant a wave of family illnesses was being reported: colds, headaches, flu, bronchitis. Three wives of hourly workers had ulcers diagnosed during this period; two sons of two different Baker workers were hospitalized for mental illness during this period.

As for the hourly workers themselves, the rumor mills were having similar effects. Duane Paddleford was losing his hair for the second time. He hadn't received any official notice of termination, but at the end of September he learned the four women office workers were being laid off the first week in October. This indicated to Paddleford that the closing date was coming soon. To his dismay that first week in October he began losing his hair again.

That first week in October also, Joe Nadeau began waking up in the mornings with sharp, shooting pains in his stomach. He went to the doctor, took tests, and was told he had an ulcer. Nadeau, a violent-tempered man, was furious at the company. Only five months before he had written in his health diary that he felt ". . . fine, always happy, busy and active, not worried about anything, busy fixing my car, mad that Baker is moving out after I worked for them for 19 years."

Now in October, bothered by his ulcer, by shooting pains in his foot—the result of a car accident some months before—Nadeau wrote that he was ". . . pissed off at Baker, disgusted because we're not getting more severance pay, sick because of this lousy mess at work, unhappy about the way they're treating us, not going to the doctor anymore unless things get worse because he charges too much, not worried about finding another job. I just hope like hell they'll lay me off so I can begin looking . . ."

Nadeau told a nurse he was staying for the severance pay. So was Jerry McNerney, who felt it just couldn't be much longer. "I'll be glad when it's over and I can get established in a new position," he told his interviewer.

Edward Szabo, who would turn out to be one of the occupational successes of the closing, disclosed that he had inside information that Baker had consulted with the union regarding possible extension of the closing date to February 28 but that the union refused to sanction an extension of less than a year. Perry DeMoss says he never heard of any such offer.

Other rumors in October:

Fred Smith, a batch mixer, says he's heard from a reliable outside source that November 1 would be the closing date. Two other men —Mel Stillwagon and Walt Bastien—also say the plant will be closing November 1. They know because they are cleaning out certain key tanks at a certain rate.

Big Dave Masiak contributes to the rumor mills on October 15. He's heard that Chrysler has cancelled their contract with Baker for all paint products, and they they're going to open their own paint plants.

Albert Lapin has heard a rumor that Ford is going to open their own paint plant and he thinks as soon as he gets laid off he'll go over there. "I'll get a job at Ford and help them get the boys in line," he says. Lapin, who is 56 years old, admits to being apprehensive about Baker's closing. "All I know is paints and cooking," he says. "I used to be a cook in Rhode Island years ago, but my feet hurt too much to go back to it." He also thinks Baker might fool everyone. "They'll stay longer than you think. Business is good now. They won't move so fast."

Lapin made this prediction two weeks before he was terminated, four weeks before the plant closed.

October 25. On this date Willis Ingram has learned that forty men will be laid off October 29. He has heard this from Perry DeMoss. Hank Cruickshank's wife has heard that fifty men will be laid off October 29. Steve Toucek says a foreman has told him the official closing date is November 1. Today, October 25, Ned Rockwell was given a list of forty men to be laid off on the twenty-ninth. He expects the list to get longer.

Monday, October 29. The list in Ned Rockwell's hands has grown to forty-eight men, including two men who retired. There is now a problem of insurance coverage for the month of November because this notice was given the last day of October. Rockwell says he cussed out Frank Robertson—everyone. He's tired and depressed. Management, he reports, wouldn't allow Floyd Rink who was leaving at noon to walk through the plant and cafeteria to say goodbye to all his friends. Floyd's been there 20 years. This upset everyone. The hillbilly is a popular character. "Floyd'd give you the shirt off his back if you'd wear it," Rockwell says. Six weeks later Rink will be in jail—not for stealing, which he'd done his share of, but for beating his step-daughter in a jealous rage. There have long been funny rumors about Floyd and his step-daughter.

November 2. Joe Black says there'll be no layoffs November 5, but a big batch are going November 12. He gets his information from Perry DeMoss. The colored, says Walter Jahnke, a pipe fitter, stick together. Jahnke thinks the UAW takes special care of the colored.

The union is giving a party on Saturday, November 6, for all the employees. Several say they won't go. Not in the mood for it. Some report their stomachs hurt. Others say what the hell good is a party when they couldn't keep the plant from closing? Pete Volak who prides himself on looking at things dispassionately says the UAW has lost contact with the working man in the smaller plant. "They look after the bigger plants because that's where the publicity is," Volak says.

Gene Vincent also blames the UAW for the closing. They wanted too much.

Jack Ramsey, whose stomach ailment has begun again as the closing draws to its final conclusion, blames management for having knuckled under to the UAW too often. Ramsey says he's not worried about getting a new job, but mostly he's looking forward to Christmas vacation. "I won't even put an application in anywhere till after the first of the year," Ramsey says.

Harold Simmons, who is ambitious and energetic, isn't sure who's to blame for the closing. On thinking it over, Simmons says he'd have done just what management did if it was his company. He thinks they made a smart move to go down to Ohio.

Joe Nadeau, who is Jack Ramsey's first cousin (the two don't get along), blames everyone for the closing, including "the federal government." "Higher taxes," he says. "They're moving to Ohio to get out of paying the higher taxes." He is furious at the Pennsylvania Corporation for its part, too. He says last year was the best year in the history of the company. "The bastards are just pushing us out."

John Kerrigan has heard that the new plant in Ohio is not to be unionized. Others have said this too.

Chester Wilson, 26 years at Baker, reports on November 4, "today the men are just walking around the plant. It looks like a ghost town."

Leonard Spiess is 51 years old and losing clumps of hair just the way Duane Paddleford is. He reports that he's heard the plant will close its gates officially December 1. He doesn't know what he'll do. Take a vacation probably. He's glad Christmas is coming.

Roy Menefee, who took another job, says all but sixteen will be laid off on November 12. They're going back to the 1940 hirings, Menefee says.

"How the hell does he know?" Ned Rockwell says irately. "He ain't even in the plant anymore."

The fact is that the men who've already left the plant are staying in close touch with the plant and with each other. Menefee works at Ford seven days a week and hates it. "You make good money," he says, "but money isn't everything. They think you never want to see your family."

Ramsey says he heard today, November 10, that one man who had resigned had committed suicide. Rockwell confirms that the man once tried to commit suicide, was hospitalized in a mental hospital, but has recovered. There appears to be little basis to the rumor, but the men take it as a tip-off that those who have resigned aren't any better off on the outside than they are, sticking it out to the end.

Barney Witenko is one who tried out a new job during his vacation period and returned. He says the work was too hard. He's staying on till the end. This is another clue that older guys will have to face heavier labor, plus no seniority, and, in all likelihood, working at night.

Milan Bobich's wife says that Nick Dudek, who resigned a month ago, came over to visit them the other night very depressed. He's got eczema. He says he's been refused employment at two plants till his skin clears and he felt he made a mistake giving up his severance pay. He didn't have the skin condition before he quit. "At least," says Mrs. Bobich, "he doesn't have a family to worry about."

November 15. Among those laid off today: Ramsey, his cousin, Joe Nadeau, and Albert Lapin. Lapin and Nadeau came to work drunk. Nadeau kept drinking all day in the plant and swearing at everyone—supervisors and fellow workers. "He's the most upset of any man in the plant," Jerry McNerney reports. Lapin, older and weaker, kept drinking all day too, openly but quietly. McNerney reports, "I had to take him home. He couldn't stay on his feet. His wife was very upset when she saw us bringing him home. Said he'd never done anything like this before."

Mrs. Lapin and McNerney put Lapin to bed. He was sick for five days. Mrs. Lapin reports he kept saying over and over: "The plant is all closed. There's no one there. Not even the union. There's no need for the union. Everyone is gone."

On Monday, sober, he got out of bed and started putting on his work clothes. "Where are you going?" Mrs. Lapin asked, astonished. "To work," Lapin said.

December 1—only forty men left. Henry Burns has heard a rumor that the company is only going to give Ohio a try for a year. If things don't work out they'll reopen Baker. Since he's heard of no plans to sell the old plant, Burns thinks this could very well be true. So do others.

Walter Jahnke thinks such rumors are stupid. He's a pipefitter, one of Robertson's skilled maintenance boys. Robertson is helping him get a new job. Jahnke will work to the very end, pick up his severance pay, and move into a new job at Detroit Diesel as a pipefitter. Baker was a good place to work, he says, there are other good places to work. Jahnke is not worried; he knows where he stands. "A pipefitter can always find a job," he says.

Jack Ramsey isn't worried either. Tall, handsome, hard-bitten, only 42 years old and well spoken, he too has a trade.

"I'm a truck driver. A truck driver can always find a good job. I'm not worried one bit. As a matter of fact, I'm looking forward to a little vacation. I won't even start looking for work till after the first of the year. I've got a lot of chores to catch up around the house."

More than two years later Ramsey, a skilled truck driver, will still be catching up on his chores. He laughs, with an edge of bitterness. "Oh, I'm looking for work. I went around yesterday and put in six applications. But you know what the trouble is? Everytime I get a chance to take a job I want, I'm sick. To tell you the truth, my health won't let me take a job since Baker closed."

Everytime I Get a Chance to Take a Job I Want, I'm Sick

Name: Jack Ramsey
Age: 44
Birthplace: Welland, Ontario
Education: high school
Employment: 1945–46, Acme Cartage
              1946–65, Baker Color Company: truck driver
              1965,   unemployed
Married: Daniella DeLucca; no children
Residence: Livonia, Michigan
Health: bursitis, ulcer symptoms, prostate infections, headaches for
    which he takes tranquilizers, ingrown toe nail, eye weariness in
    morning, twice hospitalized for double hernia repairs.

"And that's a lot of bull shit about his being too sick to work," says his cousin, Joe Nadeau. "Jack's a lazy bum just like his old man was. His old man was a college graduate and went to work as a grease monkey and retired at forty and lived off Jack's mother. And Jack's the same kind of queer bird. He's retired and living off his wife."

"Joe and I never got along," says Ramsey, grinning. "It doesn't surprise me his saying that. He tells one lie after another. Just last week I drove around and put in a bunch of job applications. But like I told you, it's got to be the right kind of job."

"What's the right kind of job?"

"As good if not better than I had at Baker. It's got to be days, and within 10 minutes' driving time of the house. I found a good job at ABC Trucking but no sooner did I show up for it than the hernia acted up again and I had to go back to the hospital. Now I got to take it easy for a few more months."

Ramsey is not terribly unhappy about "having to take it easy." He has the right kind of house in which to take it easy, a lovely brick home that cost the Ramseys upwards of thirty thousand. Ramsey, who is handy, has done a lot with it. He has panelled the basement and laid a vinyl tile floor there; he has put in a bar with indirect lighting all around it, though neither he nor his wife drink or entertain much. He has wired the house for hi-fi so that you can hear music in every room. In the living room there is wall-to-wall carpeting and tasteful modern art prints from J. L. Hudson's hang on the walls. The furniture is Danish modern.

Ramsey grins. "Pretty snazzy for a truck driver. Well, it's my wife. She's got the know-how in the family. My job is the outside."

Jack is particularly proud of the lawn and garden and of his roses. He has more than a dozen varieties: American beauties, JFK's, Bloodworths, English Country, Lebanon, and others. He planted each rose bush and cares for each.

"I always liked gardening," Ramsey says, "but right now you've caught me at a bad time. My bursitis doesn't let me do as much as I'd like to."

Ramsey dates the bursitis—and for that matter most of the rest of his health troubles—to the beginning of the closing. Back in 1963 he got stomach pains. They went away in the course of time, but just before he was laid off they came back. Now he goes for a check-up twice a month—on Thursdays. He laughs. "Tina and I alternate." he strokes the dog in his lap. "She goes every Wednesday, I go every other Thursday. We're a couple of hypos, I guess. I don't know whether I gave it to her or she gave it to me, but when you live together maybe it just happens like that. She's not feeling so well now. I took her to the vet last week and he said she's got a liver ailment of some kind. Maybe the living's too good, huh honey?"

Tina, a small, white, overfed poodle, barks playfully up at Ramsey. She sits in his lap and as he talks looks up from time to time and listens. Ramsey fondles her and the dog buries her face in his lap.

"It's funny, maybe not so funny, but I can remember pretty good the very first time I saw her. It was a crazy night—the night we got the letter about the plant closing. Back in '63. The day guys were talking about the letter when we got to work that day and the second shift just sat around most of the afternoon and evening and gassed about it. Ned Rockwell stayed on to tell us what he thought it meant and he thought just like everyone else thought; no matter what they tell you now, they all thought the company was bluffing. I was about the only guy there who didn't think so. Hell, that place was an old folks' home. They should have closed it up years ago.

"That night, I couldn't have loaded more than a dozen pallets. Old Morgan was mad at all of us but there wasn't anything he could do. I got off about midnight but I didn't feel like going right home. I guess I didn't feel like breaking the news to my wife. She never thought much of Baker or of my job there. Driving trucks. She left me alone though, and I left her alone. For a while we separated, back fifteen years ago. I don't want to get into that. We got together again and that's that. We've been under one roof ever since. She's always had her life and I've had mine. Sometimes I tried to make her understand why Baker was a good place to work. Like a family. Sure you goofed off, but when an emergency happened you all pitched in. I'm no electrician, but I helped rewire a whole building after the explosion. I'd been there 19 years and never got laid off once. Even during the recession in 1956 when the auto companies were laying off people right and left, Baker kept us on. They made work for us—scraping and painting the plant, cleaning up, working on trucks. We weathered the recession. It was a good place to work. There won't be another one like it. My wife never could or would see it that way. All she saw was that I was a truck driver there.

"Anyway, that night I didn't much feel like going home and telling her that the company was threatening to close down Baker, so I parked my car on Grand River, not far from the plant, and stopped in a bar for a drink. I'm not much of a drinker but I had a couple. I knew deep down they weren't bluffing in that letter, but it was still hard to believe, if you know what I mean. I mean Baker had been in Detroit before General Motors, before Chrysler, before Ford even. It was just hard to see how they could pick up and leave.

"I left the bar about one o'clock and walked back to the car. On the way I passed this pet shop window. I'd gone by this a hundred times and never really looked in. Pet shops are free shows. There was a monkey, some guinea pigs, and this litter of poodles. And everyone in that window was asleep except this one pup—and she was sitting there like a little lady, watching me watching her." Ramsey laughs. "I guess you could call it love at first sight."

"I just stood there and looked at her and remembered how it was when I was a kid and we had dogs. My old man liked dogs. He liked gardening too, and he was handy too. He could make real antique furniture. You won't believe this but he was an honest-to-God college graduate and you know what he did? He worked all his life in a gas station. Did I say all his life? That's a laugh. He retired at forty. I'm forty-four. He quit at forty. He had family money and he spent it on himself. He died only last month. . . . We got on pretty well. He left me his coin collection, and it's a good one. I figure it's worth about $5000, maybe more. At least that's what a guy in a store down at Woodward and Kirby appraised it for, a couple of years ago. I even added to it once. I bought a Hungarian coin I saw advertised for $50. My wife got sore. Said it was a kid thing and why wasn't I making real money instead of using real money to buy this kiddie money? You couldn't expect her to understand it. Hell, sometimes I don't even understand it myself. I should have sold the whole collection. I sold an old American coin from Massachusetts, a Pine Tree shilling, and a guy gave me seventy-five bucks for it. I heard he turned right around and sold it for two hundred which shows you what a chump I am. I didn't tell my wife about that. There's a lot of little things I don't tell her anymore. And I guess she does things I don't know about either. She's got her crowd. They play bridge, go to the movies. I don't have a crowd now that Baker's closed. I call up Duane Paddleford once in a while, and Big Dave Masiak to see how that goldbricker is doing. Once in a while my cousin Joe and I get together but we don't get along. I saw John Kerrigan downtown once. He's doing OK, I guess. Mostly Tina here keeps me company, don't you, honey?"

The dog barks; Ramsey chuckles.

That night in 1963, according to Ramsey, if it had been daytime and the store had been open he would have bought the puppy right then and there, but it was past 1 A.M. and he had to get home. He figured his wife would be asleep by now.

She was. And he didn't have to tell her about the letter. When he woke the next morning she was gone to work, so he didn't have to tell her about it all that day. And when he came home at midnight that night they had another thing to talk about—the dog. He'd gone out and bought her that morning. At first his wife was angry about not being consulted, but she had to admit the dog was cute, and since he promised to train her, feed her, walk her, she couldn't object too much.

It was a day or so later—he can't remember now—when Jack Ramsey told his wife about the plant closing.

"She shrugged," Ramsey says with a grin. "Baker didn't mean one damn thing to her."

Ramsey says his health got better over the next two years, but he started feeling poorly about September of '65. He never once thought about quitting early and looking for a new job. None of the old-timers did. Times were good and if the company was going to screw them, hell, he'd collect every last cent of that severance pay.

Furthermore, Ramsey says, he wasn't going to rush into a new job right away. Their house was paid for, Mrs. Ramsey was making good money at the advertising agency; they had no kids. Any new job was going to have to meet his requirements: as good as, if not better than, Baker; day shift, truck driving, and within ten minutes' driving of his house. Sure, that excluded a lot of trucking firms, but not all.

Meanwhile he had a lot of things to do around the house. He wanted to lay a new vinyl floor in the basement. He was going to use the severance pay to buy a color TV. And there was Christmas to get ready for.

He stayed home all that week after being laid off. He had a birthday; he was 41 that week, and his parents came over to dinner on his birthday. He and his father watched the new color TV. They didn't talk much about what kind of job he'd look for now.

During the holidays he got sick. A strep throat and his bursitis began bothering him again. He went to a doctor and got some shots.

"But let's face it," Ramsey says, and grins, "mostly I loafed. Like I'm doing now. I slept a lot. I got up, made myself breakfast, I'd putter around, nap till noon, make a sandwich, and then go out and look around the hardware store for things. Then I'd come back, watch TV, nap till dinner. My wife would come home and we'd eat and watch TV together if she wasn't going out. Then I'd walk the dog. That's how I get my exercise in winter."

Christmas 1965 came and went. After the first week in January—Ramsey doesn't remember the exact date—he went over to Kohn Trucking which was about five minutes away and put in for a job.

They called him a week later and he worked for three days and then got laid off along with some others.

"They telephoned me four days later and said to come back in, but I told them I'd got a new job meanwhile. Hell, I wasn't going to give them another chance to lay me off. I made a promise to my-self to get something as good or better than Baker. Three days on the job and they lay you off. That wasn't any Baker for sure."

He didn't put another job application in anywhere until March, and then about March, he says a cold settled in his prostate gland and he got an infection and was laid up for a month. They called him about the job but he couldn't take it because he was sick. He changed doctors that spring because the one he had been seeing wasn't doing much for him.

He got his exercise walking the dog, playing with her and he worked on his garden, which had really become beautiful since he now had some time to give to it. People used to stop their cars to look at his roses.

He tried keeping in touch with some of the Baker guys. He kept in touch with Paddleford especially. He heard from Duane about other guys at Ford. Duane was doing well. His hair was growing back. He'd heard, though, some of the other guys weren't doing so well. His cousin, Nadeau, was working his balls off on his six months probation at Chevy. Afterwards, if he knew Joe, he'd goof off for twenty years. Ramsey felt sorry for some of the older guys who had kids to support and a house to pay off and were now at the bottom of the seniority barrel.

The wife didn't bug him about not working. She went her way; he went his. They hardly talked anymore. She was going out with her friends three nights a week. Since he wasn't feeling so good with the prostate and the bursitis, and just a couple of months ago the hernia business again, he was having restless nights. So they agreed that she ought to get a good night's sleep and she moved into another bed-room.

The new doc he was going to said he had an inguinal hernia and it should be taken care of. That was in the fall of 1966. Ramsey had it operated on in mid-November, almost the anniversary of his termi-nation from Baker.

He took a long time recovering. He tired easily. And he thought a lot about his father's early retirement. In December Ramsey was 42.

By the spring of 1967, he was recovered from the hernia operation. But it still hurt everytime he lifted something. The doc said it
might have to be corrected again but to give it more time. So he gave
it more time. That spring and summer he should have been working
on his garden but it wasn't much fun bending over. The bursitis. He
gave up the roses in the summer of '67.

The only thing that gave him any pleasure was the dog—Tina.
You couldn't really explain to anyone how smart and affectionate she
was. She came into his bed each night when he went to sleep and
slept stretched across his feet. The wife never said anything. She'd
give the dog a Milk-Bone once in a while but she never walked or
ever played with her.

Every once in a while he'd go for a drive in the Buick and put in a
half-dozen job applications, but then the hernia would start acting
up, and he'd have to stay home and take it easy. While he sat around
he thought a lot about the old days at Baker. About Big Dave, Ned
Rockwell, Matt Gargan his supervisor, Duane Paddleford, his cousin
Joe who had made it at Chevy and was now goofing off, about all the
guys, the times they had, the pinochle games, the explosion, the
emergency work, the never ending debate about whether the company was bluffing or not, the bull sessions, the gossip—there would
never be another place like Baker.

And then suddenly, as happy as he was remembering the old
times, he'd get nervous, turn off the TV, which he wasn't watching
anyway, turn off the hi-fi, which he wasn't hearing anyway, and Tina
would sense something was wrong and lick his fingers. Once he
shoved her away and she looked at him and tears came into his eyes.
"I'm sorry, honey. I didn't mean to hurt you. You forgive me, won't
you?"

She ran off into the bedroom and he had to go after her and tickle
her and they played a little and she came out of it.

But lately she wasn't feeling so playful. There was her liver ailment. And the vet thought she was showing a little arthritis in her
hind feet. She didn't like going to the vet but he coaxed her with
some chocolate dog nibbles.

He went to his doctor on Thursdays; she went to the vet's on
Wednesdays. They went together to each doctor. The vet thought
there wasn't much he could do for her. Work on her diet a little,

vary it. She needed more exercise. Ramsey told the vet he was willing to walk her but she liked playing inside.

On Thursdays he went to his doctor. He'd run through three doctors since he got terminated. This new guy gave him pills for the bursitis. And when he asked him what he thought he should do about his hernia's acting up again, the doctor said these pills would take care of that too.

"What the hell kind of pills are they anyhow?" Ramsey demanded.

The doctor told him they were tranquilizers.

That was the last straw. Ramsey grabbed the dog and they left the doctor's office. He'd find another doctor. When he got home he flushed all the pills down the toilet. He was furious.

"We don't need those kind of pills, do we, Tina?"

The dog barked.

He laughed, shakily, and sat down. The dog jumped onto his lap and he stroked her and gradually his rage subsided.

"The most important thing in life today," says Ramsey, with a smile, "is life itself. I wake up every morning happy that the sun is shining or the rain is falling. I wish good health for all of us. Including you."

Final Days

At the end everyone had his own closing. Jefferson Barrett's last days were spent sitting in an empty warehouse listening to his radio and addressing Christmas cards. He would call in to the security service operator each morning to let her know he was there. Then he'd call the main plant in the afternoon just to chat with someone. Sometimes Frank Robertson would come by late in the afternoon on his way home and they'd chat, but there wasn't much to say. It was lonely but pleasant those last few days, sitting in the empty warehouse working on his Christmas cards and listening to the radio.

On his last day, December 30, Robertson took Jeff Barrett and the other supervisors out to lunch.

"He called out to the warehouse the day before and said for me to wear good clothes, that he was taking me out to lunch. I closed up the warehouse that last day at 11 A.M. and came over to the main plant. All the supervisors were there in their good clothes. There was some joking about it being too cold to go fishing. I turned in my I.D. card and my keys. They'd turned theirs in too. Then we all went over to lunch at Gremlins on West Morton. There was about a dozen of us. Robertson bought us lunch on his credit card. There were no speeches. We'd already had a party on December 11th over at a night club on Plymouth Road. Robertson got up and made a speech about how much he appreciated our service through the years. There was a photographer there who took group pictures. Our gold clocks or watches were presented to us. I had chosen a clock. Three weeks later over at Gremlins for lunch there were no speeches. We all just ate between 12 and 1 in our good clothes. Afterwards we shook hands and went our separate ways. I came back home. The girl that was taking care of my wife was surprised to see me. I sat there and talked with her and my wife. I just sat there all afternoon talking in my good clothes. My, it felt funny."

That was December 30, 1965. Just a few weeks after the last of the hourly workers had been laid off. Most of the hourly had gone on the Fridays of November. It was maintenance people, the union committee, and a few old-timers who were permitted to stay on into December.

"The manner of choosing who'd go and who'd stay," Frank Robertson recalls, "was determined by seniority within a given area and after that by who would still be needed to make paint. I'd meet with the supervisors and the superintendents and we'd go over lists of men, who was staying, who was leaving. It wasn't easy. But we were able to go on making paint until the day before the end."

Those last weeks, however, Robertson was less concerned with the hourly people than with his salaried personnel. "The hourly had the union looking after them," Robertson says, "the salaried had no one but me. And this brings up one of the most degrading experiences of the closing for me. Because General Office was always responding to union pressures, they didn't have time for the salaried people. The salary people who were being terminated didn't know till way late in the game what their annuities or severance pay were going to be. It made them very uneasy, to say the least. I tried time after time to get answers from General Office and they gave me one excuse after another. The actuarial figures weren't ready, and so forth. I kept after them about this and finally in the last few weeks I got the answers. Now at least I could call somebody like Esther Lindquist, who'd worked in accounting for fifteen years, a widow who was putting her kids through college and still paying on her house. I could call her in and happily say, 'Esther, I've got the figures you've been waiting for.' And I could say, 'Esther, when we terminate you, which we think will be about such and such a date, your severance pay will be this and your annuity will be this.' There were some thirty-odd people like Esther. I called each of them in and gave them their figures. Well, twice the company informed me that the figures they had given me and which I had passed on to two people were wrong—too much money was being given to them—and each time I had to go back and call these people in and tell them their amounts were to be reduced. It was humiliating and degrading. And it made all of the salaried people suspect me and suspect all the figures I'd given out. Some of the confusion was caused because social security benefits went up about this time, which meant that the amount of money the company was going to pay for a period of time went down. Twice I had to call people back in. Now those people ought to hate me. They just all ought to hate me, don't you think?"

He is silent, waits for assent, gets it.

"And then there came a third case. They wrote me and told me a third mistake had been made and I was to call another person back in and tell him he was going to get less money than he thought. That was it. I called Wysse Allen in Pittsburgh and told him no more. I told him that unless he personally assured me that this was it, I was not going to go back to that third person. That all the were now in and that they were final.

"Allen apologized. He said he was wrong in approving those sets of figures and if it was any comfort to me, the man who drew them up was no longer with the company. But it didn't matter because it wasn't any comfort. I'll have a deep-seated resentment as long as I live for what they put me through. Those moments at the end when I had to go back and tell people they were going to get less money than I said they were, those moments were even worse than the lie I lived at the beginning of the closing when everyone was congratulating me on becoming plant manager and none of them knew that I'd been picked plant manager to bury our plant. It was a nightmare at the beginning and the end, but especially at the end."

It was during this time, in early December, that Robertson first knew he was getting sick. His skin felt as if it had been sunburned, his lips were dry. He felt hot. When he moved he had a burning sensation all over his body. He called his doctor from the office and told him of this odd sensation. The doctor, an old friend, urged him to stop in for an examination on the way home, but Robertson couldn't. Things were ending up at the plant. Only days were left. Finally on Friday, December 17, one week after the last of the hourly workers had been terminated, Robertson went to visit his doctor.

A nurse took his temperature. It was 103. The doctor came in and Robertson recalls his standing against the doorjamb and saying: "Why didn't you wait till you were almost dead?"

He gave Robertson a thorough office examination but strangely could find nothing wrong. He checked his throat, sinuses, chest. He ended up prescribing a heavy dose of antibiotics and asked Robertson to call back in a couple of days. Three days later Robertson's temperature was still high. The burning sensation was still there and to it had been added diarrhea and general weakness. The doctor put him in the hospital for two days and more tests were administered. He was taken off the antibiotic. Indeed, it was at this time that he was told that in all likelihood the antibiotic had done too good a job, killing many helpful bacteria in his system.

He came out of the hospital on Wednesday, weak and depressed. But Monday, the 27th, he was back at work. This was the week he terminated the supervisors and had a farewell lunch with them. After that week, in the new year of 1966 there were only two people from the production staff left at the plant—himself and Tom Morgan. The plant was an empty shell.

"With a little imagination," Robertson says, "you could still hear the echoes of the fork trucks, the machines, the tankers changing gears as they rolled into the yard, the swearing of the men loading and unloading. You could still smell the smells—the paint, lacquer, thinner, oils. They took a long time leaving."

Robertson didn't do much in his office those days but finish off records. There was no report to write to General Office on the closing, nothing was ever set down in writing. But a lot of work records had to be checked, signed, and stored away, and in forty-two years a man accumulates a lot of personal mementos—mementos from conventions and business trips, pictures of old friends and bosses, personal letters, pen and pencil sets. Every night Robertson took home a carton of personal belongings. At night he sat and listened while Doris talked and worked on her doll collection. She talked about Arkansas, about selling the house in Detroit, about getting away from it all—the past, his problems—about starting a new life. He was still sick each night—vomiting, diarrhea. There had been a diagnosis of what ailed him—mucous colitis. It was something he might have to live with the rest of his life. It could be controlled with medication. He needed to take a rest, a long rest. Well, they were going to retire him in February.

It was during this period—after the plant had closed but before he formally retired—that Robertson received a visit from Dr. Sidney Cobb of the Institute for Social Research. Cobb, he says, informed him about the health research study he had been undertaking since May with the union's cooperation and sought permission to look at the work records of certain hourly personnel to get a profile of past sickness and absenteeism. Robertson had heard about the study from two or three different people and could see no objection to it. He agreed to let Cobb look at what records he could find that hadn't been stored away.

Dr. Cobb has written of this visit: "Robertson and Morgan received us. Robertson was very courteous and agreeable. He never thought he had to clear our request with the Pennsylvania Corporation. If this health study could help the men, he would cooperate with it in any way he could. He talked a lot about the plant and the men. How much it and they had meant to him. He talked a good deal about the old days when the Baker brothers were making japan colors and carriage paints. He described the original plant at 24 Baltimore Avenue, a two-story brick building and next door to it a wooden frame house in which the offices were located. He recalled the day that the Pennsylvania Corporation had bought out the company, the day they moved from Baltimore Avenue to the present site. He recalled his own days as a laborer and how he had worked his way up.

"Mr. Robertson told us quite a number of stories about the closing. Some of the most painful to him were about the refusal of employees to take other jobs when they were offered them. He expressed his personal feelings about the effects of paternalistic policies that he had administered over the years and especially about their tendency to leave a man ill-equipped to deal with the vicissitudes of the cold hard world. It is my impression that this was not an independence-dependence issue but rather an issue of the strength of the cathexis and the magnitude of the loss created by the separation from the plant. Robertson was concerned that the severance pay held men for longer than they should have stayed at the plant. I was forced to disagree with him in that I think only a relatively small number of the men stayed solely for the severance pay though, of course, this is difficult to estimate. Most of them stayed out of loyalty to the company, some stayed simply out of fear of the unknown, and naturally some stayed out of a desire for the severance pay. It is worth noting that some of the men who were in the company have remained dependent beyond their termination. Mr. Morgan reports that nearly every day men who have been terminated come to him and ask for advice and help.

"We were given a free hand to abstract such information as we might desire from the personnel records."

Frank Robertson himself was terminated on February 28, 1966.

He put in a full day's work finishing up on the records. Then at three-thirty he put on his hat and coat and walked through the plant alone. He walked through every building. Through Buildings 2 and 4—the heart of the plant production; through the labs with their ovens and test ball mills and mixing tanks; he walked through the filling and mixing and canning rooms; he gazed at the small assembly lines in the filling rooms—30 cans a minute—York would do more than 150; he walked through Building 12, the lye tank; through Building 18—the grinding department with its huge ball mills from which pastes were put into drums and transported to Buildings 2 and 4; he walked through the deserted shipping and receiving sheds; through Building 7 with refinish sales' meeting room where sales employees could meet, sometimes with mechanics from around the state, to discuss new methods of putting refinish on a car; he walked through Building 13—the resin department—through the filter press room, around the storage tanks, the huge electric kettles; he walked through Building 17, the tankhouse where Ned Rockwell had held sway for so many years; through the thinner and lacquer building.

"It was a quiet and lonely walk—but that's the way I wanted it," Robertson says. "I wanted to fix the plant in my mind. Some of the happiest days of my life had been spent in those buildings and I wanted to remember them. I knew I would never go back there again."

Finally, Robertson walked back across the yard to the office buildings where the sales offices were. There he shook hands with everyone—secretaries, salesmen, the two janitors. There were some tears, he remembers, but he didn't cry.

He shook hands last with Jack Whitsell, the office manager of industrial sales. Whitsell was to be in charge of the empty buildings until they were sold.

"She's been a grand lady, Jack," Robertson said softly. "Keep her face clean."

Then he took a carton that contained the last of his personal belongings, went out to the main gate, signed out, shook hands with the guard and drove out of the plant for the last time.

He was sick all that night and stayed in bed the next two days, getting up only occasionally to watch Mrs. Robertson glue sugar cubes onto her doll house. On Monday he called a real estate agent and told him he and Mrs. Robertson wanted to sell their house. They were moving to Arkansas.

"We were burning bridges," Robertson says with a rueful smile, "something I'd advised others against doing. But I had to do it."

Odd as it sounds, the farewell to the plant that Robertson recalls most clearly and feels most deeply was not his lonely walk through the deserted buildings, or the quiet goodbyes to the sales staff. He remembers most vividly the laughing, swearing, drunken farewell that took place more than two months before when he bade good-bye to the last of the hourly employees.

All that were left of the hourly on their last day—December 10, 1965—were maintenance people, the members of the union committee, and a few old-timers. At 11 A.M. Robertson walked over to the maintenance department to say good-bye to his favorites. "They *were* my favorites too," he says. "They knew every inch of the plant, every pipe, every electric line, every tunnel, every machine. They knew this plant as only men who build and repair things can know them."

They were waiting for him too. About fifteen of them—old-timers, each with more than twenty years' seniority, standing in a semi-circle, waiting to shake his hand. "Well, boys, this is it," he said. "There's no more work to do this afternoon. We're taking the afternoon off."

"We figured you had an idea like that, Frank," one of the men said. "We're way ahead of you."

They'd been banking the fires for two days, putting the plant slowly to bed. They had already closed everything up, figuring that Robertson would give them Friday afternoon off.

"Good," He paused. Words came hard. "I want to thank you boys for your loyalty and hard work through the years and especially during this long and hard closing."

He'd got through it and everything would have been all right then if suddenly one of the maintenance boys, a tough little Italian who'd worked there for more than twenty-five years, hadn't suddenly burst into tears. Tears ran down his face.

"He grabbed my hand. 'Now, Tony,' I said, and I couldn't talk either. I patted his hand, shook hands with the others, and turned and walked out before I broke down too. I went over to the cafeteria. And there was Ned Rockwell and the members of his union committee sitting there drinking coffee. Some things never change, I thought, smiling.

" 'Well,' Ned says, 'there you are. We were wondering when the hell you were going to show up here.'

"I laughed. They laughed too. I told them I'd come to say good-bye and to tell them they could take the afternoon off.

" 'We know about that too,' Ned said. And he grinned. 'And we got an invitation for you too. We're all going across the street, us, the maintenance gang, whatever old-timers want to come along, and we're going to get good and drunk and cuss this rotten old place out, and we want you to come along and have a drink with us.'

"I stood there a second, I hadn't expected this, and I didn't know whether I could take it. But they were all there looking at me, men I'd hired, fought with, praised and punished.

" 'I'll be privileged to come along.' I said.

"So after lunch we went solemnly across the street, and they bought me a drink, a bourbon old-fashioned, and then I bought them all drinks and we fell to talking, to remembering things, sometimes how they were and more often how they weren't. Everyone told his own story, the funny things, the angry things, stories about guys who'd left fifteen to twenty years ago, and what happened to old so-and-so who had worked in S and R and used to pitch horseshoes behind the boiler room, incidents out of the past came tumbling out, fights, ball games. Perry DeMoss came in and had a drink and pretty soon he was claiming he was the best second-baseman that Baker ever had, and on it came: old Christmas parties; old secretaries; rush orders from Chrysler that had kept them hopping week-end nights; the big snowstorm in 1952, and the time Ramsey and Paddleford backed a truck into forty drums and the drums went rolling every which way and Ramsey laughed and laughed; and the time the trucks got stuck in the yard during an ice storm and the drums started rolling off; Steve Toucek's fight with what's-his-name. . . . And on it went like that, stories that were partly true, maybe even mostly true. I knew then, watching the men drink and listening to each man tell his tale, that each of them had his own Baker, each had his own plant, and each had his own memories to last him the rest of his life. It had been a good place to work—for all of us.

"I stayed about an hour and then I got hold of the manager in the corner and told him to let them stay as long as they wanted and to put the bill on my name. Then I ducked out. No one saw me go.

"When I got home, Doris was waiting for me. She said: "How did it go?"

"It went all right," I said. "I bought them drinks. They'll have a good free drunk on the company. God knows they deserve more."

"We started at 1 P.M. about." Ned Rockwell recalls with a grin. "We bought old Robertson a drink right out and then he bought. He bought for all of us, but we didn't know that at first. He left. No one saw him go. About six o'clock someone says where the hell did Frank Robertson go, and the barmaid says 'He went home but he said to tell you he's paying for all the drinks.' Well then we really got down to serious drinking. What time did I get home, honey?"

"About two in the morning," Mrs. Rockwell says with a smile, embarrassed for him, but a little proud too.

"She's got to know," Ned says with a laugh. "I don't remember a damn thing except for the early part. His buying. His sittin' there, small, funny, and quiet—listening. Him and me, sittin' together. Two different kinds of guys who'd really been doing the same job." Ned laughs again, but there is a bitter edge to the laugh. "Yeah, I felt that then, and it was true then, but I sure suckered myself out with that feeling."

"What do you mean?"

"You know, at the end he was giving everyone recommendations for new jobs and he came over to me and he says, 'What are you going to do, Ned?'

"And I say, 'I dunno. But I've been thinking about opening a janitorial business.' I was, too.

"He doesn't say anything, but a few days later he takes me aside and he says: 'There are lots of brooms, mops, buckets and soap cartons that the York plant isn't going to need and they won't bring in much for the company at an auction. I want you to have them, Ned.'

"I thanked him and took all the mops, brooms, and buckets. I still got them out in the garage. A couple of days before we closed, it was almost like he had an inkling of things to come, he comes over to me and he says, 'Ned, I've written recommendations for damn near everyone in the plant except you. Don't you want one?'

"Sure I wanted one, I knew that. But . . . I couldn't take one from him. Him and me, we'd put that old plant to bed together. The men—they were our men. We'd mothered it and fathered it and done a good job—together. We were equals and we both knew it. How could I have taken a job recommendation from him? I couldn't. I said to him, 'Hell, man, what am I going to need a recommendation from you for if I'm going into business for myself?'

"He didn't say anything for a moment, then he smiles and says: 'I guess you got a point there, Ned.'

"We let it go at that. I didn't get a recommendation from him. I suckered myself for sure, didn't I, honey?"

"You did right," Mrs. Rockwell says quietly.

"Right like a dumb-dumb," Rockwell says, and laughs. "That old Baker plant."

"Have some more tea," Mrs. Rockwell says.

Winners and Losers

The plant was closed. If one dates the beginning of the closing from the first official letter sent out by the company in November 1963, it had taken a little over two years to close the Baker plant. In those two years, men stayed at their jobs, production increased, and even after the explosion, production efficiency was as high as it had ever been. Although the plant blew apart at one time, it never fell apart.

What later happened to the Masiaks, the Ramseys, the Mc-Nerneys, to Ned Rockwell, Henry Burns, Duane Paddleford, Frank Robertson—is another story.

Although the analysis of the health data from Dr. Sidney Cobb's study will go on for at least another two years, Cobb's research so far reveals that out of 54 men still left in his study, the Baker closing and its immediate aftermath precipitated 3 cases of ulcers, 8 cases of arthritis, 5 cases of hypertension that required hospitalization, 2 cases of labile (fluctuating) high blood pressure, 6 cases of depression severe enough to require medical help, 1 case of alcoholism, and 3 industrial accidents suffered by men in new jobs they disliked. In addition there were two cases of alopecia (loss of hair)—Leonard Spiess lost his hair once, and Duane Paddleford lost his twice.

Dr. Cobb is inclined to place part of the blame for the high degree of sicknesses among the men (much higher than it is to date in any of the control groups) on the undue length of the closing. He feels that two years is too long a time in which to close a plant. "No man," he says, "should be forced to lose his hair twice."

Down in Arkansas, Frank Robertson, sick with guilt from his own role in the plant closing, misses—indeed, for his own sanity, must miss—Cobb's point. "Two years," he says, "isn't too long a time. If a man can't get a job in two years, he's only got himself to blame. Isn't that so?"

"The stronger men will always cope," says Cobb. "They will get out and manage whether a plant closing takes two years or ninety days. These men can see the handwriting on the wall and can do something about it. The others can't, and they get hurt."

So far, for the writer of this book, at any rate, there is no evidence that men who resigned early to take other jobs ended up any better off than those who stuck it out to the very end. Orvie Blackburn (who chose not to participate in Cobb's study) was one who saw the handwriting on the wall and quit early and he was the only suicide among the hourly.

The difference between success and failure might seem to lie in a mixture of luck, job skills, the kind of wife a man had, his age, intelligence, and emotional make-up.

Pete Volak, at 36, was young, energetic. During the last years at Baker he moonlighted, as many did, driving a linen supply truck for his brother-in-law. Pete stuck it out to the end, then dropped the moonlighting when he went to work at Riis-Moran, the other big paint plant in Detroit. Like most of the Baker men who got jobs at Riis-Moran, Volak was laid off when work slowed down in the spring of 1966. He began driving the linen truck for his brother-in-law full-time, and found out he really liked it, liked getting away from the fumes of a paint plant, and he found he was making more money full-time with the linen supply truck than he had ever made at Baker. Volak was lucky to have had a brother-in-law in the linen supply business.

Edward Szabo is fat, arrogant and lucky. Along with Willis Ingram, who has done so well in the numbers game since he left Baker, Szabo is a genuine success story.

Szabo always had a part-time interest in politics. He was president of his P.T.A., and did campaign work for the Democratic party from time to time. But for the plant closing, Szabo would have been a kettle operator all his life. Now, thanks to well-placed friends, he is purchasing agent for the city of New Boston, making a good salary, and looking forward to even greener fields through his now ever-increasing political connections.

A sidelight to this is that Mrs. Szabo is not as happy as she used to be. The man who holds political office is not the same man she knew as a kettle operator. The Szabos have separated.

Another job success whose marriage is in trouble is Harold Simmons. Simmons, like Szabo, is doing better now than he ever did at Baker. At Baker he had been an electrician. The job did not satisfy him but, on the other hand, working conditions were good, he had time and energy to play ball with his sons, coach them in the Little League, time to do things with his wife. He says today that if they hadn't closed the plant, he'd still be back there making his three dollars an hour. Simmons, ambitious, energetic, stayed on till the end and then took a job as an air-conditioning engineer because he wanted to become more than a technical man. The air-conditioning job didn't suit him—it wasn't big enough—and in January of 1966 he took a job as a dispatcher at the Consolidated Gas Company. It was an important and difficult job. He was responsible for the remote control of all gas valves between Chicago and Detroit. It was complicated and taxing work and for two years Simmons wasn't sure he could master it. During those two years he saw little of his family.

Mrs. Simmons, who had a history of nervous disorders, was no longer able to count on him. She claims now that her husband's new long hours weren't only for his job. "He didn't have any time for social life, for anything, if you know what I mean," she says. Mrs. Simmons says she began following her husband after he left work and one evening she caught him in his car with another woman. Simmons will neither confirm nor deny this. He will only say that the reason he and his wife are now getting a divorce is probably his fault. He says that his wife has always been emotionally unstable but where he used to have time to help her weather her crises, now because of his new job, he no longer has the time.

In some cases wives were hit harder than their husbands by the Baker closing. Cobb's nurses report that out of fifty-four families, three wives came down with ulcers during this period, two with arthritis. There was one case of hypertension and a case of asthma. One woman was hospitalized for mental illness during this period, one for tuberculosis, and one for skin cancer.

The nurses report that four marriages seem to be in trouble since the plant closed, and there have been two divorces.

In addition, children of Baker employees have been affected by the closing. Two brothers, 17 and 18, went into a mental hospital one month after the plant closed. Their father was one who came down with arthritis during this period. One 16-year-old girl, unmarried, became pregnant, one 15-year-old girl was severely beaten by her step-father and required hospitalization. Again the control groups have showed no such parallel upsurge in family illnesses and social problems.

If the wives suffered alongside their husbands—and in some

cases more than their husbands—it is also true that many of them provided the buttressing strength that enabled their men to weather the change. Joe Nadeau who left the plant in a drunken rage on his termination day, had a wife who worked, who supported him emotionally, who made decisions for him. Nadeau, who is extremely prone to psychosomatic illnesses and had ulcers and headaches the last three months of the closing, has made it on his new job thanks mainly to a tough and supportive wife.

Leonard Spiess also has a good wife, but he was too low on self-esteem to weather the change. In January of 1966, he took a job in a chemical lab. He worried about his health in the new job and, sure enough, he got a rash from the fumes, a rash that spread everywhere on his body, including his mouth and nose. His only hope was that the company would put in a blower to blow away the fumes. "I thought maybe they'd find it cheaper to put in a blower than pay for my treatment at the clinic. But I guess they found it cheaper to fire me. I don't blame them."

Unfortunately, during this period, Mrs. Spiess took sick and had to be hospitalized, and Spiess refused to look for work until his wife's recuperation period was over. When she had gone back to work, Spiess found a job as a school janitor. It's a job he hates for he doesn't like kids. His family situation is now poor. He and Mrs. Spiess go for long periods without speaking. Spiess, marginal in self-esteem and intelligence, is not doing well.

Although the majority of the Baker men have weathered the job change they are almost to a man worried about their retirement. Indeed, most, like Henry Burns, don't see at all how they'll manage through this period. Burns, a hard worker, was 59 when the plant closed. Albert Lapin, 56 years old, is another who sees no retirement ahead. Lapin was one who refused to believe the plant would close. He kept assuring everyone they'd stay longer than people thought. And if they closed, he'd add, Ford was going to open a new paint plant and they'd value older experienced workers "like us." Today, Lapin is working as a part-time janitor. Years ago he used to be a cook in Rhode Island. "All I know is paints and cooking. My feet hurt too much to stand and cook and I'm too old to get a job in a paint factory."

Like Jack Ramsey, Lapin tried to fill his unemployed period with household chores. They didn't last more than a month. His wife, sick now with backaches and arthritis, is sympathetic with him. "They understood his problems at Baker; they gave him the easier things to do there."

Lapin took a job at a gasket company but the machines frightened him. Two weeks later he quit. Now he has the part-time janitor job and is drinking more than he should. At Baker he had been a lab helper, an unskilled job.

The fact is that men with skills did better than men without skills. Walter Jahnke, a pipefitter, had no trouble getting a new job. Gene Vincent was an electrician who quit early and took a job at Massey-Ferguson which he didn't like. "The supervisor was always hanging over my shoulder. At Baker they left you alone." Vincent's job skills were marketable; they left him mobile. Three weeks later he took a job at Cadillac Motors, which, while not as pleasant as Baker, is OK. He'll stick it out there.

If men with skills did better than men without skills, it should also be noted that men with skills tended to have white skins, and most of the Negroes were unskilled workers. Although Willis Ingram had success par excellence in coping with the closing, most of the other black hourly workers have fared poorly.

Most of the men with rigid personalities have also fared badly. Cobb's study points out that while it helps to have a marketable skill, it helps equally to have the kind of personality that can adjust to change. Inflexible people—Ned Rockwell is a prime example—have a hard time absorbing change. Henry Burns, born at the wrong time, is also cursed with a rigid personality. He was one who should have quit early and taken a new job to be eligible for retirement. He refused to move until he had to, and then it was too late.

Willis Ingram, compared to these two men, was flexible. He knew his way around the jungle and he was willing to use that knowledge. Rockwell *knows*, but he can't use his knowledge because of his rigid personality. Ingram is able to use his knowledge.

Another Baker employee who coped successfully with the closing was Glen Littler. Today Littler, a former kettle operator at Baker, says that the closing at Baker was the best thing that ever happened to him. He was making $3.15 an hour as a kettle operator. During the closing he had three weeks' vacation time coming to him. He used the three weeks to go to Milwaukee to take a truck driving course. When he was laid off on November 19, he was employed the next day by Farrand Trucking.

"I should have got out of paints fifteen years ago," Littler says. "The only reason I started in at Baker was because my father worked there. And it was a good place to work then. But now I'm away from the fumes, I don't have to moonlight, and I'm making more money than I ever did before. Listen, Baker did me a favor by closing."

By taking two years to close, however, Baker didn't do Littler's wife a favor. During the closing time, Mrs. Littler almost collapsed completely—hypertension, angina pectoris, cardiac insufficiency, and asthma. Littler is worried about her and says he'll move anywhere in the United States if the climate will be better for her. He has just bought his own truck and is on the verge of going into business for himself. "I can drive a truck anywhere," he says cheerfully, considerably buoyed by his own success in maneuvering since the plant closed.

For Floyd Rink, the hillbilly who was refused permission to say good-bye to his friends his last day at work, the Baker closing may have precipitated a crisis that might have been avoidable under different circumstances. Rink is working at Ford today; and he is, as he was at Baker, a good worker. But soon after he was terminated from Baker and before he found his new job, Rink went to jail for beating up on his sixteen-year-old step-daughter when he found her with a boy in a nearby park. Rink had to be subdued by two policemen; the girl was hospitalized for a week. In the court trial it came out, in Mrs. Rink's reluctant words, that Rink had been "getting satisfaction from the girl since she was eleven." A fast talking and often charming southerner, Rink, according to his wife, had been jealous of her daughter's boy friends since she started dating at fourteen. After Baker closed, Rink had plenty of time to keep an eye on his step-daughter. He spent days and nights following her around. Now Rink is out of jail and working at Ford; the step-daughter has gone to live with a relative in another city.

"It's hard to say," says Sidney Cobb, "exactly what the effect of the plant closing was on someone like Floyd Rink. He might have gone berserk and attacked his step-daughter at anytime. I think there might have been less chance of it if his life had been in an equilibrium."

Cobb separates the men in his study into winners and losers—those who coped and those who didn't do so well. Cobb describes three main classifications of unsuccessfuls: (1) those who had constructed defenses that didn't help them, (2) those who were passive to start with, whom the closing immobilized, and (3) those who were the bottom of anyone's human barrel—the marginal people.

Those who constructued what Cobb calls "maladaptive defenses" —defenses that weren't helpful—were largely rigid, compulsive types who denied the plant was going to close. When finally faced with the actuality of their own impending termination, they usually said things were really OK, there was nothing to worry about. Cobb calls this a "reaction formation," the last step in the denial pattern in which people do and say the opposite of what they mean to do and say. They end up doing specifically the wrong things by getting involved in a whole series of opposites. If they're unemployed, they refuse unemployment compensation; if they're sick, they won't go to a doctor; if they're worried, they insist there's nothing to worry about. Steve Toucek, terminated, denies it by refusing to accept severance pay. Burns, faced with unemployment, takes a vacation. So do Jack Ramsey and Albert Lapin and several others. Ned Rockwell, needing a job recommendation from Frank Robertson, turns one down.

All these men had rigid personalities; they were compulsive people who lived by rules, rules they set up to make things all right. This imposition of their own sense of orderliness on an essentially disorderly world provided protection against inner emotions, against anxiety, but did nothing to provide protection against life itself. At best it gained time for a few of them. And in only one case did an irrational defense work. Before the plant closed, Willis Ingram told anyone who'd listen to him that he was not worried about a new job—he had an invention he had patented that would take care of him. He was extremely secretive about this invention. Right after the plant closed and Ingram was set up in his numbers game, he blithely announced that the invention had been stolen and he wasn't interested in it anymore. The invention, Cobb feels, may have been a truly life-saving invention of Ingram's mind, for having it left him emotionally intact to cope with his impending job loss.

Ned Rockwell, on the other hand, invented nothing to tide him over. His only defense against anxiety and depression was long, hard union work in which he cast himself, along with Frank Robertson, in the role of father of the men. This posture worked for Rockwell until the plant closed, and then there was nothing left for him.

A second category of workers who fared poorly were those who were so depressed and anxious that they were immobilized. They sat and waited for events to overtake them. Duane Paddleford, Jerry McNerney, Joe Nadeau, John Kerrigan. Some of these have since found satisfactory jobs, others have not. All suffered physically from the plant's closing.

Finally, there was the least successful group—the marginal people, marginal in health, intelligence, skill, and age.

Big Dave Masiak, Albert Lapin, Leonard Spiess, among others— people who just could not help themselves, people whom Wysse Allen would call "born losers" but who, nevertheless, had an occupational home at Baker and will never find another one again.

Dr. Cobb believes that one measure of a civilized society is the extent to which it takes care of its losers, whether they are born or made. Toward this end he has definite feelings about how the world can be improved for those whose jobs are abolished.

He feels strongly about community agencies taking a role in a plant closing. "Whether they'll admit it or not," says Cobb, "plants do take responsibility for certain less able people in their employ. You'll find a personnel manager transferring a man who can't lift heavy items from assembly to lab duties. Or giving someone like Willis Ingram, returning from a hospital, light janitorial duties. No personnel officer will say he's doing this out of a sense of social responsibility, but the point is that they are taking the responsibility, and—even more important for our purposes—they know their people. The people who are less able to cope with job change are identifiable. What must happen now, I feel, is that the responsibility for these less able people has to be taken over by the community in advance of the closing. Employees who are marginal in their performance because of physical, mental, or moral defects must be identified to a community agency whether it be a state employment commission or a kind of family service agency, which will then take specific responsibility for getting these men suitably reemployed."

Cobb feels too that retraining programs should be available to people about to change jobs, not just to the unemployed.

Along the same line he says that government employment agencies at both the state and federal levels must stop their absolutely pernicious practice of refusing to help a man until he is unemployed. In Bronson, Michigan, a town of 2200 population where Cobb is studying another plant closing, the men there have been told by the state employment commission that their applications for employment would not be activated until their old jobs were terminated. In Ann Arbor, Michigan, population 90,000, the writer of this book after telling a state employment interviewer that his plant job was folding up in two months was told to return to the agency two weeks before he was to be terminated. In Detroit, he was told it was best, for a lot of reasons, "to wait till your job is washed up, or come in a couple of days before. We can't send you out to lots of jobs without a dismissal slip signed by your employer."

Cobb's argument is that, far from persuading men to wait till they are unemployed or near unemployed, these agencies should be working to prevent workers' becoming unemployed in the first place. "It's easier to prevent a fire than fight one," Cobb says. "What we need are unemployment prevention services in our government agencies helping men make smooth transfers from one job to another."

Similarly, Cobb is against the idea of severance pay.

"Severance pay," he argues, "is an instrument of the devil; it is used by the company to persuade the men to remain on the job until the last day. I am convinced that this is the wrong thing for a man to do. It would be much better to have bargainers negotiate for a 60 to 90 day period during which a man may have a certain amount of time off for job hunting and during which he may quit at any time he gets a new job, instead of negotiating for severance pay. Possibly there should be a penalty payable by the company to the union for each man who is not reemployed by the date of the final closing. This should be large enough to make it worthwhile for the company to put some real effort into helping the men get reemployed. The union in turn should put the money so acquired into a fund that can only be used for helping the employees of plants that close."

There is no doubt in Cobb's mind that the Pennsylvania Corporation thought it was acting fairly and generously in giving the Baker employees two years' notice. And there was no doubt that two years sounded like a good deal to a union official accustomed to plants closing up overnight. But one lesson of Baker's long closing is that men of a certain educational and cultural level have a short sense of time. Two years is forever. So much advance notice gives men all sorts of opportunities to put up unrealistic defenses. It can give them and their families a chance to deny reality, to become vulnerable to crippling psychosomatic diseases. "Potentially useful people can hurt themselves over a period of two years," Cobb argues. "A closing should probably have a minimum length of 60 days and a maximum length of 90."

Cobb also believes that a company ought to be required by law to continue health insurance benefits for six months after a closing or until the man in question has been employed in a situation providing coverage. The Baker study shows that this is a period when health expenses go up. If insurance is not available, the effects on the men can be catastrophic.

Finally, Cobb supports the principle of the portable pension or some change in the social security system whereby older men whose jobs are terminated do not lose their retirement benefits. This is something for which unions must fight, he feels. A portable pension would be based on seniority rights. A man would carry it from job to job. Thus a Henry Burns on the hourly level or an Otto Mueller on the salaried level would not lose their twenty or thirty years of pension rights when in their last working year they were forced to take a different job.

"Change," says Cobb, "is necessary for progress. And it is imperative that we not adopt laws and regulations which would seriously inhibit change and progress. However, for a man displaced by automation there is no progress. Instead there's often pain, humiliation, and despair. A plant closing is a genuine social emergency and it will be one measure of this country's greatness how well we respond to a phenomenon that will become increasingly common in the years to come."

Epilogue

Sometime in the summer of 1966 a new chapter in the Baker story opened; the first of the industrial health compensation suits was instituted. None of the men knows exactly how it got started, but Ned Rockwell, who still keeps tabs on the Baker men, believes it was little Jimmy Jackson, a batch mixer, who first sued. Jackson, who had a lung condition for years, either found a lawyer or was found by a lawyer, and together they claimed his health had been ruined by working more than twenty years among the fumes of a paint factory. Jackson sued and to everyone's amazement collected over $2,000. Jackson's cousin, Larry Walker, was the next to sue. No one knew that Walker was sick but he was having a hard time keeping a job, and the word went out that Larry had collected a couple of grand too. By then the word was really out, men were telephoning to one another. At one point Ned Rockwell heard that at least ten guys had collected and Big Dave Masiak had collected $10,000. This was not true.

Late in 1966 a big labor-oriented law firm in Detroit took charge and began sending out letters inviting discharged hourly employees of Baker who felt they might have health claims against the company to come down and discuss such claims with one of the firm's attorneys.

Translated over the phone between the men or in chance meetings on street corners, in shopping centers, etc.—this meant that anyone who had put in twenty years or more at Baker could collect big money.

Since Baker had been full of old-timers this meant quite a few people. As one man after another collected, more men contacted the lawyers.

Not everyone made it. As Ned Rockwell points out you had to show that having worked in a paint plant was preventing you from earning a living now. He's heard that Alvin Teeter, who was a fork truck driver at Baker and was driving a fork truck at United Paint, put in for a few thousand and didn't get a penny. "There the dumb-dumb was," Ned says, "right back in another paint plant."

But there were those who had collected: Willis Ingram whose

tuberculosis had reactivated itself while he was at Baker collected $4,500. Ned himself is putting in for $2,000. Masiak, contrary to rumors, hasn't collected yet, though he now has a claim in for $5,000 and if he doesn't get it then, according to Rockwell, "everyone else better forget about it." Jack Ramsey is thinking about putting in a claim; Henry Burns won't have anything to do with it. "More getting something for nothing," he says contemptuously. Altogether, though, more than twenty suits have been processed and more are being filed.

Perry DeMoss is wistful. "I don't know," he says. "I hear some of those guys are collecting big dough. I put in twenty years before I became a union rep, but I hear you've got to sign your name to some bad health. I feel pretty good. I get headaches like everyone else, and I got diabetes, but all in all I feel good. I've never lied on paper like that. But the money could sure come in handy. I don't know what to do."

Wysse Allen, the former vice-president of the paint and brush division of the Pennsylvania Corporation, is angry when he hears mention of the industrial health suits. "I'll tell you what it proves— it proves that if you treat men fairly, give them lots of notice, give them severance pay when you don't have to, they'll turn around and throw a lot of fraudulent health claims at you. The lesson of the Baker closing to me is: Next time make every man being terminated sign a health waiver before he can collect his severance pay."

Mike Harrah, the corporation's lawyer in all the closing negotiations, smiles. "Health waivers wouldn't have done any good. It's a losing battle for a company which closed a plant and laid off 500 or so workers to fight industrial health suits in a big industrial state like Michigan. They'll just have to think of these settlements as part of the cost of closing."

Despite the rash of compensation suits, which Harrah acknowledges could run into a lot of money, he feels the closing as a whole was a kind of miracle. The company kept producing to the end, the men got a fair deal. He wishes all plant closings were that civilized.

Today, Mike Harrah and Howard Green—the corporation's two-man negotiating team—have been broken up by death and occupational mobility. In September of 1967, Harrah took a job with a large mail-order house in Chicago where he has been promoted and now has the title of Associate General Counsel. In January of 1968,

Howard Green dropped dead of a heart attack while visiting the new resin plant in Newtonville, Ohio.

"I was shocked to hear of it," Frank Robertson says, "but not surprised. Howard was a tired and beaten man. I think the Baker closing took as deep a toll on him as it did on any of us. He loved the place too, even though he'd moved to General Office."

As for the union negotiating team of Arthur Phelan, Perry DeMoss, and Ned Rockwell—it still exists but, of course, without Rockwell. Perry DeMoss says that he and Art Phelan still work together on contract negotiations and grievances and despite some of the mistakes Phelan may have made in not communicating with the union committee during the Baker closing, he still has a lot of respect for Phelan. "He's won a lot for us at the bargaining table," Perry says.

Like Harrah, Arthur Phelan has been promoted and also now carries the title of Associate General Counsel—for the UAW. He has few memories of the Baker closing except that he still thinks the company was fair-minded in giving two years' notice and that there was really nothing anyone could do. The idea that two year's notice can be as devastating to a man's health—can immobilize him as effectively—as two days' notice is an interesting one to Phelan, one he hadn't thought of, and one he would like to explore further. Phelan still gives off the air of the scholar—the reflective, articulate, rational man.

Perry DeMoss has not been promoted. He is still in the same office at the West Side Local, and still is worrying about his own salary and his inability to up it. He still worries that the smaller plants he represents will never match the economic gains of the Big Three auto plants, though some progress is being made. "A man with five years' seniority," he says, "is now becoming eligible for pension benefits. We're writing this into the latest contracts." A development like this would have helped someone like Henry Burns in the Baker closing. DeMoss still feels boxed in by his job, but he also feels he is lucky to have it and he enjoys the work. He is much respected by his coworkers as a shrewd, tough, and cautious bargainer. The York plant is still not organized though soon after Perry got word of this to Solidarity House, the Organizing Department there asked him for all the records on Baker. Apparently they are working on the York plant.

About Baker, Perry has many memories, some good, some bad. But he still says "we" when referring to the plant. He feels particularly bad about the long lapse in his friendship with Jeff Barrett, the plant's first Negro supervisor, who was a good friend of his before Barrett went over to salary. He says he wants to get together with Barrett soon.

The third member of the negotiating team—Ned Rockwell—has fared as poorly as any man can. In the Spring of 1968, a rumor went around that Ned had tried to commit suicide by taking an overdose of sleeping pills. This was supposed to have happened late in 1967.

Ned sneers at it. "Listen, if I wanted to bump myself off, I've got three guns in the closet and that's how I'll do it. Like old Orvie Blackburn did it."

"I'd like to know how stories like this get started," Mrs. Rockwell asks, upset.

"Dumb-dumbs talk," Ned says. "Red Shehan told me that he'd heard that Georgie Borchard had committed suicide. So I called the Borchards and Georgie answers the phone, grumpy as ever. Hell, with a disposition like Georgie's he ought to have done it but he didn't. Dumb-dumbs talk, that's all there is to it. Maybe it's the Blackburn thing catching up with people."

"Well," Mrs. Rockwell says, "I'd still like to know who starts rumors like this. What actually happened was pretty different all right."

Ned shrugs. He changes his position in the easy chair slowly, gingerly. His back has gone bad on him. His hair, in a year's time, has grayed so it is hard to believe he is only 42 or 43. He looks closer to 60. As he talks, his wife watches him closely.

"I hated that job at the tool and die shop," he says. "They treated me like dirt. I got that job at Saxton's three weeks after Baker closed, through her brother. He likes it. Says there's no better place than Saxton's. It's his Baker; you know what I mean? Well, that's all right, he's a die maker. But I was unskilled labor and they let me know it. The foreman comes up to me one day and says to me, 'You know something? You're dirt. We can get a dozen guys like you off the street anytime we want.

"I used to have a terrible time getting him up in the mornings to get to work," Mrs. Rockwell says.

Ned smiles sheepishly. "I suppose we might as well tell him what happened that morning. I had a bad night sleeping, and about four in the morning I took a couple of sleeping pills. Well, about six the kids started getting up and making a racket getting off to school. They woke me up and I still had another half hour to sleep, so I took two more pills, forgetting that I'd just taken two a couple of hours ago and I locked the door too."

"I was up with the kids," Mrs. Rockwell says, "getting them off to school. Then at six-thirty I knocked on Ned's door to wake him up. There wasn't any answer. So I opened it, but it wouldn't open. He's never locked the door before. And I can't hear him breathing or snoring or anything. I banged on the door. And I still couldn't wake him or even hear him. Well, I called my brother who only lives a couple of blocks away and I was scared to death. My brother came in and he broke the door down. We couldn't wake Ned up. So we called an ambulance and took him to the hospital and they pumped out his stomach. But it was only a mistake."

"That's no way to go—with pills," Ned says, with an amiable, helpless grin, the grin of Otto Mueller, of Big Dave Masiak. "They say pills suffocate you."

"The only reason I got scared was that it was getting harder and harder to get Ned up to go to work at that place."

"It was a lousy dump." Ned shifts position carefully. "I made good money though."

"You were sick so much it didn't amount to what you made at Baker."

For a while Rockwell was operating a crane at Saxton's, but then something the crane was lifting slipped off and struck him a glancing blow. He took twenty stitches in his forehead and was out of work for three weeks. He points to the scar across his brow. Then he got pneumonia twice during the year there, and an ulcer attack that sent him to the osteopathic hospital.

"It's a damn good hospital," Ned says. "One of the best and I been in quite a few lately. I got good treatment in there and I was determined they weren't going to get me out so quick. Hell, at one point she and I were in at the same time. We lost a baby in March of 1966. It would have been our ninth. I wanted that kid. Christ, I'd lost everything else—Baker, the committee—I wanted another kid."

"He did too," Mrs. Rockwell says, and smiles. "But he wasn't the one who had to produce it."

"Then she had to have a hysterectomy. It was touch and go with her for a while. I stopped worrying about the kid and started worrying about her. But she's all right now. It's just me. I know a lot of my troubles are psychological. But Christ, they're real enough. When she was having our babies it was me throwing up every morning, not her. You remember?"

Mrs. Rockwell smiles. "I remember all right."

"We've had a string of hard luck all right since Baker closed. You could tick it off. . . ."

In June of 1966, Ned decided to run for township trustee. In July, he had to go into the hospital for his hypoglycemia and his ulcer. He was beaten in the August primary by another man named Rockwell, mostly, he feels, because he was in the hospital all the time. Late in August he went back to work. In November he had his crane accident and was back in the hospital.

"Like I said," Mrs. Rockwell says, "Ned was making more an hour there than he had at Baker but because he was sick so much we were getting less."

"That place would make anyone sick," Ned says. "The way they treat all the unskilled men stinks to high heaven. The shop steward was a real dumb-dumb. A Polack. I told him he wasn't doing anything for the workingman. We finally walked out in May of '67. The union rep didn't want us to. A real phony of a rep. And that's a lousy local. Worse than our old West Side local, and that was bad enough. I went to the meetings. A guy gets up to ask a question, they shut him off. I got up and told this union rep what a phony I thought he was. He told me the next time I said that in public I'd get a fist through my face. I told him anytime, anytime. The guys were with me, but they couldn't come right out and say so.

"I always got along with the guys. I call them names: dumb-dumb Polacks, hillbillies. I tell them this country would be all right if we only got rid of all the Polacks and the hillbillies and just kept the real Americans." He laughs and shifts again to ease his back. "I'm what they call a nickel immigrant. My old man came over across the river from Canada.

"Some of the guys wanted me to run for shop steward, but I had enough of that at Baker—I still got all the Baker records in my garage. I look at them from time to time. But I'm on the outs with the union. I'm on the outs with the West Side Local. Perry DeMoss's a good man but he looks out for Perry first, and well, that's natural. Maybe he's the smart one and I'm the dumb-dumb. The whole thing's changed since it first started; the union used to be something different. Maybe if I could have gone into the union movement when it was getting started, when it was really doing things, when a guy could speak up and say what he thought and not have to follow a party line. But now the reps and the big phonies in Solidarity House—they're just looking out for themselves. I'm on the outs with all of them."

"Seems like Ned's on the outs with everyone," Mrs. Rockwell says, with a wink.

Rockwell laughs. "Maybe. Even my brother-in-law's not speaking to me now. I led the walk-out at the tool and die shop. We walked out of there last May. He didn't want to. He says I just wanted to cause trouble. Hell, I wasn't out to cause trouble, but when you see bad working conditions and poor dumb idiots getting screwed you got to do something about it. We stayed out for three months. It was during that time we almost bought a farm. You didn't know we almost bought a farm, did you?"

"It was me who put the bug in Ned," Mrs. Rockwell says. "I always wanted to get out of Detroit. Our oldest boy is seventeen; he could have helped on the farm."

"Some guy at work had this uncle who had a farm outside of Kalamazoo. Says he gets thirteen hundred dollars from the government for the soil bank just to do nothing, and he gets eight hundred bucks from renting 40 acres, and he could make a living farming the rest. We drove out to Kalamazoo to see the old man, but he'd changed his mind about selling. While we were out there we looked up the United Farm Agency there and we found a pretty nice place. We made all the arrangements to buy it but then we couldn't sell this place. And a couple of weeks later the strike at Saxton's ended and I went back to work. For four days. The foreman was treating me like dirt again so I quit and got another job.

"Now I'm in assembly at Chevy. I work at a clipping machine, putting rivets into a piston part. The stuff flies all over, gets in your hair. But I like it better than the tool and die place. The pay's better too; we're not making ends meet—but who is? I work with another guy at the machine, a Polish guy. He's a good worker. But I'm almost up to him. I'm just working hard now and minding my own business.

"We got a colored boy moved onto the machine with us about two months ago. I'll call the Polish guys Polacks, and call southerners hillbillies, but one word you'll never hear from me or anyone in my family is the word 'nigger'. I've worked with too many colored guys not to know some of them are damn fine people, and others, hell, there's skunks and dumb-dumbs wherever you go. But this colored boy on the machine with us now, he's a smart kid, and I can joke with him. Let me give you an example. About six weeks ago my back started locking on me. The doctor says it's a spasm. I don't know. It'll hit me out of nowhere. I can hardly move right now. Once I get to work this afternoon I'll feel better. But now I drag myself around like an old man. At work they call me "Pops"—how do you like that? Me, Ned Rockwell, who never took anything from anyone whether he was the vice-president of a corporation or a lye tank cleaner—they call me Pops. This colored boy too. A man's skin don't tell you anything about what the man inside is like. Let me tell you, for instance, about this kid.

"My back locked on me while I was working the machine and I just fell down to the floor and lay there. This boy he squats right down by me and damned if that son of a bitch isn't grinning at me. 'You know, Pops,' he says, 'you look like a guy sun bathing on the beach. And that's something a black man like me can't ever understand. You see this skin, Pops?—black. You white guys just hate it like poison. And yet every year you white guys spend millions of dollars buying suntan lotions and creams and go out and lie in the sun just to get your skin dark, so it must be you really want black skins, don't you think so, Pops?'

"By then, even though my back still hurts, I'm laughing, and he gives me a hand and I get up on my feet and go back to work at the machine. We work together. He's getting to be good at the machine. I'm a good worker too. The foreman says that next to the Polish guy, I'm the best man at the clipping machine."

Down in Arkansas, Frank Robertson says he is beginning to feel a little better and the Baker experience is beginning to fade from his mind. "Time is a wonderful healer," he says. He feels that he's emotionally ready to go back to Detroit for a visit. He has lots of friends there and wants to see how they're doing. If Mrs. Robertson feels better they may even go back this summer.

Robertson has recently taken up from his basement and put in view some practical mementos of the old Baker plant. He has placed in his carport two green and white Baker trash barrels and a couple of Baker fire extinguishers. Also in his carport he has hung a Green Cross safety helmet, and on a post between his Oldsmobile sedan and Mrs. Robertson's Mercury hardtop he has nailed a round outdoor Baker Company thermometer. The thermometer has a smiling face painted on it. Around the face, just outside the degree markings are printed the words:

BAKER AUTO FINISHES
ALWAYS BETTER
WHATEVER THE WEATHER

The needle points to 61 degrees. Cold for Arkansas in the spring, but as Robertson himself points out, a lot warmer than Detroit.